942

OUR
LIVERPOOL

By J. P. Dudgeon

Tactics
Dickens' London
The Art of Making Furniture
The English Vicarage Garden
The Garden Planner
Village Voices
Enchanted Cornwall
The Country Child
Dear Boy
The Spirit of Britain
In the Public Interest
A Tale of Two Villages
Emmerdale
The Girl from Leam Lane
My Land of the North
The Virgin Guide to British Universities
Courses for Careers
Breaking out of the Box
Kate's Daughter
Child of the North
Lifting the Veil
The Woman of Substance
Captivated
Neverland
Our East End
Our Glasgow
Our Liverpool

OUR LIVERPOOL

Memories of Life in Disappearing Britain

J. P. DUDGEON

headline
review

First published in 2010
by HEADLINE REVIEW

An imprint of Headline Publishing Group

1

Cataloguing in Publication Data is available from the British Library

ISBN 978 0 7553 1715 8

Typeset in New Baskerville by Avon DataSet Ltd,
Bidford on Avon, Warwickshire

Printed in the UK by Clays Limited, St Ives plc

Headline's policy is to use papers that are natural, renewable and
recyclable products and made from wood grown in sustainable forests. The
logging and manufacturing processes are expected to conform to the
environmental regulations of the country of origin.

HEADLINE PUBLISHING GROUP
An Hachette Livre UK Company
338 Euston Road
London NW1 3BH

www.headline.co.uk
www.hachettelivre.co.uk

Contents

The great crime which the moneyed classes and promoters of industry committed in the palmy Victorian days was the condemning of the workers to ugliness, ugliness, ugliness: meanness and formless and ugly surroundings, ugly ideals, ugly religion, ugly hope, ugly love, ugly clothes, ugly furniture, ugly homes, ugly relationship between workers and employers. The human soul needs actual beauty more than bread.

D. H. Lawrence, *Nottingham and the Mining Countryside*

'Johnny Todd'[1]

Johnny Todd he took a notion
For to cross the ocean wide.
And he left his true love weeping
Waiting on the Liverpool side.

For a week she wept full sorely,
Tore her hair and wrung her hands
Till she met with another sailor
Walking on the Liverpool sands.

O fair maid why are you weeping
For your Johnny gone to sea?
If you will marry me tomorrow
I will kind and constant be.

I will buy you sheets and blankets,
I will buy you a wedding ring.
And I'll buy you a silver cradle
For to rock your baby in.

Johnny Todd came home from sailing,
Sailing o'er the ocean wide,
There he found that his fair and false one
Was another sailor's bride.

So, all you lads who go a-sailing
For to fight the foreign foe.
Never leave your love behind like Johnny,
Marry her before you go!

Jung's Dream

Mathew Street . . . the Grapes . . . the Cavern . . . the Beatles . . . the Liverpool School of Language, Music, Dream and Pun, and alongside it a statue of the psychiatrist Carl Jung, set in the wall and inscribed: 'Liverpool is the pool of life.'

The centre of Liverpool rocks. Forty or fifty years ago it rocked for the world, the universe even. Since then the Cavern has been knocked down, Peter O'Halligan's School of Dreams has transmuted into an Irish pub, and the statue of Carl Jung has been nicked. But the centre of Liverpool has not stopped rocking, there is another Jung in place, and in the nearby Grapes, famed as the pre-pub for Cavern all-nighters since the early sixties, you'll still find someone who was 'on the inside', who was once a personal friend of the fab four, who drank with them and who has written a book about them, which he is prepared to sign for you if you part with £13.

In my case, the on-hand guru was Sam Leach, self-styled 'original promoter of the Beatles', whose book, *The Rocking City*, laid out in piles on a table by the bar, describes him as 'almost certainly' the one who got Brian Epstein to the Cavern in the first place, and quotes John Lennon as saying that he was once 'the pulse of Merseyside'. As I pulled out £15 from my pocket and Leach relieved me of it, his apology that he had no change faded into the distance as the Christmas barmaid leant generously over the bar towards me and asked what I would like.

The night unravelled far too well to worry about the £2 that the distraction cost me, and anyway I should have been prepared, for one of my first interviewees, Sonia Strong, had said before I had even sat down, 'Have you noticed the girls? They are absolutely gorgeous. They all look like they've come out of magazines.' The writer John Cowper Powys, who died in the year the Beatles broke upon the world, wrote of his periodic visits to the city as 'among the happiest of my life . . . I lived in an atmosphere of complete freedom as far as sex was concerned . . . these wonderful Liverpool girls. One girl, the daughter of a seafaring family, had limbs so slippery-smooth as to be hardly human.' An earlier writer, Edgar Wallace, simply sighed and said, 'Liverpool, what a place to commit adultery.' I have lost count of the number of people I met who came to Liverpool and stayed because they found love. Love is in the Liverpool soul, something to do with the prevalence of seafaring men perhaps. Absence makes the heart grow stronger, every night is a homecoming, love is in the air, and at the risk of quarrying a fourth cliché, and with due respect to the habitués of Brassey Street (and the Beatles), money can't buy it – unless you're a footballer of course.

Liverpool rocks. By the end of the evening I felt I must have arrived at the Grapes along psychic tramlines, so right did everything feel without and within. Had I perhaps become attached to the famed ley line into Mathew Street, which thanks to Grapes regulars I now knew all about, that conduit of psychic energy first detected by cultural mythologist, 'post-punk' and 'British house' pioneer, art world subversive and general anarchic influence, Bill Drummond?

Drummond didn't arrive in Liverpool until after May 1965, when beat poet Allen Ginsberg famously placed it at 'the centre of consciousness of the human universe', but he knew what Ginsberg meant, which was why Drummond argued for the ley line passing along Mathew Street, via the bust of Jung.

Carl Jung was the first to show man how to unlock the unconscious, which he did by exercising a talent for illustration. He expressed what was going on in his own unconscious in mandala, the imagery of Hindu and Buddhist art. The illustrations came first, automatically, irrepressibly. Only later did he understand their meaning. He would draw a new one every day. At first he wasn't aware why he was drawing them, let alone what he was supposed to understand from them, but gradually he became able to interpret them. Really, his whole theory of psychology, which is daily being ratified in modern neuroscience, stemmed from this process.

It was in 1927, during this intense period of Jung's inner

life, fourteen years after he first plunged down into the dark depths of his unconscious, and eleven years after drawing his first mandala, that Liverpool first found its way to his surface consciousness.

> I found myself in a dirty, sooty city. It was night, and winter, and dark, and raining. I was in Liverpool. With a number of Swiss – say half a dozen – I walked through the dark streets. I had the feeling that we were coming from the harbour, and that the real city was up above, on the cliffs. We climbed up there. It reminded me of Basel, where the market is down below and then you go up through the Tottengasschen ('Alley of the Dead'), which leads to a plateau above and so to the Petersplatz and the Peterskirche. When we reached the plateau, we found a broad square dimly illuminated by street lights, into which many streets converged.[1]

Millions have found their way from the Mersey into Liverpool in this way, this city that has been open to the world since the eighteenth century. Originally, there were two streets leading from the river up into town, Chapel Street and Water Street. Jung clearly disembarked at the bottom of Chapel Street, his reference to the 'alley of the dead' perfect because it was in this street that bubonic plague first broke out in 1558.

To get to 'the plateau above' he would have had to turn right off Chapel Street and walk across what is today Exchange Flags and High Street into Castle Street, thence into the 'broad square' he described, which corresponds to present-day Derby Square, the highest point of the city. This was where Liverpool Castle once stood, built on a specially constructed plateau. The castle offered a third way down to the river, but more especially it overlooked the Pool to the south, the original tidal inlet where boats moored, long before the docks were built. Again, Jung accurately confirms the Pool as the focal point of life in the city, which it was in the old days, and which is as remarkable as the rest of his description, because he never was in Liverpool.

All who write about Liverpool mention Jung, and you can't be in the city for long before his name comes up. Fewer have actually read what he wrote, or realise that he never came to Liverpool, not in this life. It was a *dream*, which he experienced at a particularly low point. When, at last, his dream vision departed from real, topographical Liverpool, it proceeded to a level hugely meaningful for him.

In his dream, the Pool is round and located not to the south of the square but in its centre. In the centre of the Pool is a small island. In the centre of the island is a magnolia tree.

> While everything round about was obscured by rain, fog, smoke, and dimly lit darkness, the little island blazed with sunlight. On it stood a single tree, a magnolia, in a shower of reddish blossoms. It was as though the tree stood in the sunlight and were at the same time the source of light. My companions commented on the abominable weather and obviously did not see the tree. They spoke of another Swiss who was living in Liverpool, and expressed surprise that he should have settled here. I was carried away by the beauty of the flowering tree and the sunlit island, and thought, 'I know very well why he has settled here.' Then I awoke.

What we have is an image of the perfect mandala, a succession of concentric shapes, including two unbroken circles, the common centre – 'the source'. It represents man at peace with himself, inner harmony, wholeness, the masculine and feminine in balance, with thoughts, sensations, feelings, intuition functioning perfectly.

> The dream represents my situation at the time. I can still see the greyish-yellow raincoats, glistening with the wetness of the rain. Everything was extremely unpleasant, black and opaque – just as I felt then. But I had a vision of unearthly beauty, and that was why I was able to live at all. Liverpool is the 'pool of life'. The 'liver', according to an old view, is the seat of life – that which 'makes to live'.

Jung awoke from the dream with the feeling that he knew precisely why the Swiss had chosen to settle here in Liverpool, and delivered for all ages his assessment of the spirit of the city, which was in the depths of depression, as he was in 1927, but gearing itself up for a moment of catharsis that would rock the world.

The reason why Liverpool, and not Bradford or Manchester, is a *locus* in this way, is that Liverpool is well acquainted with the shadow of its unconscious and, in a remarkable way not dissimilar to Jung, has redeemed and transformed it through its art.

Powys and Wallace and others, including Liverpool's own artists, notably the sculptor Arthur Dooley, and millions of non-artists too, have been struck by its feminine side – by the beauty certainly, but by the toughness as much as the softness, and the maternal qualities, which have brought its children through. The result is that Liverpudlians are a 'true' people, they *are* their environment in a way many city dwellers are not, with strong roots embedded in the past. Love there may be, but it is on their terms.

True people are thin on the ground in post-modern Britain. Over the past fifty years the authorities have done their damnedest to rub them out of Liverpool, first by uprooting the people and scattering them to the four winds on the edge of town, which has created the savage face of the city most often reflected in the media, and then, most recently, by dizzying them with the idea that style – the clothes you wear, the car you drive, the food you eat, and the way you organise your life visually – is all that you really are.

It is an idea hard to resist as you wander through the spectacular 42-acre 'Paradise Found' development in Liverpool One, where retail is the relentless focus: 1.6 million square feet of 'designer' shops, thirty new buildings, two major department stores, a park, two hotels, a bus station, a cinema, over 600 housing units, 3,000 parking spaces, all made possible by a massive injection of £920 million from the Duke of Westminster's Grosvenor Estates. But the most impressive aspect of the city's 'European Capital of Culture in 2008' celebration – by far – was not 'Consumer Liverpool', it was, in the widest sense of the word, its art.

CHAPTER ONE

The Pool of Life

———

No contemporary map of Liverpool exists earlier than the eighteenth century, and there's no record at all of any settlement before the thirteenth. This is difficult to credit, given the city's subsequent reputation as a revolving door for the world's peoples, and, in particular, its proximity to Ireland, a nation of travellers and settlers like no other.

In the fifth and sixth centuries of the first millennium AD, holy travellers poured out of Ireland and founded communities up and down the coast of Britain, in Cornwall in particular. How could they have missed Liverpool, with Dublin but an inspirational breath away?

If they did come to Liverpool, what would they have

done? Generally, the *modus operandi* of these missionaries was to set up ascetic cells close to water, before their often far less holy followers rooted down, their settlements growing into villages, towns and sometimes even cities.

The sixth-century founder of Glasgow, for instance, was an Irish traveller, St Kentigern, or Mungo as he was also known, with a shade more 'Sauchiehall' street cred. He founded a cell, a place of worship, which grew into a monastery on the banks of the Molendinar, a river that flowed into the Clyde. Eventually superseded by Glasgow Cathedral, the Irish cell was the original beating heart of what became the mediaeval town.

Had such a holy Irish visitation come to Liverpool in the same era, one would expect to find a similar cell close to the Mersey, and sure enough Liverpool's first map does show a place of worship, the Chapel of St Mary del Key, on the banks of the river at the west end of Chapel Street. Did this chapel supersede an earlier monastic cell perhaps? Certainly the site on which the chapel was built lies at the heart of old Liverpool. All the surveys agree that Chapel Street was one of the original streets of the city, and eventually St Mary's was superseded by the Church of Our Lady and St Nicholas,[1] its name aptly embracing those of the chapel and the patron saint of sailors.

A lack of evidence that Liverpool had any sort of life earlier than the thirteenth century has had the frustrating consequence of making the Wirral, on the opposite side of the Mersey, look the cool place to be in those far-off days. For there is plenty of evidence that people did settle in the Wirral, and by preference, initially turning up their noses at the frog-inundated marshlands that became the more famous Liverpool some while later.

It is frustrating because there has long been rivalry between Liverpool and the Wirral. 'Strange people over here, very quiet and very English,' wrote Pat O'Mara, born in Bridgewater Street, Liverpool, in 1901. 'The Mersey separated us. It was an effective separation.' It is part of Scouseology that the Wirral is alien and distinct. 'If I had my way I'd brick the f***ing Mersey tunnels up' and not let them in, was the prize-winning anti-Wirral tirade that spawned a play in Liverpool only a handful of years ago.[2] The Wirral includes Caldy, where Premiership footballers and, as I write, Rafa Benitez live, and Heswall, where Paul McCartney's brother Mike has dwelt to my certain knowledge these past thirty years. Mavis O'Flaherty, an Irish matriarch from Toxteth, told me that the Wirral is the place where 'people, if they have got a little bit of money, go over and buy a house'.

'But it's not all posh,' I exclaim. Birkenhead's not posh by any means. A strong working-class tradition emanated from Cammell Laird's internationally known shipyard there, and Port Sunlight, brainchild of the soap-manufacturing Lever brothers. Even today, land at the east end of the Great Float (originally 110 acres of water and more than four miles of quays) has been developed into the Twelve Quays, from where cargo and people are transported between Merseyside and Ireland, in preference to Liverpool. Ferries can save an hour on an Irish Sea crossing from here.

Nevertheless, the Wirral did seem posh to working-class Liverpudlians in the last century, because, like Mavis, all

they saw of it were the beaches at New Brighton, Egremont
or Seacombe, once or twice a year:

> When we were growing up, we would go over on the ferry
> for a day out, go on the sand. So you've got New Brighton,
> Hoylake, West Kirby, which is still lovely. I was there last
> week, walking along the prom . . .

Here was a real beach and the open sea, light and a vast
area of water meeting the sky. It must have been mind-
boggling to a girl brought up in the dark, closed-in, sooty
working-class streets of Liverpool.

The Wirral also has Birkenhead Park, which, more than
a century ago, according to George Bradshaw, author of
the famous Victorian guide *Bradshaw's Railway Companion*,
was 'owned to be one of the finest in England'.[3] It was
designed by Sir Joseph Paxton, and so inspired landscape
designer Frederick Law Olmsted that he used it as a model
in his design for Central Park in New York City.

When I ferried across the Mersey recently, plugged in
to the compulsory Gerry Marsden loop, I fell into
conversation with a woman who was taking her grandchild
out for the day, just as she had taken her daughter, and she
herself had been taken seventy years earlier. 'When my
daughter was four,' she said, 'I used to take her on the
ferry to play on the little beaches on the other side – they
have all gone now. My brother-in-law used to work on the
Mersey dredgers – he's in America now – and his grandson
is coming over for a couple of days in August. I shall take
him on the ferry – my sister would like that.' Times have
changed, but habits have not. 'When you go to the

THE POOL OF LIFE

Cavern,' the lady said as we parted, 'remember Cilla Black. I'm her husband's [Bobby Willis's] cousin – that's my claim to fame.'

Today, the beef about the Wirral among city-proud Liverpudlians has to do with disloyalty. Dinah Dossor, an artist of the sixties, said: 'Very early on I realised that most of the people I knew worked in Liverpool and paid their rates to the Wirral, which is not on . . .'

Phil Key, sometime Arts Editor of the *Liverpool Daily Post* and a resident on 'the other side', is unrepentant:

I've lived there for thirty years. Used to come in to work in Liverpool about nine o'clock in the morning and didn't leave until about midnight. So I spent most of my time in Liverpool, but it was just nice to get away from it for a few hours, put my head down and get back in the morning.

To me [the Wirral] is a part of Liverpool to a large extent anyway. I remember some sports writer on the *Liverpool Echo* telling me once, 'I've been all over the world, Phil, and I've worked everywhere, but the Wirral is the best place to work and live.' I suppose that's true. You've got the city on the doorstep and you've got the open country. It's quite handy to be able to nip across the Dee into North Wales, and you've got the Mersey on the other side, so it's a nice little mixture of everything. People say it's posh, but it's not all that posh. On the Dee side, where I am, I suppose it's a little bit posher, but Parkgate [Neston] used to be a bigger port than Liverpool. That's where Handel sailed from to Ireland to do the first performance of the Messiah. You can check that. They always say he put the finishing touches to it in Parkgate.

Bounded on its east side by the Mersey and on the west by the River Dee, the Wirral was, it seems, first choice at the very start. Evidence of habitation, including flint arrowheads found on Hilbre, one of three islands at the mouth of the Dee,[4] goes back to Neolithic times (4,000 to 2,000 BC), and the Wirral's strategic importance ensured continuous interest after the Romans built a city of some significance at nearby Chester. Subsequently, in the first millennium, Benedictine monks of St Werburgh in Chester settled a cell on Hilbre, and in 1150 founded a Priory at Birkenhead.

The priors of Birkenhead were forever sailing to and fro across the Mersey, doing deals with traders on the north bank of the river and no doubt spreading the Word over a glass of monastic mead. It seems likely that Liverpool's first ecclesiastical monument, the Chapel of St Mary del Key, was indeed of monastic origin in this era. St Mary's Tower, which survives in the grounds of Birkenhead Priory today, was originally part of Birkenhead's first parish church, and it is very likely that St Mary's del Key was a sister foundation, a parish outpost, as was the way.

The Birkenhead band of brothers were not the only monks to explore the Liverpool side. We know that another ecclesiastical expedition, from the Abbey of Saint Peter and Saint Paul in Shrewsbury (also Benedictine and sixty or so miles to the south),[5] made a particular impression on a settlement of proto-Scousers at Walton,[6] just to the north of what became Liverpool city centre. Walton is one of the oldest areas of settlement on Merseyside, its name, like that of Wales to the south, calling to mind the 5th century Saxon name for the Celtic inhabitants of Britain, the 'Walas' or 'Wealas'. Walton may have once been known as 'Walas-town'. In 1200 it was gifted to Richard de Meath by King John, the principal promoter of the east bank of the Mersey over the Wirral, and the man on whose shoulders rests the burden of Liverpool's entry upon the world in 1207.

Liverpool did not officially become a city until 1880, but King John created the basis of it almost seven hundred years earlier. History's reason for his interest is that he needed a base for the English troops he was sending to Ireland, but he set up more than a garrison town and already had recreational interests in the area, so who knows what in that context may have expedited his plans. His royal deer park at Toxteth, just to the south of the eventual site for the new town, raises our interest in a place that would be an interesting element in the Liverpool mix for a millennium.

George Lund, born in Liverpool in 1948, has looked into how Toxteth got its name. 'The first settler was a Viking man called Tokey, and "teth" means "settlement", or "landing place". Well, they couldn't call it Tokeyteth, so they substituted an "x" and called it Toxteth.'

The earliest Viking raids occurred in the 790s, and the invading Normans of 1066 were themselves descended from Vikings, so the Viking influence remained even after the death in 939 of Athelstane, grandson of Alfred the Great, who is generally credited with driving the Viking hordes out of Lancashire. A sense of the significance of the Vikings in the evolution of Liverpool is demonstrated today, as I write, in a DNA research programme being carried out by Professor Stephen Harding of Nottingham University.

Viking descendants still in the area are being genetically identified and summoned for lucky girls to interview.

Toxteth was a busy enough place to merit mention in the Domesday survey of 1086, but in spite of the access to Ireland which its vicinity to the Mersey afforded, it found no favour with King John as a nucleus of the new Liverpool. As a result it was more than five hundred years before a township was established and the Chapel of Toxteth in Park Road (now Liverpool's oldest building) was built.

Toxteth nevertheless has an amazing history. Urbanisation of the royal deer park continued in line with Liverpool's growth through the eighteenth and nineteenth centuries. Georgian mansions sprang up in the Canning area at the behest of wealthy merchants, and in time commodious Victorian houses appeared on the Granby side of Prince's Road. Later, after the glory days of Liverpool commerce were over, these dwellings and other smaller ones in the so-called Welsh streets, south towards the Dingle,[7] were given over to a huge working-class, mixed-race community, which would find its expression in the 1950s and sixties in a unique 'Liverpool 8' culture and become the envy of urban youth across the country, with clubs such as the Ibo, the Federation, the Crew Club, the Sierra Leone, the Nigerian, the Yoruba, Gladrays, the Silver Sands and the Somali, as well as trail-blazing black organisations including Young Panthers, Liverpool Black Organisation, Liverpool Black Sisters and L8 Action Group. Toxteth, at its zenith, marked out Liverpool-born black people as being at the very forefront of change on a world scale, a fact that so troubled the then recklessly conservative Establishment that they brought the whole scene to a violent close, triggering the infamous riots of 1981.

Another interesting location, which King John might conceivably have considered as his headquarters, was West Derby to the east of Liverpool city centre. Here, on Castle Field, Castle Lane, close to Croxteth Park, stood the principal seat of power in the region from the first millennium until the focus passed to Liverpool. The Pipe Rolls of 1213 records a garrison at West Derby Castle of 140 foot soldiers, 10 knights and 10 crossbow men. In 1232 it was taken by the Ferrers family, who held sway in the area and became the first Earls of Derby, Liverpool's aristocracy. William II de Ferrers, the 4th Earl, was a particular favourite of King John.

It is a surprise to outsiders to find West Derby in Merseyside, rather than, say, in Derbyshire, but the Hundred of West Derby was the administrative name of an area that stretched throughout West Lancashire and reached back into the mists of time. The Ferrers provided the Earls of Derby from 1139 until the 6th Earl forfeited his property toward the end of the reign of King John's son, Henry III. Two centuries later the Earldom was revived when it was awarded to local man Thomas Stanley after he picked up the crown of the slain Richard III at the Battle of Bosworth Field, dusted it down and placed it on Henry Tudor's head.

The Stanleys seem to have had something of an eye for the main chance. Thomas's grandfather, Sir John, and his brother, William, had more than a few scrapes with the law as young men. There was a charge of forced entry in 1369 and a little problem of murder seven years later, after which John was declared an outlaw. Thomas Clotton, his victim, was a Wirral man, and a pardon was forthcoming after some heroics by his assailant in the French wars, but it seems that the debt owed to Clotton's family didn't just go away. In Manchester University's John Rylands Library there is a 'quitclaim' by Alice, 'widow of Thomas de Clotton', to William de Stanley dated as late as 1410. By then, however, John was well away, having married the fabulously wealthy Isabel de Lathom, whose family's lands in south-west Lancashire encompassed the administrative and judicial centre of the county.[8] Marriage to Isabel in 1385 brought with it Knowsley Park, where the Stanleys still live as the Earls of Derby today.

Perhaps West Derby Castle was never a realistic option for what King John had in mind. Certainly, the politics of the time concerned conflict between the landed aristocracy (the likes of the Ferrers) and the new merchant class, the rise of which the King's plans would encourage. In any case, John seems to have wanted to start afresh and with that in mind his eventual choice of location was in many ways ideal. He commandeered a spit of land south of Walton, north of Toxteth, and west of West Derby at a relatively narrow point of the Mersey estuary, where there was an adjacent inlet or pool, which formed a natural harbour.

Thereafter, the Liver Pool ('the seat of life – that which makes to live')[9] was well set to be the fount of almost everything.

As far back as we care to go, a mile-long pan of water enlivened the back of what is now Canning Dock. Fed on its west side by the ocean-driven Mersey tide, and inland by rivers of divers sources cascading in opposing directions down the low and irregular range of hills on which the future city would be built, the hiatus at ebb tide in the Pool was such that, eventually, a pair of enormous gates would have to be erected to be opened for an hour or two at high tide in order to let ships out and in.

Strip away the miles of dockland, the shell of the western boundary of this part of Liverpool, and imagine for a moment the shoreline as it was in 1207. No Canning or Albert Docks, no Mann Island, Pier Head, or Royal Liver, Cunard or Port of Liverpool Buildings, no Museum of Liverpool. Envisage only the river, a long strand or beach of mud and sand, and a crush of creaking, groaning sailing ships rocking in their berths in the Pool of Life.

Now, look farther eastwards, past all this. Vaporise Chavasse Park, Canning Place and the bus station. Fly up Common Shore and Frog Lane, or Paradise Street and Whitechapel as they are now, dismiss Williamson Square as a mere phantasm, and imagine a body of water stretching uninhibited into the distance past the Rat and Parrot, Nandos, the Marriot Hotel, Yates's famous landmark, and that's the Royal Court up there, isn't it? No more. It is hard to imagine, but the Pool extended to the entrance of the Mersey Tunnel at least.

For all its tidal problems on entry, the Pool, around 130 metres at its widest point, was a natural harbour. King John saw that at once. Even when, five hundred years later, they turned it into a wet dock – the first anywhere in the world – it could offer sanctuary to a hundred ships.

The king made it the focus of his plans for the new town, marking out four streets to the north of it in the shape of a cross. Today we can recognise the two running north to south towards the Pool as High Street, earlier named Joggler Street, and Castle Street, which also probably had an earlier name, as Liverpool Castle was itself a while coming. Intersecting these east to west were Dale Street and Water Street. Water Street was originally named Bonk Street – not fun-loving King John's little joke. 'Bonk' meant 'Bank' in those days, so historians tell us, and certainly Bonk Street did find its way to the river. On the ridge where these four streets met, a stone cross, known as High Cross, was erected, and the new town's stocks.

King John also authorised a weekly market and an annual fair to be held on Castle Street, which enticed traders to gather from far and wide. In a wise move likely to identify the place as belonging to the people, two stone pillars were erected, demarcating a place of sanctuary. If you stood between these pillars, you were safe from arrest. The position of one of them is still visible on the north-west side of the street.

The land around and about was then carved out into 'burgages', on which houses might be built, and in 1229 members of the new mercantile class, which all this activity was fast creating, were given leave to form a Merchant's Guild, the elected boss of which, the so-called Reeve, became Liverpool's first official headman.

Suddenly, from almost nothing, Liverpool was a community of around a thousand souls, which included not only traders, but fishermen, farmers, blacksmiths, builders, carpenters and millers. A mill was erected south-east of the Pool, beside one of its feeding rivers.

This was an incredible fast-track happening in

Liverpool's pre-industrial dawn, and people from the Wirral couldn't get across to the new town fast enough. They instituted a regular ferry service in the very year of the Royal Charter, 1207, no doubt vying for position in the court of the English king, as he set Liverpool on the road to transformation from 'a cluster of mud hovels into an opulent city where ships sail every ocean and whose trade has spread to every land'.[10]

As the town established itself, the Wirral seems not to have kept pace, at least up to the mid-eighteenth century. Particularly, Hilbre and Wallasey to the north were desperate regions. Inhabitants turned to smuggling and wrecking. Boats were lured onto the rocks, and cargo destined for trade with the growing town was removed. It was said that there was 'scarcely a house in North Wirral that could not provide a guest with a good stiff glass of brandy or Hollands'.[11] Stories are legion. The trade centred on a sixteenth-century public house known variously as the Half-way House, the White House, Seabank Nook and Mother Redcap's after its characterful licensee, said to be 'a comely, fresh-coloured Cheshire-spoken woman . . . a great favourite with the sailor men'. Located on the promenade in Wallasey, between Caithness and Lincoln Drives, and tucked safely away behind the natural barrier of another tidal pool (since filled in), Mother Redcap's was built with three-foot thick walls and a massive iron-studded door, which, if opened forcibly, triggered a trapdoor that consigned any unsuspecting revenue man to a deep cellar below, something hopefully adapted since its transformation into the old people's home it became.

Historians complain that Liverpool, meanwhile, had been dragging its feet, and should not have taken so long to capitalise on the fortuitous start it had been given. But these are post-industrial historians writing. Why should the Liverpudlians of the day have been so finely tuned to the commercial and enterprising spirit of more modern times? Indeed, looking back, the assumption that industrial wealth is what life is about is not one with which the Liverpool working man has much reason to agree.

Back in the thirteenth century, people were content to trade for wine with nearby France. Others were happy simply to drink it and sail out into the Mersey and Irish Sea to fish, while yet others bought skins, hides and yarns from Ireland (whence the best spinners of yarns have always come) and sold them to Manchester men, forging a partnership that would turn that city into the leading textile manufacturer in the world once the rat race really got going. Local iron, wool, coal, knives and leather goods were also popular fare at this time.

In fact, although the town's population didn't reach two thousand until the seventeenth century, good progress was made following King John's death in 1216. In the early 1230s, a castle had been built at the south end of Castle Street, and became the new fulcrum of power in the area. Sited on a specially constructed plateau (today's Derby Square, where the Law Courts and Victoria Monument are), it marked the highest point of the city. To the south it overlooked a dovecot and orchard leading to the Liver Pool, while to the west, under an 18-metre wide moat cut out of solid rock, ran a passage down what is now James Street to the river.

Also, three more streets had been added to the north side of the king's original plan, making a group of seven in all, shaped in an 'H', as my old map overleaf shows. Joggler Street now led north into Mylne Street (today's Old Hall Street). Chapel Street led east up from the river by the Chapel of St Mary del Key, across Joggler and Mylne Streets into More Street (later Tithebarn Street). The point where they intersect was marked with a cross, known as White Cross, like the one between Joggler and Castle Streets.

Joggler Street has since been replaced by the Town Hall, Exchange Flags and High Street, but its name begs some sort of explanation. A clue lies in the large open space on its west side, evident in old maps – made for street theatre and official proclamation, apparently.

For centuries, in Liverpool as elsewhere, before the advent of 'house' theatres, travelling players would put on impromptu shows in the street. Appearing as if out of nowhere, they would draw a crowd with the performance of some play or mythic masque or rite. Respected nineteenth-century historian William Fergusson Irvine[12] suggests that Joggler Street got its name from this practice, not after 'jugglers', as one might suppose (particularly as it is often seen on maps as Juggler Street), but after the generic French mediaeval term for minstrels or players, '*jongleurs*' – not so strange to English ears after the Norman invasion.

Players and jesters were as common a sight in mediaeval Liverpool as they would be in the 1960s, with wit no doubt as quick as anything you could expect from the Scaffold almost half a millennium later, but often with

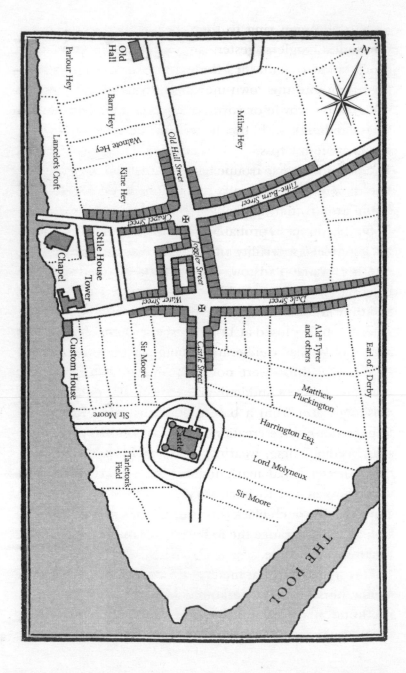

Old Hall

Parlour Hey

Barn Hey

Walnote Hey

Lancelot's Croft

Kilne Hey

Old Hall Street

Milne Hey

N

Tithe-Barn Street

Chapel Street

Juggler Street

Stile House

Chapel

Tower

Water Street

Dale Street

Custom House

Sir Moore

Castle Street

Ald" Tyrer and others

Earl of Derby

Matthew Pluckington

Sir Moore

Castle

Harrington Esq.

Tarleton's Field

Lord Molyneux

Sir Moore

THE POOL

an earthy, Pagan ring to their play. So many 'players of interludes, jugglers, gesters and wandering people' were there, and so fantastic, that some were banned from 'bryngyng into this town monstrous or straunge beasts or other visions voyde or voyne'.[13] On one notable occasion, 'the wanderers with the hobby horse' were put in the stocks at High Cross.

The hobby-horse troupe had failed to procure a licence, but it would have been a foolish townsman who pelted them with rotten vegetables. For the *masque cheval*, or hobby horse rite, is probably the oldest Pagan institution of all, essentially a fertility rite. I once caught sight of it in another town, Padstow in Cornwall, where May Day celebrations are famously true to mediaeval tradition. A group of us had gone there for a drink the night before. After the pubs closed at 11 p.m. other tourists left for their lodgings. We had deliberately hung back, sensing that the natives of Padstow were not finished. Sure enough, in the darkness we were suddenly made aware of scuttlings and swishings, and from a basement area in the tiny square appeared a bizarre creation – no pantomime horse, but a man-become-horse, wearing a jet-black hoop and skirts, with African tribal markings on the 'rider's' mask. The vision proceeded to buck and flail in a circular motion through the pitch-black streets. It was very weird, quite unlike its appearance the following day in full Technicolor for the tourist trade.

It is significant that mediaeval Liverpool locked up the hobby horse, for in literature, myth and psychoanalysis, the horse is a symbol of the 'voice of nature' with which artists, healers and gurus seek to make contact, but which rational man has tried to dominate and exploit throughout history.

In *Gulliver's Travels,* Jonathan Swift satirises our ignorance on this matter, transporting his hero to an island where the horse-like Houyhnhnms enslave mankind (seen as ape-like Yahoos) rather than the other way round. Gulliver later transforms himself into a Houyhnhnm, literally 'becomes horse', releasing himself from the morbid material concerns of man.

In Jungian psychoanalysis transformation follows a similar journey of discovery. In his dreams the subject may be led by a horse (symbol of the instinctual side of man) into a wild land remote from men ('the unconscious'), where lie the keys of paradise. Paradise to the Jungian is a balance between the 'male' and 'female' sides of man, not a genetic distinction but one between the 'conscious, practical, rational, civilised' and the 'unconscious, natural, instinctual, primitive'.

In ancient myth this 'feminine' side is the subject of one of the oldest stories of the *Mabignogian,*[14] belonging to the second millennium BC, in which the goddess Rhiannon 'becomes horse' for Pwyll, Lord of Dyved, who is engaged in a struggle for his soul. Like the later Roman horse goddess Epona, Rhiannon is a re-creation of the matriarchal moon goddess, known to have been worshiped in Sumer in Babylonia as long as 10,000 years ago. She was a three-in-one deity: the caring, instinctual mother; the source of love that first coupled male and female at the beginning of the world; and the ruthless protector, a figure capable of terrifying destructiveness, readily consigning to the Underworld those who threaten her or those in her charge.[15]

I was astonished recently to hear a successful woman journalist in her mid-thirties, now a full-time mother of two boys under five, talk about the transformation of her old self who wanted to control everything to her new maternal self as a letting-go, as 'entering something universal . . . Once you are in it, really *in* the relationship with your child,' she said, 'you become like an animal. You will do anything, absolutely anything, to defend him.' Motherhood had revealed a side of her where instinct prevailed.

This primitive, rather frightening response to maternity immediately put me in mind of Jung's description of his own mother. 'She held all the conventional opinions a person was obliged to have, but then her unconscious personality would suddenly put in an appearance. That personality was unexpectedly powerful . . . and frightening . . . and usually struck to the core of my being, so that I was stunned into silence.'

The voice of nature, the unconscious 'natural mind' as Jung termed it, is 'the sort of mind which springs from natural sources and not from opinions taken from books; it wells up from the earth like a natural spring, and brings with it the peculiar wisdom of nature'. It may be heard in anyone who journeys into that 'wild land remote from men', and at its most impressive finds expression in the sublime and beautiful economy of great, transforming art.

In psychology, the moon goddess is an important structural element or archetype of the collective unconscious. It does not have to be motherhood that gives her voice. It is just that, perhaps because of women's adaptation to procreation, the ultimate creative act, they do seem to offer privileged access to her, which is why the male artist often turns to a woman for inspiration.

He may begin by being attracted to her romantic or maternal aspects, but is soon looking for her ruthless 'natural mind', or for an image of his own in hers. Only when he finds it does he experience the goddess's magnetic pull. There are strong sexual associations, a confusion of inspirational with sexual energies, and there is no guarantee that things will end well.

It is the same with the hobby horse, the ultimate symbol of fecund inspiration. Margaret Alford, acknowledged authority on the tradition, claimed the rite was the most obscene she had ever witnessed.

Mediaeval Liverpool imprisoned the hobby horse, the instinctual, inspirational, feminine side of Liverpool's psyche. The town suppressed her and opted instead for the male voice of reason, commerce, and industry. But locking the hobby horse up in the stocks would ultimately make no difference.

The horse would continue to be revered and treated with utmost respect by the dock-side carriers and wagoners who employed it, one legend being, as we shall see, that carriers treated their horses better than their own families. Again, for all the macho world of dockland, throughout history we will see that it is the city's loving and fiercely protective women who are unassailably powerful, while at moments, as for example in the 1960s and '70s, and since the mid-1980s, the goddess has erupted in Liverpool more or less continuously in a creative explosion of transformational art.

When it was announced that Liverpool was to be the

'European Capital of Culture in 2008', some people in Britain mocked the decision, thinking of the poverty, unemployment and instances of violence which generally characterise the British media's picture of the city. But in America, which thinks of Liverpool's adventurous sea-going past, its art, its poetry, the impact of its music revolution in the 1960s, and of course its beautiful women, the decision seemed a perfect one. It is in these aspects of the city's history that we will see its relationship with the moon goddess most clearly.

Seamen know her, they watch as she rides alongside the ship, skipping over the white surf, always just out of reach. This is Pwyll watching the moon goddess Rhiannon 'dressed in shining gold brocade and riding a great pale horse', racing on her white mare just out of reach. She appears to be travelling at a steady pace, but the horseman that Pwyll sends after her, cannot catch up with her. This happens time and again. Finally, on the third day, Pwyll himself climbs into the saddle and pushes his horse 'to its utmost speed', but always the moon goddess remains just beyond his grasp.

This sense of something out there, just out of reach, is the subject of the 100 cast-iron, life-size figures in Antony Gormley's *Another Place* sculpture spread along 3km of the foreshore and stretching almost 1km out to sea on Merseyside's Crosby beach. The figures look out over the ocean, not inland at what is known. The work has been associated with emigration, but it is the *pull* of the ocean, that great symbol of the unconscious, which dominates this piece, and the moon is behind that, in science as well as in imagination.

The moon is time itself in a port city, which is just as well, as many of Liverpool's city clocks do not tell it correctly. Á friend informs me that the clocks in Naples are worse: 'In every single station on the way to Pompeii the clock tells a different time. And if it has two faces, each one will tell a different wrong time.' It doesn't matter, because in all port cities time is governed by the moon's gravitational pull, and the pull of the moon is rarely as strong as it is on the Mersey, as the National Oceanography Centre explains:

> In most tidal rivers the change from ebb to flood is a gradual process. The ebb current downstream slows, there is a period of slack water and then very slowly the flood tide starts flowing upstream. In a few rivers however, the behaviour is remarkably different. The onset of the flood tide is marked by a distinct and sometimes very vigorous wave – a bore. Two such rivers that produce bores are the Dee and the Mersey. They are at their best when very high tides are expected above 10 metres at Liverpool, which occurs on only a few days each year. However lower tides can produce good bores if other factors are favourable such as a period of dry weather reducing fresh water flow in the rivers. The Mersey bore may be seen in the lower estuary opposite Hale Point about 2hr 25 min before HW Liverpool. From the park at Widnes West Bank it may be seen passing under the Runcorn road and rail bridges about 1 hr 50 min before HW Liverpool. Under good conditions the bore may be seen as far as Warrington passing under the rail bridge south of Bank Quay station about 20 min before HW Liverpool. It passes rapidly

through the town centre and arrives at Howley Weir just
before HW Liverpool.

Such is the moon goddess's pull on the imagination of
Liverpool's boys that they grew up with 'going to sea' the
romantic adventurous alternative to working the docks,
whilst girls like Caroline Langley readily identified with her
'shimmering' allure. Caroline was born in 1894 of
Norwegian father and English mother. She worked as a
nurse at Parkhill Isolation Hospital in the Dingle, the name
given to Toxteth Park in 1836, after Dingle Brook, which
rose at High Park Street. Many a night Caroline would look
out over the Mersey as if she were the figurehead on the
prow of a ship:

My hospital (Parkhill) was at the very end of South Hill Road.
There was a beautiful house on a hill. The administrative
block, where the doctors kept offices and kitchens, was
there. A Nurses Home had been built on the opposite side.
Dingle Lane ran down the side of our Nurses Home. The
wards were all on a slope down to the river's edge. It was
really a small pox hospital – small pox was rife in those days,
and then of course TB was rife as well. The small pox people
were moved and then we were all TBs. We had all been
trained, there were no probationers. But there were sisters,
and a wonderful Matron, Miss Campbell.

I did a lot of night duty. I can remember the Night Sister
coming from the house at the top, and the dock wall (of
the Herculaneum Dock) was just at the side there, and it
was rough grass all round us, you see. She used to come
and swing a lantern, come down and visit us at each of our

wards at night. I think she and I must have had the same, if you like, 'romance' in our minds. We used to come out and stand in the pathway, and out in that beautiful river lay *The Conway* and *The Indefatigable* [two training ships for boys]. *The Conway* was a sailing ship, of course, and *The Indefatigable* was steam. And the moon used to shimmer all over . . . The first thing I used to do when I was on duty at night, I used to look which way the tide was going, because the ships used to turn around, you see. All along the Oglet shore – it was the courting place. Oh how I loved my Dingle. I loved that hospital. I knew every dock in those days and if I got any chance to get round by the tar and rope where I could smell the sea, it was very wonderful.

I had to leave it because my sister was drowned. I had to fly home. I went to the hospital on the 1st day of January 1914 and my sister was drowned sometime in the middle of 1915.[16]

This is the trouble with the moon. Follow her and there is no guarantee that things will turn out well. In *The Mabignogian*, Pwyll, desperate to make contact with her, at length cries out to Rhiannon, who pulls up and introduces herself as the daughter of Heveydd the Old. Their 'romance' begins, but Rhiannon is no ordinary woman, and this is no ordinary romance. When she bears Pwyll a son, Pryderi, the boy disappears and there is a suggestion that she has eaten him. Believe me, Pwyll's real problems have only just begun.

Liverpool's romance with the moon goddess fared little better at first. In the eighteenth and nineteenth centuries, male greed so strong that it distorted the town's moral sense corrupted the relationship, pulling the mind of its people down into the bowels of the Underworld, the very heart of darkness.

CHAPTER TWO

Heart of Darkness

———

It had all started so well. Liverpool was, obviously, well placed geographically for trade across the Atlantic, and poor communications eastwards with the interior, via road and river, only served to encourage plans in the direction of the New World. The earliest recorded voyage to the West Indies was made by the *William & Thomas* in 1641, although others probably went before that. The expedition seems to have suffered the odd hitch, because John Moore of Bank Hall, who had a financial interest, went to court over it.[1] We know, too, that the voyage was followed in 1648 by one to America, which returned a cargo of 30 tons of tobacco to the town.

Tobacco, however, would never be Liverpool's particular

thing. Glasgow, further north and with a similar seaboard looking out towards the Americas, would see to that. By the 1760s the Scottish town was the foremost tobacco trading port in Britain, in 1771 declaring an incredible seven million tons of the stuff imported in one year.

In 1666, however, London was hit by the Great Fire and suddenly London merchants and money men began to see Liverpool as a possibility for investment, particularly with an eye on America and the West Indies, where English colonisation would grow. The refining of sugar from the West Indies began in Liverpool in 1667, when Allyn Smith, a baker and sugar refiner from London, rented from Sir Edward Moore a piece of land in Cheapside, off Dale Street, on which he erected a building 'forty feet square and four storeys high'.[2] Into this industry Henry Tate, a local Liverpool greengrocer, ventured in 1862, famously setting up his own stall. The company steadily expanded, buying up the opposition, and reaching a production peak of 550,000 tons of refined sugar a year a century or so later. In 1981, the Love Lane factory, by then Tate and Lyle,[3] was closed by order of the Common Market because production was too high, food-mountain economics which hit the local community hard.

For all its success, however, sugar trading with the West Indies and refinement in Liverpool was not the great catalyst of Liverpool industry. According to John Holt, a schoolmaster and parish clerk of Walton, who with Matthew Gregson, a Liverpool upholsterer and antiquarian, gathered a priceless collection of contemporary records of the eighteenth-century slave trade, in which the town would become pre-eminent, it was salt.[4] In 1790, Holt wrote:

> The Salt Trade is generally acknowledged to have been the
> Nursing Mother and to have contributed more to the first
> rise, gradual increase, and present flourishing state of the
> Town of Liverpool, than any other article of commerce.

In the early 1600s, salt was Liverpool's number-one export, in demand as a preservative, particularly in places where fishing was a significant industry, such as Cornwall and Newfoundland. There's an interesting remnant of it in the small fishing hamlet of Dungeon, between Hale Head and Oglet on the foreshore of the Mersey just below John Lennon Airport. Local historian Mike Royden used to play there as a youngster:

> An intriguing name, it conjures up images of nooks and
> crannies and deep pits, with stone walls covered in green
> slime and the constant dripping of water. Well, it did for
> me, living nearby! It was an unusual place, with its inclined
> approach road sloping down to an overgrown grassy
> platform, with sandstone blocks and masonry rubble
> strewn around. There were also those strange pyramid
> shaped stone blocks, piled high against what looked like a
> quayside. And not a manacle to be seen. In fact, much of
> the stone work and raised areas were the visible remains of
> a salt refinery erected by early industrialists in the late
> seventeenth century.[5]

Royden's reference to the manacle reminds us of the emotive power of the slave trade, and how it has eclipsed other aspects of the town's history. The refinement of salt from sea water was an important industry in Britain from the fourteenth century and makes Dungeon a significant site historically, as Royden points out. The original process was pretty primitive. Sea water would be trapped in shallow pools and allowed to evaporate through the summer months into a concentrated brine, which would then be further evaporated in pans, heat provided originally by wood, but later by coal. Indeed, by the end of the seventeenth century hundreds of thousands of tons of coal were burned in the process annually. Well into the twentieth century salt was in high demand as a preserving agent, as Tommy Walsh, who was born in 1930 and lived in the back of a corner shop in Blundell Street, recalls:

Oh fascinating, fascinating, memories! The things that we didn't sell! For example, things like toilet soap, never heard of it; toilet rolls, never heard of them. You know, the *Liverpool Echo*, that was what that was for! We used to get a block of salt and we would cut it and make bricks. I can remember packet salt being introduced. We all agreed it wouldn't take on, not a chance! The seamen bought an awful lot of the salt, but we didn't sell it only to them, there was salt for the people as well. The shops had fridges, but none of the houses did.

In the eighteenth century, salt-refining methods underwent a revolution and with it so did Liverpool's trade overseas in iron, coal and a host of other commodities, because the salt industry improved communications with the interior. Liverpool had been refining salt from sea water for centuries, laboriously evaporating the water in shallow pools and pans. The breakthrough came when they began mining rock salt in Cheshire, salt production rocketed, and it became clear that the navigation of the River Weaver, which led coal to the salt fields, had to be improved and there was a clear need to open up a canal network to the Lancashire coalfields. Coal was essential to the refining process undertaken at Fordham Bridge, at Dungeon and in the centre of town by Salthouse Dock (originally South Dock), which opened in 1753. The improved river opened in 1757, the Sankey Canal from the St Helens coalfield to the Mersey at around the same time, the Bridgewater Canal from the Duke of Bridgewater's collieries in Worsley in 1763, and the Leeds-Liverpool Canal was begun in 1770. Salt production increased from 14,000 tons in 1752 to 186,000 in 1820.[6] More especially, Liverpool was now open as a port to whoever wanted to deal with them from the interior.

The town began to prosper rapidly with the growth of English colonies in North America. In 1673 a new Town Hall was built, raised above an arcade on pillars, where merchants could buy and sell – Liverpool's first Exchange. By 1698 there were twenty-four streets in the town, and the traveller and writer Celia Fiennes described the architecture as 'mostly newly built, of brick and stone after the London fashion':

> The original was a few fishermen's houses. It has now grown into a large, very rich trading town, the houses are of brick and stone, built high and even so that a street looks very handsome. The streets are well paved. There is an abundance of persons who are well dressed and fashionable. The streets are fair and long. It's London in miniature as

much as I ever saw anything. There is a very pretty Exchange.
It stands on eight pillars, over which is a very handsome
Town Hall.

A year later, on 3 October 1699, the first slave ship out of
Liverpool, the *Liverpool Merchant*, scooped up 220 people
from the west coast of Africa and sold them in Barbados. It
was followed pretty swiftly by at least one other. In October
1700, the captain of the wholly inappropriately named
slave ship the *Blessing* took instructions to sail first to
Kinsale, in Ireland, to take on provisions, then on to
Guinea, the 'windermost port' of the Gold Coast, there to
dispose of the cargo and purchase slaves. Thence to
Barbados to dispose of 'the Negroes to best advantage',
load up with a cargo of sugar, 'cottons' and ginger, and
return to England. Alternative destinations, such as
Jamaica and the Leeward Islands, are suggested in the
event that the *Blessing* meets with 'no Encouragement'.
Coming upon the original sailing directions in the
Liverpool Record Office sends some electrifying images
through one's mind. The *Blessing* is the first slave ship on
which any detail is recorded. The following is an extract
from what I could make out for sure from the actual
handwritten order:[7]

Mr Tho Brownbett – Leverpoole 10 Oct 1700 & Mr Jn
Murray Gent – You being Capt and supercargoes of ye
good ship *Blessing* by god's grace bound for Guinea Orders
to you are as follows . . . on the first fair wind & weather
. . . make the best of your way to king-sail . . . Kingdom of
Ireland where apply your self to Mr Arthur JEeise Merch

there who will ship on board such provision and other
necessaries as you shall want for your intended voyage & if
you find we have omitted any thing in our Orders to him
you may take any thing as shall be necessary for your
voyage. Make all despatch there . . . with first fair wind and
weather make best of your way to the coast of Guinea,
where make to the Windermost Port of the gold coast so
you will have opportunity of the whole coast to trade &
purchase slaves . . . [Thence] to Barbados [and] dispose of
the Negroes to best advantage . . .
     Signed
     Yr Loveing friend

Leaving aside the enormity of the order, one is struck
immediately by the illiteracy of the dealer. The same point
interested an observer in 1760:

Though few of the merchants have more education than
befits a counting-house, they are genteel in their address . . .
Their tables are plenteously furnished and their meats well
served up, their rum is excellent, of which they consume
large quantities in punch made when the West Indian fleet
comes in mostly with limes, which are very cooling and
afford a delicious flavour. I need not inform your lordship
that the principal exports of Liverpool are all kinds of woollen
and worsted goods, with other manufacturers of Manchester
and Sheffield, and Birmingham wares etc.[8] These they barter
on the Coast of Guinea for slaves and elephants teeth and
gold-dust. The slaves they dispose of at Jamaica, Barbados
and other West Indian islands for rum and sugar for which
they are sure of a quick sale at home. This port is admirably

well suited for trade being almost central in the channel so
that in war time, by coming north about the ships have a
good chance of escaping the many privateers belonging to
the enemy which cruise to the southward . . . since I have
been here I have seen enter the port, in one morning, seven
West India ships.[9]

Clearly, trading with the West Indian colonies for sugar in
the 1600s now made it easier a century later for Liverpool
to enter the slave trade, and it wasn't long before African
heads began to adorn the Custom House and the frieze of
the Town Hall. This remained apt well into the twentieth
century when Clifford O'Sullivan, born in Liverpool in
1913, was sailing the time-honoured route to the slave
grounds of the eighteenth century with the Elder
Dempster line.[10] Only the cargo out of Africa has
changed.

Elder Dempster were a very hard-working company. We
weren't paid overtime, but I never remember being worried
about it, we just carried on . . . I first joined Elder Dempster
in 1936 as 4th officer of a passenger ship – the old *Accra* –
she was lost during the war. I progressed through the
fleet . . . and then eventually [became] Master of a cargo
ship.
    Elder Dempster traded in West Africa. They had several
trades: we went from the UK to West Africa, from the US to
West Africa, from the continent to West Africa. It was always
to West Africa, taking general cargo there, from a pin to a
motor car, and bringing back all the West African produce,
such as cocoa, coffee, mahogany logs, oil – manganese oil,

rubber palm oil, groundnut oil – palm kernels, groundnuts, piassava, ginger . . .

We used to load in particular in Liverpool for West Africa. We'd load for anything up to thirty ports [along the West African coast], starting in Dakar in Senegal and working our way all the way down – Zambia, Sierra Leone, Liberia, Guyana, down to Nigeria, the Cameroons, Angola and into the Congo.

The ships all had about four decks . . . lower hold, lower tweed, upper tweed and shelter deck – so that the cargo could be divided up for the various ports . . . Dates were given for the [African] exporters to produce the goods on the dock. If they didn't produce it by that date, then it was left behind and sent on the next ship. Elder Dempster always had another ship coming, about ten days after . . .

Once we got to Sierra Leone we would pick up our labour. We would pick up anything between sixty and eighty Kru boys, the Kru boys being the indigenous Kru tribes of the Liberian Coast.[11] They were a very nice people, very good sailors, very good workers. They would come aboard with their mammies and their girlfriends – seeing them off – and they'd all be drunk. As soon as we'd go away, the mammies would go ashore, and off we'd go . . .

The next day they'd be sober and work like the Devil. They used to work all hours God made and they were paid two shillings a day. They got three meals a day, rice and meat for breakfast, meat and rice for lunch, rice and meat for dinner. And they were happy people – very rarely did you have trouble with them. Nowadays, they've all gone back to their tribes, gone back to Liberia. Because once the countries in West Africa got their independence and became free of the British Empire, then, mid-1950s, the Union stepped in: you had to use the labour from the port you were in. So, it was the end of the Kru boys.

When we got further down the coast, most of the ports were 'surf ports': we used to [drop anchor] out in the surf, anything from a mile to a mile and a half offshore, and the boat boys would come out paddling their surf boats.

There would be twelve men to a boat, eleven actually in the boat and one ashore who would be doing the cooking. So there would be five men paddling each side and one man, the bosun, standing on the end with a big oar, steering. He would have two iron clappers in his hand, and he'd beat the clappers to keep time for the boat boys paddling the canoe . . . ['shantying' – singing]. The rivalry that used to go on between the boat boys and the Kru boys, each trying to outdo the other all the time![12]

Liverpool slave traders first petitioned Parliament for free and open trade with Africa in 1749. Records show that by the 1780s the city was the European capital of a trans-atlantic slave trade responsible for transporting nearly 1.5 million Africans into slavery in America, although it has been estimated that an accurate estimate of the trade between 1451 and 1870[13] is 10 to 12 million. By the 1790s, Liverpool controlled 80 per cent of the British slave trade and over 40 per cent of the European trade, and this continued until the Abolition Bill was passed in 1807. Of course, the story didn't stop there, because slavery continued in America until 1865, and Liverpool merchants simply moved from dealing in slaves to dealing in slave goods, cotton in particular. Continuing improvements in communications with the interior of Britain meant they could supply Manchester and the cotton-mill towns of Ashton-under-Lyne, Blackburn, Bolton, Burnley, Bury, Darwen, Oldham and Rochdale as well as the Rossendale Valley, and make fortunes in the process.

It is important to understand what being a slave meant. The slave 'could do nothing, possess nothing, nor acquire anything but what must belong to his master'.[14] Slaves were expected to put in up to 'twenty hours of unremitting toil, twelve in the [cotton] field, and eight indoors to boil or grind the cane – believe me, few grow old. But life is cheap, and sugar, sir, is gold.'[15] A law passed in Georgia as late as 1829 made teaching literacy to a black person an offence punishable by a fine and imprisonment at the discretion of the court. Slaves were also bred for sale, like animals on a farm. Enslavement knew no bounds:

There's something more than wrong when a nigger takes the risk of having himself nailed into a box so that he can be put on the railway with a label addressed to somewhere in the North . . . A slave, though he's shaped just as we are, can, under the law, be yoked like an ox or branded like a mule . . . The Fugitive Slave Law penalised to the extent of five years' imprisonment or a 5,000-dollar fine, anyone who aided a slave's escape.[16]

The middle passage of the so-called triangular trade was the cruellest, after the slaves had been picked up from Africa and were being transported across the Atlantic to the West Indies. Captains used different systems of packing them on the boats, the men secured by leg irons, the women and children separated from them and prone to sexual abuse by the crew. Some captains went for 'loose packing', which generally meant that a greater percentage actually survived the crossing, while others went for 'tight packing', which had a lower percentage survival rate, but a higher initial intake, which could turn out to be the better commercial proposition in the end. Ships' captains were not above throwing slaves overboard 'in order to collect the insurance if it was found that the price of slaves had dropped in the Caribbean. "Brown sugar" was the commodity usually entered in the log book when this happened.'[17]

It seems the business wasn't undertaken with guilt, or even any sense of impropriety. It *made* the professional reputations of Liverpool men such as John Gladstone, who begat a famous Prime Minister and who also worked sugar plantations with two thousand slaves in the Caribbean. For Foster Cunliffe, three times Mayor of Liverpool, slave trading was a family business. He and his two sons had four slave ships and over a thousand slaves working for them. The Hayward brothers, Arthur and Benjamin, so profited from the African trade, as it was known, that they funded a bank on the proceeds. In 1883, it was taken over by the Bank of Liverpool for the then gigantic sum of £400,000, and after that by Barclays.

The anti-Abolitionists argued strongly that Liverpool could not afford to do without the trade. To make this point was one purpose behind the collection of slave-trade statistics started by John Holt and Matthew Gregson mentioned earlier. As one of Liverpool's principal tradesmen, Gregson was in favour of the slave trade, and he produced tables showing the number of ships employed in the African trade, the number of men in Liverpool laid off from work because of Parliament's 'restrictions' on it, and calculations of the potential losses to Liverpool should the trade be abolished altogether, running into many millions.

Yet others sought to excuse the trade by likening slaves to ordinary white sailors. One of the letters against Abolition in the Record Office begins as follows:

> We are here astonished how it could enter in the Heads of your Humanity men to think of Abolishing the Slave Trade . . . It is a matter of too much importance to this Kingdom . . . our flagg will gradually cease to rise triumphant on the Sea's. Humanity is in fashion . . . The Orator shines – the Subject is sublime – it impresses with an idea that the Orator feels all he says . . . Its granted there are Abusers . . . [but] would you because there are abusers abolish? . . . the Effects such a dangerous Experiment would have on our Naval Mercantile Trade . . . What are poor sailors but slaves . . . on board a Man of War, many of them taken by force from an aged father & tender mother – or loving wife and children . . . he is then kept in a state of perpetual Imprisonment – if he has a Wife she cannot see him on board if she is a woman of Delicacy or feeling . . . on board is often a Scene of vile hardship – fully as much as or more so than a Slave Ship – his State is more deplorable than a new Negro . . .[18]

Some, it seems, didn't see anything immoral in trading in white slaves either. In his history of Liverpool, Ramsay Muir[19] quotes Captain Hugh Crow of Liverpool telling how some Irish vagrants were put up for sale in Charleston, Carolina. A group of black slaves pretended to bid for them, which led to panic in the Irish camp. One of the Liverpool merchants to benefit from this white trade was Liverpool slave trader, Bryan Blundell.[20]

There was one occasion of an apparent rush of conscience. John Newton, slave-ship captain of the *African*, found God, wrote the song 'Amazing Grace' and joined abolitionist William Wilberforce, preaching against the trade in Liverpool. Eric Lynch, who was born in Liverpool in 1932 and has run a 'Slave Tour' of the city for thirty years, finds this hard to believe:

I will tell you the true story about Newton. His father was a slave trader and he was an ordinary seaman on a ship. Somehow or other he comes to Liverpool and he becomes great friends with one of the leading slave traders in Liverpool, a man by the name of Joseph Manesty. Manesty introduces him into a very rich family in Liverpool and they have a daughter, thirteen years of age. In them days, a child of thirteen years of age could be married, and Newton took one look at her and fell in love with her, but he is just an ordinary seaman. He works his way up and eventually becomes a captain of a slave ship. Now previous to this, Newton had a very foul mouth and people used to say to him, 'One day the devil will take you because of your foul mouth,' and he used to laugh it off. On one of his voyages, his ship was loaded with slaves. He's the captain now, and there's a terrible storm and he thinks he is going to lose the ship and all the slaves, and lose his life. So he falls to his knees and he prays to God. If God saves him and his ship, he will alter his ways. The storm abated, no doubt he sold the slaves. Thirty years later, he joined the abolitionist movement, became a preacher, and wrote the hymn 'Amazing Grace', which can be played, if you play a piano, on the black notes only. It's a fact. He married the girl and lived to be an extremely old man. When he died, among his papers were found documents that proved he was still receiving money from the slave trade.

It is true that all Liverpool's MPs in the late eighteenth and early nineteenth centuries, except for William Roscoe, were in favour of the African trade, and generally the Liverpool slave trader was part of the respected Establishment, and is often still celebrated in the city's street names.

John Gladstone, Felix Doran and Joseph Manesty are among the slavers who are remembered in this way today. Slave-ship owner Doran lived in Lord Street and seems to cling ghost-like to the area, giving his name to Doran's Lane. Bannister Tarleton, the Liverpool MP who fought tooth and nail against Abolition, has his eponymous memorial in the busy retail centre of Liverpool One, while Manesty's Lane, also part of the modern city centre, recalls Joseph Manesty, who owned John Newton's boat.

Many of Liverpool's philanthropic institutions were founded on fortunes amassed from the trade, a fact that speaks not of the slave trader's need to quieten conscience but of how it was compatible with Christian values in the minds of many at the time. Even the beautiful Bluecoat School for poor children, the only eighteenth-century building extant in Liverpool today, was founded by a slave trader – Bryan Blundell, the one who, according to Ian

Law, was happy to make slaves of blacks *and* whites.

The racism and cruelty of some captains is rarely on record in court files for obvious reasons, but sometimes, as here shortly before Abolition,[21] there was a result of sorts for the African victim.

When the Captain in pursuit of his voyage had arrived in Jamaica, he hired the Plaintiff, an African negro, in the capacity of captain's steward, and a man named Robinson as Second Mate. The ship sailed for Liverpool, and on the 4th of June, 1805, the steward being on deck with Robinson, whose watch it was, asked leave of the latter to go below, in order to make the cot of the first mate, which was granted, and at the same time, by the desire of the first mate, gave him some grog. Presently afterwards the Captain enquired what he had been doing? And when the chief mate heard that the steward had told the captain that he had been given some spirits, he was so irritated that he threw him into the sea.

Robinson, by jumping into the boat, rescued him from a watry [sic] grave. Soon after the captain ordered the steward to be fastened to the ring bolts of the deck, with his hands tied behind him, for eight hours, the captain throwing buckets of water over him. The next day the captain charged him with stealing money from one of the passengers, which the steward positively denied. The captain then made a cat-o'-nine tails with a new log line and flogged him, until being exhausted he commanded both the chief mate and second mate to renew the torture. While the wounds were yet fresh, this inhuman monster ordered the brine to be taken from a beef cask and to be rubbed in the open sores. To add contempt and derision to this horrid series of atrocities, he

> was thrown into a turtle tub of water, under which his head
> was at intervals immerged [sic] by this barbarian . . .

The man was then put into 'double irons' and exposed naked to the elements. Still persisting in his innocence of the crime – the passenger in question, who had lost a guinea and some silver, was perpetually drunk 'and actually died drunk' – the same torture was repeated 'on the 11th, 13th and 14th of the same month'. When the ship arrived in Liverpool a surgeon attended him and he was taken to the Infirmary. The surgeon, a Mr Lindsay, told how 'a large portion of the flesh came away over the surface of the back, sixteen inches square. After this there was a prodigious accumulation of the fungus, or proud flesh. Now healed there was a 'considerable contraction of the muscles of the back'. The victim was awarded £500. There is no mention of what became of the captain.

The racist aggression is the point of the story, but it was unclear to me whether the African was a slave or actually employed by the bullying captain. Eric Lynch told me that 'even during the period of slavery, there were black African men working on the slave ships. They were slaves, but they were working on the ships. Germany, France, Belgium, Holland, Sweden, Denmark, Spain, Portugal, they all had forts around the coastal areas of Africa, and these coastal areas were being bled dry of Africans. Slave-ship captains employed black men as pilots because they knew how to navigate up-river from the coast [to find new stocks of slaves], and many of those black men were then put to work on ships. Given half the chance, if you are taken as a slave, where would you rather be, down below chained up in the hold or working, even if it was under the lash, out in the fresh air?'

One irony of Liverpool's appalling record in the slave trade is that in 1699, a year before the first slave ship sailed from Liverpool, the town was officially given moral and spiritual recognition at the highest level and made a parish. The parish church of St Peter's, consecrated in 1704, later became the city's Procathedral, before the Anglican Cathedral was finally built, in Hope Street, between 1904 and 1978. Hitherto, the town had been part of the parish of Walton, still regarded by many as the original Liverpool. St Peter's was the first Church of England parish church to be consecrated after the Reformation, but it was soon hosting the slave trade.

Advertisements in *Williamson's Liverpool Advertiser* and the *Liverpool Chronicle* offer evidence of slave sales operating in Liverpool in 1766 and 1768 respectively, highlighting, for example, the plight of eleven negroes up for sale at 10 a.m. 'at the Exchange Coffee Shop in Water Street' and of 'a fine Negroe [sic] boy of about 4 feet 5 inches high. Of a sober, tractable, humane disposition. Eleven or twelve years . . .' at the Merchant's Coffee House in St Peter's churchyard. The publicity for the sale, on 15 December 1768, titillates a very un-Christian interest, for the sale was 'to commence at 7 o'clock by candlelight by order of Mr Thomas Yates'. Imagine the fearful feelings of this boy, caught in the flickering candlelight.

There is a golden cross on the ground in front of Top Shop in Church Street today, indicating where St Peter's stood before its demolition in 1919.[22] I found myself standing in front of it with Liverpool-born Ramsey

Campbell, who is generally regarded as Britain's most respected living horror writer.[23] Discovering that he was about to publish a disquieting new novel, set in his home town and entitled *Creatures of the Pool*,[24] I suggested that we walk the area together.

Ramsey, who has a keen sense of the contiguity of time, looked first at Top Shop, part of the Liverpool One 'designer' development, and then down at the golden cross on the pavement at his feet, and said, 'Confusing isn't it? What Church Alley leads to now is more shops. Tie Rack – "Students 15% off"! What would you do with a cheap student?'

We'd met at Derby Square, site of the old castle, parts of which disappeared between 1660 and 1678, the rest in the 1720s. As the Town Hall and Exchange Arcade went up, the mediaeval castle came down, sure sign that a new dawn had broken, but what the new dawn had broken onto was the slave trade, the diabolical heart of darkness, for which Mr Kurtz's last words – 'The horror! The horror!' – at the end of Joseph Conrad's brilliant novel of Africa, *Heart of Darkness*, seem a fitting legend.

The African trade got into the psyche of Liverpool. We know this because it was all of two hundred years later that Liverpool, in cathartic fashion and in the person of Lord Mayor Joe Devaney, made a public apology for what they had done. Joe told me how it came about.

What happened was that in August 1999 the late Bernie Grant came to Liverpool on International Anti Slavery Day and delivered the most inspirational speech on the importance of apologies. Then, in the Autumn, Lord David

Alton, a Liberal Democrat Councillor, came to talk to me about slavery, and I said, 'Look why don't we apologise?' So Myrna Juarez, a young Liberal Democrat Councillor, with my help put down a motion. I fully supported it. Some people, including Eric Lynch, really objected that they hadn't been the main architects of this, and when we did it at the council meeting, there was genuine discord, genuine objections to the fact that we were doing it – not that we were apologising, but that we were doing it so quickly. The important reason we did this so quickly was because it was late in 1999. The motion was unanimously passed at a special meeting on 9 December 1999. The apology for the city's role in the slave trade was the final act of Liverpool City Council of the second millennium.

Well, the thing is, it's easy to apologise, but we were taking a big chance really. We could get sued for reparation. That's why the Government won't do it, and why America won't do it. They won't apologise because with apology comes compensation. But I thought it was important, and I wanted to back it up, the apology, with a programme of action. I have said from the very beginning, the legacy of slavery is racism in this country, and also the poverty and deprivation that goes with it. I felt strongly that I wanted to try to do something about that and address the issue. So, we apologised and we got some programmes out of it. I don't think we have been recognised outside the city for what we did. I also helped to set up the Reconciliation Project, which is still going on, getting young people together through art. We commissioned a wonderful, wonderful statue, which was completed in the studios of Stephen Broadbent, a well-known Liverpool sculptor.

I understood there were connections to slaves in Eric Lynch's family, and was interested in his reaction to the city's apology, which Joe had organised.

My mother was a black woman. She was born in a little village outside of Newcastle, Shotley Bridge. Her father, my grandfather, was born in Barbados. He arrived in this country sometime in the 1800s, approximately eleven years of age, on his own, without any family members whatsoever. He ran away from the ship he arrived on and joined a fair, eventually becoming a boxer. He was the first black man to be registered with the British Board of Boxing Control. His name was Felix Augustus Scott. There is a possibility that his parents were slaves – he may have been a slave child. Or he may have been a cabin boy, or something like that. Because he ran away from the ship, he must have been tied to it in some way, or stowed away. As soon as he got to England (it must have been one of the sea ports, we know it wasn't Liverpool), he ran away, joined the fair, became a boxer and finished up owning the fairground, because he married the owner's only daughter.

So Felix's wife, my grandmother, was a white woman. Not only was she white, she was Russian and Jewish. I say to people, if you think that's a bit of a mixture, start to examine your own genealogy. I love that television programme, *Who Do You Think You Are?*

My father arrived in this country as a young man, and he, like my maternal grandfather, was born in Barbados. He was actually born on a plantation. I've visited it. It's no longer a plantation, but I've visited the site. He was a free man, but there is a possibility that his parents, or grandparents, my great-grandparents, were slaves.

I was born in Newington, a street in Liverpool that runs from Bold Street in the city centre into Mount Pleasant. Bold Street was named after Johannes Bold, a slave trader, and at the back of the house where I was born was a little side street called Cropper Street, named after the Cropper family, who were anti-slavery.

I asked Eric what he thought about the apology Liverpool had made for the city's part in the slave trade. This is what he said:

A man of words and not of deeds
Is like a garden full of weeds
And when the weeds begin to grow
It's like a garden full of snow
And when the snow begins to melt
It's like a ship without a belt
And when the ship begins to sail
It's like a bird without a tail
And when the bird begins to fly
It's like a needle in the sky
And when the sky begins to roar
It's like a lion at your door
And when the door begins to crack
It's like a stick across your back
And when your back begins to bleed
It's like a garden full of weeds . . .[25]

And so you can go on and repeat this, because it is just

words and no action. There is a solution, but the problem is they won't carry it out. There is a model already set in America. One of the major leading banks there, when there was a debate about it, said, 'Yes, we are a bank, but we did not become a bank on the profits of slavery.' They said, 'We had nothing to do with slavery, and we will open our books for anybody who wants to come and look.' Fortunately, there are highly educated black people in America who went and audited the books, and they were able to prove that the bank did get their money from slavery. That bank said, 'OK, fair enough, we have made a mistake, and to rectify it we will pay for the education of black people in the poorest districts.'

Corrupted by the distorted values of the African slave trade, Liverpool went on systematically to drain, poison, and bury its natural fount, the Liver Pool. I wanted to see exactly where the original 'seat of life' of the old city had been, and what had become of it. I remembered a snatch of *Creatures of the Pool*, which Ramsey had sent me a week earlier. Gavin Meadows is taking a group of tourists on the Liverghoul Tour. There are many tours of the city, but this one is out of Ramsey's imagination (I think), although places and history are, of course, creepily real. One passage in particular I wanted to enact:

We're walking where the Pool used to be, along Frog Lane or, if you feel more old-fashioned, Frog's-lane, alongside which the ribs of half-built ships would once have loomed over us. They weren't the only reminders of the Pool. Local people dread storms at high tide, because the cellars flood.

Behind us in Paradise Street where the bridge was, the
muddy road is often blocked by families driven out of their
subterranean accommodation together with their beds and
other furniture. The swamp alongside Frog Lane has been
drained . . .

We are walking now down towards Whitechapel (Frog Lane
as it was). Paradise Street (Common Shore) is off to our
right. 'Now,' said Ramsey, 'where you see Barratt's at the
corner of Whitechapel, that's where the Pool was, basically,
and down to the river, beyond John Lewis.'

'So boats would be moored right here, where we're
standing?' I asked, wondering what height they would have
reached above me.

'Until it was filled in, certainly, and they were building
ships on the banks as well, never mind mooring them.'

Facilitating Liverpool's increasing reputation as an
ocean-going trader, Thomas Steers began walling part of
the mouth of the Pool to form a wet dock (later referred to
as Old Dock) in 1708. He completed it in 1715 and added
the aforementioned pair of gates for access. From 1737,
what would much later become Canning Dock[26] began to
emerge in front of it as a tidal basin, a dock without gates
to protect ships waiting to enter Old Dock. By 1765, there
were three graving (dry) docks.

This heralded big change. Thereafter, the waterfront on
both banks of the Mersey advanced steadily to accommodate some sixteen miles of docklands all told, spreading
from south to north on the Liverpool side with names such
as Herculaneum, Wapping, Canning, Princes, Waterloo,
Huskisson, Canada, Gladstone, each with its own story to

tell, including the famous Albert Dock in 1845, right into the 1970s when the still active Royal Seaforth Dock was built.

Once Old Dock was completed, the rest of the Pool behind it was drained and squares were laid out – Clayton Square and Williamson Square, along with the smaller Wolstenholme Square and Cleveland Square. In 1772, the Theatre Royal opened in Williamson Square[27] and suddenly Liverpool presented a vastly different aspect from the Liverpool of just a few years earlier. Broadbent, with access to firsthand records and memories only once removed, wrote:

Pleasant landscapes, fruitful gardens, and picturesque windmills dotted here and there on hill sides, could be found within a mile of the Town Hall . . . The bankers, merchants, and others of the upper and middle classes were dressed in satin small clothes, silk stockings, and cocked hats and ruffles. Their coats, waistcoats, tie (latter very elaborately worked), and breeches, were oftentimes all of one colour, the prevailing hues being of a light or snuff colour. White stocks at the throat were invariably worn; and the young men, and not a few of the middle-aged, wore their hair dressed with large curls on either side of the face with queues behind. Brown bob wigs, cauliflower wigs, and bush wigs seem to have been principally worn by middle-aged and elderly persons. Whether they wore their own hair or not, hair-powder in the higher ranks was *de rigeur*, whilst canes and walking-sticks with large gold or silver heads were in general use.

The ladies powdered their hair, which, in those days, was worn very high; and with their large hooped dresses wore very high-heeled shoes. Many of them carried large green fans to mitigate the heat of old Sol's rays. Such were some of the conditions of life in Liverpool when the Theatre Royal was built.[28]

The town was growing fat on the African trade. By the end of the eighteenth century, there were four new wet docks, and customs revenues had increased from £50,000 in 1700 to almost £681,000 in 1785. Wrote the Reverend William Bagshaw Stevens in 1797, 'Throughout this large-built Town every Brick is cemented to its fellow Brick by the blood and sweat of Negroes.'

After abolition in 1807, few scales fell from anti-Abolitionists' eyes. Trade in slave goods remained the priority – coffee, sugar, tobacco and, of course, cotton. Cotton became the city's most profitable slave-harvested commodity, with two million bales passing through the docks every year. A new Exchange was built between 1803 and 1808 behind the Town Hall on old Joggler Street, to be demolished and replaced in the 1860s, then moved to Old Hall Street in the early twentieth century. The Exchange quadrangle at the back of the Town Hall, known as Exchange Flags, where the brokers actually did their business, still survives. In the middle of it, a dramatic First World War statue of monumental proportion captures with surprising frankness the special insight Liverpudlians of the eighteenth, nineteenth and twentieth centuries had into the heart of darkness that empowered British Imperialism. Britannia has her head down. Her people are in chains. A figure of death lurks.

Set back from the line of new docks, Old Dock was now

more or less cut off from the ocean's tides, and by the end of the eighteenth century its walls were worn and its natural spring water had become polluted by the waste and sewage of the modern town. The powdered wigs had called for it to be filled in, but even now as they danced over the poisoned Pool of Life on the way to the theatre, the capping was proving less final than they had hoped.

'The drained land was described by one commentator as "building land of the worst description",' Ramsey told me. 'So why they are building stuff on it is one of many mysteries.'

Ramsey was questioning not only the original capping, but the reburial of the Pool under the official, 2008, concrete European Capital of Culture, the ironically named 'Paradise Found' development, the new consumerist zone of modern Liverpool.

It intrigued me that so much effort had been put into burying the Pool over the centuries, and that even now it is refusing to comply.

'I say in the book,' said Ramsey, struggling on up Frog Lane with me in tow, 'whenever there was rain or a high tide, the cellars in the buildings built on the Pool would all flood. We'll get to that point, though we're not quite there yet. It still seeps up the sewer round Whitechapel. It was always doing it when I was researching the book. And the Underground loop, that's always flooding, they close it off about once a year. James Street station is just down there. It comes round to Central Station eventually, goes round Moorfields, Lime Street and then Central and back to James Street. That's the actual loop. Once a year it shuts down because it corrodes.'

I felt a little spring of optimism that the pure Liver Pool, which the old town had polluted and buried out of sight, should be exhibiting such irrepressible resurrectional tendencies.

CHAPTER THREE

The Shadow Darkens

B y this time, my guide was hell-bent on introducing me to another of Gavin Meadows's stations on the Liverghoul Tour, at the eastern fringe of the old town. 'All this is the Pool still,' Ramsey panted, as we made our way farther up the south side of Whitechapel. 'Now, opposite here was the Fall Well.' He was pointing away from St John's Lane, and we both paused respectfully before moving on past the Mersey Tunnels. 'This tunnel, the first, to Birkenhead, was dug out in the 1930s. There's another further along that goes into Wallasey . . . This whole area [the Haymarket] was a market for some time . . .'

We were now at the bottom of Byrom Street, which leads into Scotland Road. In the seventeenth century this was the very edge of town. Roads out were rough affairs, ill-kept and dangerous, on account of being infested with highwaymen. In 1726 a Turnpike Trust was formed to maintain one of them as useable, but its members would have been aghast at what meets the eye today, and the eyes of Meadows and his tourist troop in Ramsey's novel:

> Ahead on Byrom Street cars race three abreast under concrete walkways and mostly vanish into the mouth of a road tunnel where the Haymarket used to be. Traffic lights dam the flood of vehicles barely long enough for all my customers to cross. A nondescript concrete lane smudged with shadows of foliage brings us to Great Crosshall Street, but there's no sign of a cross among the apartment buildings that box up students from one of the Liverpool universities. As I talk about the area – behind the apartments Addison Street used to be Dead Man's Lane, under which plague victims were buried and still are, according to the tradition that some were sunk too deep in the mud to be moved elsewhere – my father paces me on the wrong side of the road. He pedals across Vauxhall Road.[1]

Ramsey had been all ready to follow the route taken by Meadows's father in his book, in short to proceed down Great Crosshall Street, thence across Vauxhall Road into Tithebarn Street, where lie more terrible shadows, to which, in time, we will indeed come. But I was intrigued by Dead Man's Lane. I learned that the plague, probably brought by rats in the holds of Liverpool's ocean-going ships, was visited upon Liverpool on three occasions, in 1558, 1609 and 1647. I also found a report in the *New York*

Times that the town had contracted it again in 1901. The American interest is no surprise, so intertwined were the fortunes of the two cities by then.

The effect of the three earlier outbreaks had been disastrous, with mass graves dug on the fringes, as here. 'It was known as Dead Man's Lane or Sick Man's Lane to make people feel not so threatened,' Ramsey told me, 'but today it's Addison Street – much more genteel now. They'd bring the bodies in carts and dump them in.'

As we were waiting to take our lives in our hands and cross the deafening, two-times three-lane Byrom Street, my attention was caught by a red-brick wall, very old but well made, snaking around the south boundary of the estate within which, I deduced from a map, the plague pit lies. I was struck not only by the age of the wall and its craftsmanship, but by a little white font – or was it a holy water vessel? – set in the wall, like something you might see in a Catholic church. Ramsey was at once taken with it, too. 'I've never noticed it before, and it is interesting that the area of the pit is still walled off from the city in this odd way.'

Once across the road, we saw that the font was dry and full of junk. A wrought-iron handle suggested that once upon a time the passing faithful could pump water into it, but it was only a litter bin now. We found our way to the other side of the wall into St Stephen's Place, a community estate, its buildings modern, single-storey, probably council owned, oddly quiet but pleasantly peaceful. At Holy Cross Primary School we stopped and viewed a plaque, which read: 'In memory of the parishioners of Holy Cross who died during the Blitz, Liverpool, May 1941.'

We had come to find a plague pit and discovered commemoration of another epic tragedy that occurred three hundred years later. 'I didn't even notice all this,' said Ramsey. 'We'll need a second edition now.'

In Addison Street, Dead Man's Lane, we stood in front of an old people's home that had what looked like a classic Madonna figure and fountain in the garden. 'It's a whole Catholic community here,' I muttered to myself and then read the inscription. 'No, it's actually in memory of someone . . .' I could barely make out the words, but it looked like Hannah Mary . . . Suddenly the Holy Cross association made sense. I knew what we had found. This strangely peaceful little sanctuary held not two but three of the blackest moments in Liverpool's history.

I thought of the plague carts piled high, of Ramsey's description of the pit here, just where we were standing, the fear the townsfolk had in those far-off, superstitious days that the plague would rise out of the earth, however deep its victims were buried. I thought of the Blitz, when a whole community here was destroyed, men, women and children . . . And finally, I thought of Hannah Mary Rathbone, Lady of the Fountain, and the reason for the statue, the fountain and the little font:

> I can recall asking my mam who the 'Lady of the Fountain'
> was. She told me that she was an angel sent to Holy Cross
> parish, to care for and nurse the sick and destitute.

Margaret Donnelly, a local woman, was not alive when this Merseyside mother figure walked Holy Cross, one of the parishes of the notorious Scotland Road. Nor, indeed, was

Margaret's mother, although she passed on to her daughter the legend of how the poor of the parish 'saved all their coppers, week in and week out, until they had enough to erect this fountain and statue in her honour'. They had transformed a place of misery into one symbolic of inspiration.

Hannah Mary was born in 1817 into one of the wealthiest families in Liverpool. She married John Hamilton Thom, the Unitarian minister of the ancient chapel of Toxteth from 1829, and founder of the Ministry of the Poor, through which she became acquainted with, and dedicated her life to, those who lived in 'the squalor of the overcrowded courts and cellars of Holy Cross, which saw some of the worst overcrowding and verminous filth in the city'.[2]

In recent memory, Liverpool's Irish Centre placed a plaque in Lace Street, two streets from Addison Street, because it was 'a good example of one of the streets [where people] suffered so much in the 1840s . . . crammed in, with large numbers of people living in each single room'. That some starved to death at this time is a matter of record:

In 1846 a policeman found Martin Finnegan collapsed in the street and unable to speak. He was taken back to the cellar in Lace Street, where he 'lived'. His bed was straw on a mud floor, with no covering of any description, and he died during the night . . . Mary Meganey lived in the Vauxhall Road . . . She was found dead in bed, and at the inquest it was revealed she had had only a cup of tea in three days . . . On May 8, 1847 eight-year-old Luke Brothers died and the post-mortem report stated there was not 'the least particle

of food in the stomach'. On the mud floor of the room in
Banestre Street in which Luke died were five other people, all
suffering from typhus . . .³

In 1600, Liverpool's population had been around 2,000. By
1700 it had risen threefold, but in the next hundred years
it climbed to 77,000, following a great influx of Irish, Welsh
and Scots from about 1795. By 1831 numbers stood at
205,000, yet the great Irish immigration sparked by the
potato famine had not even begun. Another 1.3 million
people arrived from Ireland from the mid-1840s.

By 1790 around 10 per cent of the poorest townspeople
in Liverpool lived in dark, damp cellars with no sanitation.
The first courts – multiple dwellings in cramped,
inaccessible *cul de sacs* – appeared in 1803. Many of them
sprang up off Scotland Road. Families of ten or more
would live in a space one person might balk at today. There
was little ventilation or light, one tap served the whole
court, and there was no sewage system other than a central
open gutter, down which rain washed the effluence in a
torrent to a small grid at the bottom, often blocked and
creating a foetid lake in which children played.

Small wonder an outbreak of cholera in the spring of
1832 claimed 1,500 lives. The epidemic did, however,
precipitate the rise of another archetypal Merseyside
matriarch. Kitty Wilkinson had invited her neighbours to
wash their dirty bedding and clothing in her hot boiler, a
machine few possessed in those days, and noticed that the
survival rate of sufferers from the deadly disease was far
greater among those who had taken up the offer. As a
direct result, public wash-houses were established all over

Liverpool, an institution of importance not only to the physical health of the town, but also, as it turned out, to the spirit of the community, for it was a place where the women of the area could meet, as Tommy Walsh avers.

> We didn't know it then but the Liverpool wash-house was the first wash-house in the country. Kitty Wilkinson founded it.[4] The women used to come in to our corner shop going to that wash-house. There were things said that were very true, which became sort of clichés, like: 'She'll be the talk of the wash-house.' That was where all the conversation was, of course.[5]

By 1840, Liverpool had sixteen docks with attendant warehouses, the work of the waves of Irish, Welsh and Scots who continued to flood into the town. The contrast between the wealth of the merchants and the labourers of the town was staggering, and the former were still of course in charge. Men at ease with trading in human beings were not to be expected to care very much for the health of their workforce, or the precariousness of workers' employment, but in an extraordinary fashion, one who had no connection with the African trade, did.

From the early 1800s, Joseph Williamson had been engaged in building a number of houses of rather eccentric design in Mason Street, the Edge Hill area of town to the east of the modern Metropolitan Cathedral. After the project was finished, he continued to employ his workmen in what appeared to be utterly pointless tasks, the most monumental of which was constructing a labyrinth of brick-arched tunnels, leading in various directions and over various lengths absolutely nowhere. Williamson kept his labourers employed in this way right up until his death in 1840.

By 1842, the population of the Holy Cross area, the main labour camp in the city, was reaching bursting point. 'Between Great Crosshall Street and Addison Street, there was a ratio of 657,963 persons per square mile, double the figures for the worst quoted density figures for London.'[6] This was about to be increased by the single largest migration to Britain at any time in its history.

Three years later, in the mythically beautiful Emerald Isle, conditions of life were actually worse than in Liverpool's Holy Cross. After the fungus *Phytophthora infestans* appeared, rural Ireland was all but destroyed. There had been warnings aplenty that a nation should not depend upon one crop alone, and when the potato harvest failed in 1845, 1846 and again in 1848, people were left with nothing to eat and no way to make money to support themselves. Many wandered the countryside, begging for food or work. Some starved to death. Famine took a million lives. Reports from observers make sobering reading. William Bennett's *Narrative of a Recent Journey of Six Weeks in Ireland,* published in 1847, was written with firsthand experience:

> Many of the cabins were holes in the bog, covered with a layer of turves, and not distinguishable as human habitations from the surrounding moor, until close down upon them . . . We spent the whole morning in visiting these hovels . . . My hand trembles while I write. The scenes of human misery and degradation we witnessed still haunt my imagination, with

the vividness and power of some horrid and tyrannous delusion, rather than the features of a sober reality. We entered a cabin.

Stretched in one dark corner, scarcely visible, from the smoke and rags that covered them, were three children huddled together, lying there because they were too weak to rise, pale and ghastly, their little limbs – on removing a portion of the filthy covering – perfectly emaciated, eyes sunk, voices gone, and evidently in the last stage of actual starvation. Crouched over the turf embers was another form, wild and all but naked, scarcely human in appearance. It stirred not, nor noticed us.

On some straw, soddened upon the ground, moaning piteously, was a shrivelled old woman, imploring us to give her something, baring her limbs partly, to show how the skin hung loose from the bones, as soon as she attracted our attention. Above her, on something like a ledge, was a young woman, with sunken cheeks . . . who scarcely raised her eyes in answer to our enquiries, but pressed her hand upon her forehead, with a look of unutterable anguish and despair.

We entered upwards of fifty of these tenements. The scene was one and invariable, differing in little but the number of the sufferers, or of the groups, occupying the several corners within . . . It was my full impression that one-fourth of those we saw were in a dying state, beyond the reach of any relief that could now be afforded; and many more would follow.

Those who could, left Ireland in search of a better life. Liverpool and Glasgow were the main recipient ports, creating the Gorbals in Glasgow, and Liverpool's Vauxhall and Everton, including the main artery of Scotland Road.

> They all came through these gates, all the cattle and pigs and horses and all the rest of it that came across from Ireland . . . Deck space was sold to people who wanted to cross the sea. You could get your family across from Ireland to England for 6d in the 1840s. We have estimated the number of people who came across was something like 1,300,000.[7]

'These gates' were not at the Pier Head, the image of which so many carry around with them today as representative of old Liverpool. In fact, the Pier Head was not made suitable for passenger ships until after 1876. The gates referred to are those of Clarence Dock,[8] built specifically for steam ships by Irish labourers in 1830. The gates funnelled them in, and waves of humanity, like football crowds, poured across Vauxhall Road into the mass of little streets and courts around Scotland Road.

Four parallel roads, running north-south, form a grid – Vauxhall Road, Scotland Road, Great Homer Street and Netherfield Road cross the historic working-class areas of Liverpool, Vauxhall and Everton, which run west to east above the centre of town.

The massive migration characterised the north of Liverpool forever. There has been a north-south divide ever since. The north end is traditionally working class and poor. The south end is a bit posher, around Allerton, Woolton and Childwall, but that came later. The neat classification doesn't quite stand examination, because

Toxteth and the Dingle are in the south and quite poor, but Toxteth of course never used to be. As already mentioned, Toxteth was the site originally chosen as a base by the rich merchants. So, the distinction persists.

As in Glasgow, the Irish brought their whole culture with them, religious and political arguments included, although never to the same violent and durable degree. So the north of Liverpool is thought of as Catholic and the south Protestant, and while that distinction doesn't stand examination either – the largest Irish Protestant concentration was in the Netherfield Road – the north *was* predominantly Catholic, and Scotland Road was the stronghold, no doubt about that.

Geographical, religious, political and class boundaries, some so fine that an outsider would be hard put to recognise them even if they were divulged, are nevertheless significant in the minds of Liverpudlians, and always have been. To Joan Gibbons (née Summers), growing up in the thirties and forties in Kirkdale, only a quarter of a mile away, Scotland Road had a fearful persona. Even though she was herself of Irish descent and Catholic, her father was a white-collar worker (an insurance agent) and she had serious concerns about crossing into the territory:

> I remember me dad bought me a bike and I used to love to go on this bike, and I remember thinking of the people in Scotland Road – it's awful this – how common and they might beat me up. I used to think I've got to go past Scotland Road way. I hope nobody who's poor jumps out, knocks me off my bike and steals it. But I wanted to get along Scotland Road down to the Pier Head, where there

was a floating gangway. Once there, I used to go very slowly,
down near to the water – I was always scared of water – I
could see it, dirty, muddy water, and a huge expanse of river.
You could see that on the floating gangway. My dad never
knew I went down there.

Not all of the Irish who came during the potato famine
stayed in Liverpool. Some went on by boat to America and
elsewhere. Indeed, in 1830, with the coming of the railway
from Manchester, first to Edge Hill and then via a tunnel to
Liverpool, the town picked up a new purpose as an émigré
port for the New World.

The role of the Church in forming the post-famine
communities was crucial. First port of call for many
migrants was St Anthony's, Scotland Road, built between
Newsham Street and Chapel Gardens in 1833. But that
church was far from alone in the area. As Tommy Walsh
pointed out, 'The Catholic Church built forty parishes in
Liverpool in the forty years after 1847/1850.' The pattern
of support was there from the second half of the
nineteenth century for more than a hundred years.

Tom Best was born in 1939 in Vauxhall, not far from the
Tate & Lyle factory in Love Lane:

I don't know whether you know this, but Scotland
Road/Vauxhall Road was made up of many parishes. I was
born near Our Lady's Eldon Street. That's where the
Eldonians come from, Our Lady's Eldon Street.

The parish of Our Lady of Reconciliation de la Salette,
daughter parish of St Anthony's, the main parish of

Scotland Road, was established in 1854 specifically to cater for the migration at the time of the famine. The first church was a converted warehouse in Blackstock Street. Today the church occupies a position in Eldon Place, between Vauxhall Road and Scotland Road. Street names with 'Eldon' in them abound here. The Eldonians are famous for having set up as a housing cooperative when their homes were marked for demolition. They took control and saved their community – in 1983.

Billy Woods was born in the 1930s in nearby Aintree Street, within the parish of St Sylvester's, and is able to list not only the myriad parishes and sub-areas of Scotland Road, but give their nicknames too:

> Scottie was divided into parishes: Holy Cross, St Bridget's, Archbishop Goss, Our Lady's (Elldy), St Sylvester's (Silly), St Alban's, St Gerard's, St Alphonse's, and St Anthony's, and the parishes were subdivided into areas of streets – Ashy, Silly, Hooky, Latty, Elldy and so on.

St Sylvester's church is less than 300 yards from Our Lady's, and the whole area loosely known as Scotland Road was mapped out like this, with a pub, a church and a school for every little community, where everybody knew everybody else.

Father Thomas Newsham opened St Anthony's School eleven years after the church was built.[9] Billy Woods attended St Sylvester's School. One master, Thomas Minahan, taught there for forty-three years until the year he died. Continuity defined such communities from the start, but is virtually unheard of today. The only time Mr

Minahan was absent was during the 1914–18 war, when he was gassed. Just one of many streams of interest that the school encouraged in the community was music, all a far cry from the exclusive curricular focus of many schools today. It was the speciality, naturally, of Mr Minahan, who was an accomplished artist and pianist, as Billy recalls:

> St Sylvester's boys and masters choir constantly performed to an audience of wounded service men. Concerts were held by the choir in school halls, military hospitals and convalescent homes, maintaining the morale of the injured soldiers. St George's Hall was a venue after the 1914–18 war. A St Patrick's Day performance was given at the Grafton. The BBC broadcast many live concerts performed by the choir from 1920 to 1935. One went out on the BBC Empire Service. The girls choir also gave concerts and recitals.[10]

St George's Hall in the centre of town was built by the rich merchants in 1841, a dramatic classical building, singly the most impressive in the city and with one of the great Victorian interiors, a mighty tunnel-vaulted ceiling and Minton tile floor. The comedian Tommy Handley liked to describe it as being 'behind the Punch and Judy show opposite Lime Street Chambers', not to belittle it but to celebrate the oldest recorded Punch and Judy show anywhere.

Even today, St George's Hall is a touchstone for the city. The plateau beneath its mighty pillars is the place chosen to muster for a demo or to gather for a vigil, as happened spontaneously (with a little help from Sam Leach) after the murder of John Lennon.

I have seen it written that it was monstrous for the town

to build such an expensive totem to its trading power when just a walk away people were starving. Certainly the Hall is a part of the Establishment, but besides incorporating a Crown Court and Grand Jury Room (where Virginia Woolf's uncle went mad while famously trying Florence Maybrick for the poisoning of her husband),[11] it has a spectacular concert hall and one of the finest organs in the world.

Joe Devaney recalls a pertinent story:

> When the Philharmonic Society put on concerts in the nineteenth century and even up to the 1950s, the people were interested in music but couldn't afford to go to the Philharmonic Hall,[12] so what would happen is, as soon as they published what the programme was, the organist from St George's Hall would play that music for the ordinary people. That was a regular thing.
>
> The other thing they would do there, they would have dinners for the great and good in the well of the Hall and people could pay a small amount of money to go on the balcony – and if you go in, you can see these balconies – to watch the dinner.

Lucky people! Many were no doubt in line for the Clarion Soup Kitchen, held in the Hall in 1894, where they could actually eat something, albeit only a cup of soup and a piece of bread, accompanied by a portion of politics.

Somehow – and I intend to show how – out of this nightmare, divided world emerged a Liverpool persona with a strong sense of identity, different from 'the Pols' who, Frank Shaw wrote, 'see themselves as descendants

from the slave-trading merchants of the eighteenth century
. . . They effect the Latinate Liver*pol*itan.'

> The Scousers, whackers, Frisby Dykes, Dicky Sams, even with
> their vile catarrhal accent (in which they can be truly witty;
> it's the Irish in them), are my sort. From those vile slum
> houses stretched along the waterfront, ugly warrens facing
> our lovely Mersey, comes a strange and lovely quality, of
> courage and humour and friendliness, which I find ever-
> refreshing . . . There is a living, lusting, shouting-with-
> laughter society of real people living along the Mersey. 'Of
> these shall my songs be sung.' Their lives are tragedies –
> aren't all lives? – but they live them in terms of comedy.
> They *live*.[13]

CHAPTER FOUR

Call of the Sea

Pat O'Mara was born among 'those vile slum houses stretched along the waterfront', to which Shaw alludes. He first saw the light of day in 1900:

> I was born in Auld Harris's tenement housed in Bridgewater Street, facing the Queen's Dock, but we moved from there (as usual, evicted) shortly afterwards. Most of my early life was spent on Brick Street, a street of abominably overcrowded shacks nearby. Negroes, Chinese, Mulattoes, Filipinos, almost every nationality under the sun, most of them with white wives and large half-caste families, were our neighbours, each laying claim to a certain street.[1]

O'Mara knew well the Sailors' Home in Canning Place, once the south bank of the Liver Pool, but from December 1850 until the Home closed in July 1969, the rough, wild centrepiece of waterfront life. No self-respecting woman would dare walk anywhere near it.

> Here sailormen of every colour and race co-mingle, sign on, get paid off. When getting paid off, sailormen can leave their wages safely in the bank provided for that purpose in the Home, drawing out as they see fit. Usually, however, they take their entire pay-off and march across the way to the Flag Of All Nations, that big alehouse in the immediate foreground – so named because of the diverse flags bedecking its interior. Here they meet the pimps, and, after the pimps, the whores from Brassey Street in the South End, and Scotland Road in the North End . . . Then begins a brief and torrid festival, ending sometimes fatally and nearly always tragically.

George Garrett, four years older than Pat, was born in Seacombe in Wallasey on the Wirral, where his parents had a sweet shop. He would grow up to become an important writer and mover in the socialist cause, be feted by George Orwell, and play a big part in the late thirties in the establishment of the Left Theatre in Liverpool, forerunner of the Unity Theatre. Early in his childhood the family moved to the seamen's ghetto – the Park Lane district by Salthouse Dock – opposite the Sailors' Home.

> The road itself, straight but not very wide, which flanked the line of docks at that time stretching from the

Herculaneum to the Hornby, was, except on Sundays, daily congested by two long streams of horse-drawn traffic, two slow-moving processions moving in opposite directions at a set pace, and carrying merchandise of every description as piled-up evidence of the din and activity aboard the ships in dock, ships whose ports of call touched every part of the seven seas . . .

Everywhere, ships; more steam than sail, charging the air with smoke and noise. Coal barges, trawlers, small coasters, ocean liners and cargo boats. Tramps of all nationalities, represented by the flags that flew at every stern, but all outnumbered by the Red Ensign, which, fluttering from most of the flagstaffs, indicated Britain's far-flung trade.

Long before leaving school at the age of thirteen, I was familiar with the docks and the outsides of ships. It was a necessary part of my daily noon-hour errands to meet my mother outside the slum-school and from her receive my father's dinner, which usually consisted of cheese or meat sandwiches, and fivepence, the price of two pints of beer. Off I would dash then to whatever part of the docks my father happened to be, working as a stevedore. He was a tall, powerfully built man. For him, and the exceptionally strong men engaged in his class of work, beer and sandwiches constituted a staple diet. On they would often labour through thirty hours or more without a break . . .

Added to these regular romps were the frequent sailing-days visits to the Princes Landing Stage, but first stopping to have a gaze at the withered woman centenarian, bent and grumpy, who lived in a shack at the top of the Floating Bridge and sold toffee-apples. Muttering continually to herself, she would turn a halfpenny over in her hand at least a dozen times and make you feel you were cheating her. She dawdled so long over serving that it was sometimes necessary for me to snatch the apple from the window-box, and bolt, leaving her still muttering over the coin in her hand. Then a quick dash down to the Landing Stage where the Atlantic liners were embarking their passengers. There, merged in the police-controlled crowds, I would stand and stare, join in the hand-waving farewells and parting shouts, until the liner's siren blared a deep warning note, harbourmen rushed to cast off the mooring ropes, and the tug's tightening hawsers pulled the big ship into midstream as the sensitive crowd on the Stage quietened gradually to the drag and widening distance between, for many of the passengers were emigrants who would probably never return.

On leaving the slum elementary school, down to the docks I went to work as a steam-lad at the cargo-winches. As a result I soon became familiar with the insides of ships, and more curious regarding the men who took them away to sea and brought them back to port again. I wanted so much to know some of these men, to get on speaking terms with them if possible. They filled me with wonder as they filed down the gangways, holding up parrots, or monkeys, or canaries, or any souvenirs that showed trace of a far-off country. These men were to me somehow a race apart with a gait of their own. Secretly, I yearned to be one of them, yearned so intensely that often I was thrashed at home for staying out all night with the youthful driver of a baggage cart whose job it was to collect the sailors' bulky canvas bags from their respective homes and deliver them aboard the ship just prior to sailing time, which varied with the changing tides.

Frequently, I helped to hump these long canvas bags into the men's forecastle. To me, there was something mysterious about the bunks where each bag was dumped. They seemed hardly big enough to hold the body of a normal-sized man . . . And in that cramped space I formed an opinion that men brought thus close together often become pally . . . My eyes were constantly on the look-out for a likely place in which to stow away.[2]

James Johnston Abraham describes the fo'c'sle, the living quarters of sailors aboard ship, which so enticed young Garrett, after he first entered one around 1900:

It was a long, narrow, dim-lit place, with two tiers of box-like bunks around three of its walls. Some of the men were lying asleep in their bunks; others clad only in their dungaree trousers . . . were playing some noisy game in which wooden blocks were banged with much clatter on the rough deal bench that served them for a table . . . Littered all around, in corners, in bunks, everywhere, were quaint-looking boxes fastened with elaborate locks, clothes, sandals, rubbish in buckets, vegetables, bits of dried fish and herbs hanging from 'the roof', gaudy almanacs fastened to the walls, and quantities of cheap English umbrellas tied up in bundles in every corner . . . In the stern-most corner, a few joss-sticks burning in a tin of sand before a tiny tinsel-gauded shrine, cast a faint, pervasive odour all around.[3]

George Cross was another boy mesmerised by the promise of the sea, in his case a promise never to be fulfilled. He had just celebrated his hundredth birthday when I met him, a tall, strong man even now, passing his last years painting seascapes and landscapes – (a particular passion is churches, which satisfy a historical curiosity as well) – in an apartment in the Dingle.

I was born on 18 May 1909 in Gelling Street [Toxteth]. My father was a boiler maker. He worked at R. and J. Evans's in Grafton Street. It wasn't a constant job, only when the ships came in, you know? It was more or less near constant, but there were times when he was out of work.

There were six brothers. I don't know how my mother managed, because as I say, my father he wasn't constant. But when he got a job, when he was working, we got cakes. If he wasn't working, we got no cakes.

I remember when the First War was over. I would be about nine, and all the crowd walked down Park Road towards the Town Hall to celebrate. I walked down with them. When it was all finished, I realised I was lost, and whether I was crying I don't know, but there was a woman there talked to me. She asked me what was to do, and I said, 'I'm lost,' and she asked me where I lived and I told her. She put me on a No. 27 tram car and got me dropped off at Warwick Street. Well, I knew where I was then!

I was seventeen when I first got a job on the boats. I didn't know what the job was, but the church I went to, the minister got me the job with the Booth Line Steamer Company. What was it now? A [bilge, or] 'billity' boy. Well, I didn't know what a 'billity' boy was. I went down with a nice white shirt on and me shoes polished, and when I got down to the boat I seen the foreman and he told me, 'You shouldn't have had a white shirt on. You shouldn't polish your shoes. You will go home black as soot.' The 'billity' boy was below the ship's stoke hole, where all the bilge came out. I used to clean the bilges out, stand foot astride the manhole covers, and clean the bilges out. Dirty, smelling, rats and all kinds. Then I got a job in the flour mill – from black to white. I used to come home from the ships black with the soot, you know?

I nearly went to sea. They had a ship called the *Hildebrand* and it used to go a thousand miles up the Amazon, and my mate who worked with me, he got a job as a trimmer, coal trimmer. The second in command, the second engineer, he used to pick the crew in those days, and he asked me when I was going with him. I said, 'I don't know.' It was only six weeks away, so when it came back the boss said to me, 'There's a job for you if you want to go away to sea.' So I said, 'Yes,' and he said, 'Meet at the landing stage.' I remember going home and getting a few things to take with me, and I saw my mate on the ship and he saw me and wondered why I was at the landing stage. I shouted, 'I'm coming with you.' Oh, he was delighted, but then the boss turned round and said, 'Look, you've got a job to go to. Give this chap a chance, he's not working.' They used to call them the stand-in, you know, in case anybody came off sick. I didn't know what to do. Anyway, I decided to stay. I nearly went away to sea. I would have been peas in the fishes now, because the *Hildebrand* went down.

Tempting these boys were four ships permanently moored in the Mersey. The training ship HMS *Conway*, founded in 1859, became a national institution for the training of future officers of the Merchant Navy. There were also two reformatory ships – the *Akbar*, for the reform of Protestant boys, and the *Clarence* for Roman Catholic boys.

> The process of reformation is very simple. Slummy boys, after battling aimlessly from alley to alley, are subjected to five years of strict discipline; then they are adjudged sailormen and given assistance in procuring berths on merchant ships. Only one ray of sympathy penetrates the harsh routine that is theirs . . . the weekly visit of the pastor or the priest with accompanying threats of hell-fire and damnation.[4]

The fourth was the TS *Indefatigable*, a charitable institution founded in 1864 to give sea training to boys in poor circumstances. John Masefield, a former seafarer who trained on HMS *Conway* in Liverpool, was fascinated by the ship. His first book after being appointed Poet Laureate in 1930 was called *The Wanderer of Liverpool*.

Glyn Parry, born in 1929, entered the *Conway* aged fourteen in April 1944, just before D-Day. The *Conway*, similar to the *Victory*, had wide open decks, so collapsible partitions were erected to make classrooms. Mess room tables were brought down for meals or studying.

> I'd always wanted to go to sea. My father had been to sea with the Cunard line, but he had retired in the Depression years of the 1930s . . . There were nautical connections through the family . . . I'd quite firmly made up my mind by six, seven or eight . . .
> The *Conway* at that time was anchored off Bangor; it had moved from Liverpool . . . At least one ship was sunk in the

Mersey . . . and I think the *Conway* Management Committee decided the war was getting a bit too close . . .

The hammocks were secured at both ends of course . . . a hook on the outboard hold side . . . and you simply looped an iron ring over that. For the other end, there was this iron bracket that folded down and the other end of the hammock was lashed with a rope to that bracket, and just occasionally someone would play a trick on you by getting up in the middle of the night and unloosening the knot and crash down you would go. In that same spot, right on the outboard side of the ship, you would also have your chest . . . a seaman's chest . . . One has visions of Long John Silver with his chest and his parrot. Your chest was for keeping most of your things in. There was a coat rack on which you could hang your uniform and a raincoat . . . but shoes, shirts, socks and so on, all went in your chest . . . Once a week you put your laundry into a small sack . . . there were no facilities to launder on board ship, it was enough trouble to wash yourself.

A regimented, disciplined day included a task of shinning up the main mast, over the top and back down again.

In your first term you were not required to do this, but in your second term you were required to do the lower main mast, up as far as the main yard and then you would cross and come down again. In your third and subsequent terms you had to go right up to the upper yard and come down the other side again. Once a fortnight that was a requirement. There was a safety net underneath, [but] having said that there were a number of obstructions before

you actually reached the safety net should you fall . . . It was
good exercise . . . [and] quite a sense of achievement . . .
Even on Sunday afternoons when it was quiet and you had
no formal duties a number of lads would go up the mast
and sit up there and read a book . . . I think this was one of
the main lessons that the *Conway* taught me . . . self-
confidence. I knew my limits by the time I finished my two
years on that ship and I realised my limits were greater than I
thought they were when I went there.

There was bullying in the first term . . . [and] mother
had a bit of trouble getting me to go back for a second
term . . . quite sadistic bullying in some cases too, by senior
lads . . . I think it was £50 a term plus sports gear, books
and things of that kind . . . £150 a year in 1944 was quite
a substantial sum.[5]

For a young lad, going to sea on a ship was a dream, but
one that, in dock parlance, 'necessitated a reference from
the Holy Ghost'. In 1914, with regular merchant seamen
being called up to the Navy or the Army, Pat O'Mara
saw an opportunity for himself and his mates, and finally
took it.

How thrilled I was on the morning I awoke with no school to
go to and no job to go to, nothing to do but to strike out
with the gang in search of – ships! Ships! That magic word is
everything to your Liverpool waterfront youngster, and I
think as we set out that morning to scour the line of docks,
every heart was aquiver at the important role the war had
made possible for us.

They preferred the idea of a proper long voyage to South America rather than the relatively short-berth trip to New York on the '*Lusy*' (*Lusitania*) or '*Maury*' (*Mauretania*):

> We wanted a cruise, about eighteen months, so that when we came home it would be as outstanding sailormen and with a real pay-off.

In the end, Pat got taken on to the *Restitution*, bound for Cuba.

> I made my way down Paradise Street to the spot where I knew Grossi's Sailor's Outfitter's shop stood – he would tell me what I needed and 'cash my note'. But Grossi had passed from the scene, dying from a broken heart when his Trocadero was done away with.[6]
>
> [Another, as good as Grossi, does the business] and when I walked out of his place I looked like a lifeboatman putting out to sea. Very proudly I staggered homeward along Paradise Street, sweating under the weight of sea boots, oil skins and souwester, with ten shillings in hand – the residue of my two-pound advance. [Pat's mother exclaims that she could have bought all the gear for two bob!] 'And the dirty robber never even gave him a sailor's bag!' So a pillow slip was gotten instead.

Once on board, Pat realised he knew nothing:

> I knew how to tie all the stock knots and I could splice ropes and run winches as every dock ragamuffin can, but I didn't know how to steer a ship, nor box the compass,

nor anything of the sea watches and the general routine
of the forecastle . . . These were to be hammered into me
very shortly.

Jack Brotheridge, born in 1920, was another who answered
the siren call of the sea. 'My mother and dad could not
afford a rented house and we lived in rooms, often only the
parlour with a sheet hung up to separate where the bed
was. Our first one was in Province Road, Orrell, then
known as Clondyke. Then we moved to Hornby Boulevard,
Litherland, just one room to eat and sleep in.' Orrell and
Litherland lie to the north of Everton, in the Walton,
Bootle, Crosby area, looking out over the Irish Sea. I met
Jack, aged ninety, in Limekiln Lane, off Scotland Road.

As a boy I would go down to the docks. Oh yes, there were
horses and carts in them days bringing cargo in, and there
was anything up to two hundred ships a week coming up the
river. They weren't of the size they are today. A cargo ship in
them days might be 2,000 tons. Well, now a cargo ship is
150,000 tons. There were more of them, and all the docks
that you see empty now were full of ships getting unloaded.

There were still a few sailing ships around, not many but
there was a few left. A lot of the captains and mates that
you was with on a steam ship had been sailing-ship men,
and they were far more [canny]. To leave Liverpool for China
with no engine you had to know what you was doing! You
can't imagine it, can you?

The men who had manned those ships were mostly bare-
footed, because they used to be on foot ropes out on the
yard arms. That was just before my time, but there were still

a lot of them that never wore rubber boots, even in the winter. Their feet were like iron!

They would get their first job on a boat like that when they were twelve, thirteen, fourteen, a galley boy, a deck boy. There were a tremendous amount of ships in the Mersey in them days. You see, aircraft today are taking a lot of stuff that ships used to take, and of course we exported coal, and there was factories all over Britain. Coal mines were up St Helen's way, and all over the country, and there were the Welsh coal mines. And ships burned coal. Every ship burned 100 ton of coal a day. So you would take 2,000 tons of coal.

When I was fourteen in 1934, things were really bad, but I eventually found a job as a can lad on a building site – a shilling a week, six days, and I had to walk from Litherland to Crosby – about three miles – and be there 8 a.m. sharp. After pushing a handcart to Maghull and back, I had been scrutinised by the foreman and was taken into the office and asked if I wanted to be apprenticed as a carpenter and joiner. I had to ask what they did, I was as green as grass – but accepted and acquired a few tools . . . worked hard and did as I was told. Things were changing.

Then war was declared and my dad said, 'My God, not again!' Immediately all building firms' materials were frozen, and my boss called us together and said he had no alternative but to lay us all off. He pledged to take us back when he was allowed to carry on. Dad was soon back at sea. From day one of the war, U-boats were sinking ships. Merchant ships were being lost every day, and Dad's ship was soon one of them. SS *Estralano* was torpedoed and sank in a couple of minutes. Dad and others of the crew were left in the Atlantic, clinging on to an upturned lifeboat in 40 degrees cold water. Some died, but Dad was picked up and survived.

I had picked up some casual work on the docks. There were too many skilled men out of work for me to work my trade, but [eventually] my luck changed and I got some work with the shipwrights, ships' carpenters. Then one day the foreman said, 'You're a carpenter by trade?' When I said, 'Yes,' he said, 'See that ship we've been working on? How would you like to go away on her as ship's carpenter?' I'd been to join the Royal Navy, but been told I wasn't old enough – 'We will send for you when you're twenty,' they said. Anyway, I told my foreman, Mr Spencer, that I would take the job on the SS *Mardinian*, and he said, 'Sign on right way. She's sailing today! Put your name down as born 1919 instead of 1920 and you'll be on full money and be OK.' I did that and left the morning of that same day.

The word 'carpenter' really goes back to the wooden sailing ship days, so you was the handyman really, dropped all the anchors and things like that, made good any damage to rails, battened down the hatches.

I done about thirty trips in the war. In war time you weren't told where you was going and when you was coming back, because other people might get to know, you see? Coming back you used to creep up the American coast, right up to Nova Scotia and then take the northern route, 40 degrees north of the equator, into the ice, because to go direct across the Atlantic was looking for trouble. If you went a direct route, say from the Caribbean, you would get sunk by the U-boats. They had about six hundred U-boats in the Atlantic looking for ships. But if you crept up the American coast till you got to the ice, and then come down to England round the back of Iceland . . . It used to take us twenty-four days to cross from Canada to Britain.

I've seen a few ships hit and they went down quick. Iron ore was another dangerous cargo. If you looked down the hold, it looked as though it was empty, but the weight was concentrated in the iron ore. An iron-ore ship, if she lasted two minutes after she was hit, you would be lucky. It was like hitting a bottle with a sledgehammer.

I was never hit, but I lost me father. He was torpedoed. He'd been in the first war and he was in the second. I was dead lucky. Once I swapped ships and the one I left went down the next trip. Another danger was mines all round the coast. They were acoustic mines that went off, so the hull of the ship had to be charged to reverse the magnetic field.

Once you had finished your job and she was tied up, you could get a sub off the captain out of your wages and go ashore. You used to get £8 a calendar month, it was always a calendar month. Well, four weeks is twenty-eight days and a calendar month is thirty-one, so they got three extra days out of you most months. You would leave an allotment to your wife or mother, and she could draw every week so much out of your wages. She had to go into Liverpool, into the shipping office, and present her card. So as you got to a port, you got a sub, you might get £2, something like that. Well, in a place like Buenos Aires, £2 turned into their money was quite good. And there was always a little bit of the cargo deliberately left in the hold, so that was a bit extra – there was always a character in every port who knew exactly when the time had come to give you the money and take the cargo. For instance, I was in the Mediterranean during the war, and this Army sergeant used to come on board, and if there was any cargo left over, he had Italians that he knew who would buy it. So there was always a little bit that way.

They paid you off in the pub and you could see the eyes in the bar watching every move. There was many a young fellow – we were all genned up to it – 'Eh son, do you want to go to a party?' He was whipped into a taxi, run out of town and robbed. Oh aye, there was a lot of that, and a lot of women lured men . . . 'Take me home,' and all this. It was all laid on, believe me. You had to be very careful.

The ladies of the port were very important, but also a serious problem, because if you contracted anything . . . well, they had the gravity tank. That was a tank with – what did they put in the water? – some kind of disinfectant, and if anyone got gonorrhoea, he had to . . . every day. It had a tube with a nozzle on it, and he had to . . . Well, he flushed himself out, until he got to a port where there was a doctor.

Conditions were terrible. We had to do all our washing in a bucket. You got a bucket and you had to beg hot water. You could give yourself a bath and then when you wanted to wash clothes, you washed them in a bucket. There was a toilet, 'the heads' they call them. Yeah, we had toilets . . . Once I was on a ship where we took on extra men in South America. We were going down to Punta Arenas, which is by Cape Horn. We took dockers with us and I had to build a platform out over the stern of the ship, deck it and build toilets on there. It was funny, because when we got in rough weather, you could see a fellow on the toilet and he is going up and down, maybe 40 foot! There were no women on board, so we were all right.

My first job at sea came in March 1940. Off we set in convoy, 'destination unknown'. Eventually, we broke away from the convoy and headed east. We had been going west, and the next thing – Gibraltar! We got down the Mediterranean and kept going, you know? Then we saw a ship coming in the distance behind us. We had a four-inch gun. It fired a shell eleven miles, and when we fired it, well, my ears have never been right since. We done a bit of practice. I had to man that because the carpenter and the boatswain are in the deck crew, you see? We run all the deck, everything on the deck.

So now, we didn't know what this ship in the distance was, and we loaded the gun. But fortunately it was an Australian destroyer. They come, told us to stop, and put a hundred men on board. Then we altered course and went up through the Dardanelles into the Black Sea. The hundred men were all hidden, and when we got up to the Danube, the big river that runs into the Black Sea, we went in there. There was a German ship up there and all, and she couldn't get out, but she was only a merchant ship and our gun was pointing right down at their quarters. So we tied up and at night these hundred men went up river to do some damage.

The next morning, because the ship was dead quiet, me and another fellow went ashore. We were in this dingy cellar, a kind of a pub. There was a ship blowing and we took no notice, but when we come out, the ship had gone. Our ship had gone! My first voyage!

So what the hell are we going to do? It's getting cold. We didn't know the language, had hardly any money. We were in Romania! Anyway, there was a soldier there and he was friendly enough, and he kept pointing. In the distance, I could see that our ship had anchored. We started to run down the bank, which was stupid, because by now we were up to there in water, and there was the German ship nearby. The fellow I was with said, 'Do you think they would let us stay?' Anyway, we seen a boat and we pinched it, got in this bloody boat and off we went, got swept down the bloody river. Yeah! And they played lines out for us, because we had to turn the boat, see, and row against the current to get to the gangway. If we had capsized, we would have had it.

CHAPTER FIVE

A Life in the Pens

In the 1890s Liverpool reached its so-called 'Golden Age'. It was the second largest port in the country after London, with eleven miles of docks in heavy use along the Liverpool shore of the Mersey alone. Steamers now outnumbered sailing vessels. The transatlantic ferries were 'floating palaces'. Cargo trade was global.

For most Liverpudlians it was a question either of answering the call of the sea or taking a job in the docks, neither sure-fire certain. Bill Smathers went down to the docks after coming out of the Army following the First World War. He was lucky to find work. Many soldiers arrived home to discover that jobs were scarce, life was hard and their bravery didn't count for much. Liverpool was a city with massive unemployment and a rising cost of living.

> Casual work . . . you were very lucky to get a job. And when you got a job, you had to work damn hard. Very hard indeed. In 1920 the bosses were the boss. If you said anything, then you were out. You couldn't afford to do that, you had to make a living.
>
> To get a job you had to go around and look for it when the ship docked. Your family didn't know where you were working. I'd go out about half past seven in the morning, might get a job or not. If there was anything doing up the north end, we'd jump the Overhead. That used to start from the Dingle and go right through to Gladstone Dock and finish at Seaforth Sands. People used to call it the Docker's Umbrella. If you weren't a smoker going in, God help you. You could swear the carriages were on fire, with the smoke coming out. They never had an accident.[1]

The Docker's Umbrella was the world's first electrically operated overhead railway and was designed by two prominent engineers, Sir Douglas Fox and J. H. Greathead. It ran from the Dingle in the south to Seaforth in the north, with a line underneath it for goods trains. Anyone could buy a ticket on the Docker's Umbrella and it offered an unbeatable view of miles of docklands and the Mersey beyond.

However, Tommy Walsh would take issue with Bill Smathers that the railway never had an accident:

> Yeah, the ground level and the overhead, my grandfather's

brother was killed on the ground level, underneath the
Docker's Umbrella, as we called it then. Under the overhead
railway there were two tracks and very, very heavy trains
used to go on there, loaded, from the south to the
north docks.

The Dingle station opened in 1896 and consisted of an
island platform 28 feet wide and 170 feet long. You entered
via a sloping subway from Park Road, which led to a booking
hall. After 1956 the building above ground was demolished
and replaced by a car showroom, but the subway and
platform remain and are used by Roscoe Engineering.

The Docker's Umbrella is part of the folklore of
Liverpool, and many people are still upset that they took it
down. Artist George Lund, born in the area in 1948, was
moved to Huyton in the early fifties – part of the Council's
'new broom' strategy that saw off the overhead railway. He
feels the loss even though he can't remember it.

But I do remember the big ships. And me dad used to tell
me mum it was a hive of hustle bustle of ships of all kinds in
the thirties and forties and so on. I know me mum and dad
used to go on the overhead railway, because my sister Jean
said, when she was a child, she used to go, and remembers
seeing all the big ships, the big passenger ships, the big
merchant ships, and it was bristling with life. I would have
loved to have been there. I would have been an artist doing
me drawings of all these ships, like Turner perhaps. It must
have been amazing. When the parents passed on – my mum
in 1998, my father in 2000 – I moved back here to Belvedere
Road. So, you know, the family have moved back here. I

went down to Roscoe Engineering and saw the remnants of the overhead railway. What I didn't remember of the area as a child I wanted to get a better picture of now that I've grown up, you see? They were telling me all about it, and how it was used as shelter during the Blitz. It helped with my art. You could feel lots of things about that place, that underground place, and my mind was going back to how it was.

For hardened docker Bill Smathers, feelings of nostalgia, even if he could find anything to feel nostalgic about, would have been a luxury he couldn't afford. The reality was:

You had to 'get on the stand', and if your face fitted, you got a job. You had to form a stand, inside the dock gates then. The boss would come out and put his hand on your shoulder. Well, when he done that, you were employed. You might get half a day's work, a day's work, or you might get a week's work, which was very, very seldom. Only the bosses, like the office staff, were employed permanent. The ordinary dockers were all casual workers.

This, the tally system, was the essence of employment in the docks, labelled, with compelling irony, 'casual'. You couldn't get a job in the docks without a tally. A tally was a ticket confirming employment often for half a day's work only. Dockers would turn up at the 'stands', an area demarcated for the purpose, at eight o'clock, and there'd be another scramble for work at one o'clock. It was an unfair, often demeaning system. Tallies were issued according to who you knew rather than what you could do, often who had bought the foreman a pint the night before. Sometimes, little Hitlers would throw the tallies at their disposal amongst the men, just to watch them fight for them. In the 1920s and '30s, when Bill Smathers was working, even if you got a job the money was poor.

> You got eight shillings a day. That's all and you had to work very hard for it . . . You had no mechanical gear . . . Everything was 'hand-balled'. The work was very hard and very dirty. You worked any kind of cargo that came along . . . grain, hides, sugar, tea, cotton, asbestos, carbon-black . . . You knew how to do it, so you got stuck into it. You were glad to do the day's work to get the money. There was no 'we're not working this, and we're not working that.' You just got stuck into it.
>
> You had the winch men – they were deck hands. In a discharging ship, you went down [into the hold] and you were discharging a cargo. If you had a loading boat, you were putting the cargo on, and all that cargo had to be packed, and packed tight, because if that ship went to sea and that cargo was a bit loose, in a rough sea the ship would 'turn turtle'. A lot of people were frightened of going down the ladder to discharge a ship. Well, I was used to working on the quay and working down below. It didn't make no difference. You had a straight ladder to go down . . . an iron ladder, and you had to go down a hell of a depth, down to the lower hold. People were frightened . . . and you worked in all weathers, rain didn't stop you, snow didn't stop you. You had to work.

In such a precarious system of employment, safety took a

back seat. For those who refused to overload a sling there was no work the next day, and when discharging cargo in bad weather, the cargo was more important than the man. Very often you took your life in your own hands.

Now the wet hides were quite good to work. Well, you stunk, you used to stink terrible, but there was no chance of anthrax.[2] If you worked dry hides and you got a cut on your hand, your first aid was, get a chew of thick-twist [tobacco], open the cut and spit in it. You never got a bad hand when you done that.

It didn't matter what insects you came across, you just carried on. There was beetles and rats and that sort of thing, yes – weevils. You took no notice of them. You just shook them. That was your lot. It was a job. When I didn't work on a ship, I worked for T. & J. Harrisons.[3] We were very, very slack and I got a job. And the rats! I've never seen rats like them. There were grey rats, black rats, black and white rats. I thought that's bloody funny. Well, when we got up at dinner time, there was a tray there and we had to walk in the tray, and wash our hands with disinfectant. Something funny here! Well, we got just on a fortnight's work in that hatch, and we got very curious about it. And then we found out there was plague in it. But they never told us there and then! When the ship finished, they sealed it up and fumigated it, and we had to report to hospital. But our thought was we got a fortnight's work. The ship came from Mendu, Calcutta.

But I went to one ship full of grain, and in them days they had the bucket-elevators and they used to make one hell of a mess. We used to call that a killer job, you got consumption with that. I was working at that . . . The main hatch was down and you had a piece of wood, used to call it the plough . . . you'd adjust it – the winches you see – and sit on it . . . Well, you could move a couple of ton of wheat [that way]. And I seen a black patch . . . Funny [I thought]. Anyway, I went back, took another load and I could see a fellow's head. Put my hands up and stopped the job, and I got cursed and blinded!

'What's wrong?'

I said, 'There's a stiff down here!'

Anyway, the boss came down, the police came down, and you couldn't have put a sling around him, because he'd have broken into pieces. So eventually I cleared him. We got a hatch cover, put him on and sent him up. He was a big Russian. He was about six foot tall with the back of his head smashed in. He must have been killed over in Russia, covered up with grain. We found the wooden spades.

[Afterwards] you just carried on the job. That was nothing [unusual]. You see, if a man got hurt or took a knock, you just put him aside until you could send him up . . . You stopped the job for a few minutes, or put him on a hatch cover, tied him on, and sent him up. He was always put to one side, sent up, but you carried on the job. You got used to that.

Cargo was loaded on and off boats from carts or wagons. Once upon a time the Dock Road would be full of carts, queuing for three or four days before the goods they were bringing to the docks could be transferred to a barge, or lighter, and then loaded. The booking systems couldn't cope. Bill Owen, born in 1900 in Toxteth, interviewed in

1986, recalls that his father 'had a team of horses and used to work fourteen hours a day for twenty-one shillings a week'. But his days weren't spent standing in queues down at the docks. In the early decades of the twentieth century, 'Every street had a shippon [cowshed] for cattle,[4] and stables,' Bill remembered, and carters like his father were engaged to bring hay into Liverpool to accommodate them. Horse-drawn carts were still in evidence in the 1960s. Recalls Billy Woods, born in the 1930s:

> An unforgettable sight in Great Homer Street, in the summer evenings, was the endless lines of empty carts being pulled by the most powerful horses in the world, being led by the weary carter back to their stables for a well-earned rest.

Cotton was the main cargo in the docks and the trade involved a whole range of specialist workers. Tom Best started work in the mid-1950s, at sixteen years of age, in a dock warehouse.

> I said the good thing was that you got a man's wages when you were sixteen, the bad thing was when any holidays came, Easter, Christmas, you were broke. They didn't have to pay holiday pay. That's how casual labour worked in them days, good money, but you didn't have many rights. What happened, you went down to Old Hall Street where they would come and pick the men. They had warehouses all over and they would say, 'You go to such a street, you go to that street.'
> From there I moved to the Lancashire Cotton Corporation, which was taken over eventually by

Courtauld's. My job was the bales, which would come in from all over the world, mostly American long bales, but there would also be Russian, Egyptian . . . One that was bought only every five years was South Sea Island Cotton and it was really silky.

I was in charge of a group of men. The bales were held by all kinds of bands, so you knocked one band off, cut the bale with a knife and took out a sample, which went down to the Cotton Exchange in Old Hall Street. They were looking at it for strength and texture, that sort of thing. Or they would send down a team of graders. I remember a French ship called *La Cordeleira*, it was one of the biggest cotton ships – 23,000 bales! So, there would be numerous people from the Cotton Corporation sampling and sending the samples to the Cotton Exchange. We would sort the bales out into blocks and give them a name, '54 Ajax' or something, an identity, so when the carter come in, he would have a docket to pick up 50 bales of Ajax to go to such and such a mill.

There was a Jewish guy in Liverpool, he used to trade in futures, in cotton that hadn't even grown then. He made a million in a day, and lost a million in a day. You bought bales at a certain price [before the cotton was grown] and if the crop was good, you were quids in, and if the crop was bad, well, you took a chance. Gambling really, they are selling what they don't have and taking a chance on quality and everything. Basically, I think they are in a winner's market, but you can have a bad year and be decimated.

So, I was the supervisor then of the gang that did all that and if there was any complaints, damaged bales, you know, water damage and what not, I would have to go to the various mills and report back to head office. An insurance claim would be made. Insurance was another big business in Liverpool. Everything was insured.

They had about ten different streets from north to south Liverpool with these big Victorian warehouses, six, seven, eight-storeys, and when Courtauld's took over the Liverpool Cotton Corporation, I went as manager of these. They didn't only house cotton. Bibby's were still there, Bibby's food stocks, cattle food, things like that.[5] We had to be licensed by the Watch Committee and Alderman Jack Braddock came along with other Aldermen – all were 'Aldermen' in them days, now they just call them councillors don't they? An Alderman was a freeman. If you were an Alderman, you were entitled to be buried in the local parish church. Free burial was one of the perks. So, the Watch Committee licensed me and then I had to be licensed by the Fire and Ballistics Department of the Police, because warehouses are full of flammable goods. They would have policemen who were near to retirement to go round and make sure that nobody carried matches – Fire Jacks they called them. Matches were forbidden in any warehouse, especially with cotton. They would just wait till people come down and pat their pockets. All the warehouses were insured by the Liverpool and Glasgow Fire Insurance Company. They were like the Fire Brigade, only they were a private insurance firm and had their headquarters in Bootle. The funny thing about that, if you were a warehouse keeper in Bootle, you didn't have to be licensed, but you did in Liverpool. Different authorities. Well, Bootle had their own council then.

In the dockers' all-male, macho world, muscle and loyalty to your comrades were what mattered. But Bill Smathers denies the reputation dockers have for rabble rowsing.

I didn't drink them days. You didn't have much money for drink. If you went on the drink, your family went very short. Them days you lived in the pawn shop. Things were pawned, you got money and lived on it. Then, if you got any wages, you got your things out. And so it went on. The same process carried right on, right through the piece. If you was working drunk, you'd be cleared out. Wouldn't tolerate it. Your life's at stake, do you know what I mean? If you're a docker, you're working down below hatch – that hatchman has got your life in his hands. If he makes one false move, you could be dead.

Seldom you'd see a fight aboard a ship. If it was a squabble between two men, they'd go outside. You'd form a ring and they had a fight then, but not at work. The bosses wouldn't tolerate it. You'd be cleared out immediately. I never seen a fight inside the Dock Estate.

Frank Smith, born in 1934, worked in his parents' café on the Dock Road, which they opened in 1950, and had a privileged view of the unique docker culture.[6]

My father and mother opened up the little café on the corner. That was in 1950. That was Frank's Café No. 1. Food was on the ration then. Me dad started the business with £200 and we went from there – half past five in the morning to half past six at night, six days a week. If I had any spare time, I'd go and watch Everton Red Triangle, or I'd play football of a night, or go jujitsu in the Cellar in Catherine Street.

When the ships docked here, the *Brittanic*, the *Empress of Canada*, they all had plenty of people on them. You'd get all the trade all the while. The atmosphere was terrific. Everyone was a comedian. Liverpool was full of characters. Everyone was working in the fifties. Everyone had a few bob to spend. The dockers were a law to themselves. They were all different characters. They had a code – all for one, one for all. Backed one another up. Right or wrong as well. Comradeship it was. They could have been an army. That's what upset the employers of the day.

There was no anger among the dockers because they always stuck together and no one was doing anything they shouldn't. You dare go over the picket line or cross the dock gate? Oh no, it never happened. I don't think it did, anyhow.

The docks were full of humour. Today's not a patch on what you had then. Things like, if someone was telling a story, and they thought he was telling lies, they used to turn their hats upside down. You didn't have to say anything. That's what it meant. Whatever it was, they had their own code or their own sayings. Everyone had a nickname. If you had a man who'd got married three times, he'd be 'Blessed art thou among women'. Or if you had a docker who bought the *Irish Independent*, you'd call him the 'Educated Docker'. They had names for everyone.

It was busy in the café then. The most common food order was a bacon sandwich. Every docker liked a bacon sandwich, or a sausage sandwich with black pudding. They drank tea by the gallon – drank air by the gallon sometimes – they were all good drinkers.

Maybe twenty or thirty would come in at a time. They'd

read the paper, talk football, but you had fellas who run for
Liverpool Harriers. They had their own football team – they'd
play for the Pen, as they called it – and you had professional
boxers down here. We had a lot of billiard players. They
were fit men, had to be at that time.

Famously, when Arthur Askey was asked why Liverpool had
produced so many comedians, like Tommy Handley, Billy
Bennett, Robb Wilton, Billy Matchett, Ken Dodd and Beryl
Orde, he said, 'You've got to be a comic to live in Liverpool.'
And it was humour that kept spirits high against all manner
of exploitation, whether in the docks or elsewhere. The
humour of Jimmy Tarbuck and Tom O'Connor stems from
the docks. Tom O'Connor came from Bootle and his father
worked in the docks. Harmless, witty word play is at the
heart of it – a pair of spectacles might be referred to as
'horn-rimmed testicles'. A man called Richard Richards
would be Dickie Twice: 'I said, "Mam, what's this Dickie
Twice?" And she said, "Well, it's his name, Dickie Twice."
"Oh," I said, "he's Mr Twice," and she says, "No, no. It comes
from his name," and I said, "What do you mean?" She said,
"His mother – great imagination – called him Richard
Richards."' Such was one little girl's introduction to it.

The nicknaming of dockers was an extension of this, or
vice versa. We have Frank Shaw to thank for recording
some of them. There was 'Sam Goldwyn', who was always
saying, 'Lissen lads, I'll put yer in the picture,' and 'Lino',
who was always 'on the floor' (short of money). 'Harpic'
earned his because he was clean around the bend; 'Pontius
Pilate' because he was always washing his hands. 'The
Parish Priest' worked every Sunday (overtime pay for

Sundays was so high it was called the 'Gold Nugget'), and 'Wonder Boy', a looter, was forever looking at cargo, saying, 'I wonder what's in this, I wonder what's in that.'

It was dangerous to pick up anything idly in the docks. With labour so cheap and plentiful, any excuse for debarment was taken. As Shaw says, 'Dockers were treated like dogs, which bred a deep resentment still felt today by their prosperous grandsons. All they had to sell was their muscle.'[7] But their exploitation also bred the humour that kept their spirits high.

Like so much in this city, Liverpool humour is essentially tribal, much of it unintelligible to outsiders until some level of integration is achieved. For example, who would know that 'getting off at Edge Hill', the last stop before the tunnel into Lime Street on the Manchester–Liverpool line, Britain's first, is actually a reference to pulling out on time in the sexual act, known elsewhere as the rhythm method?

Local references aside, Phil Key found that when he arrived in the city more than forty years ago he wasn't always sure whether what was being said was a joke or something abusive:

The people were very friendly, but you had to get used to the sense of humour, which can be very aggressive. You know, they just insult you in an amusing way and as long as you could give as good as you got you were all right.

Mike Berry, who was born in Liverpool in 1938, went the other way, leaving for middle class, conservative Tunbridge Wells and found himself in hot water:

You will appreciate that Liverpool's humour is robust. A lot of the verbal abuse was almost terms of endearment. In this part of the world (I've lived in Tunbridge Wells now for twenty-two years) I've made some big mistakes by assuming that people would know I was joking and then realising they didn't. But that's life.[8]

CHAPTER SIX

Macho Liverpool

In spite of Bill Smathers' protest that dockers couldn't afford to drink, Liverpool men did, just as Glasgow men did, and working-class men everywhere did. It was the great palliative and, in a tragic and largely invisible way, the final degradation. Often the wages were handed out in a pub and stayed there, and often the men who paid the wages had an interest in the pub. Money went on a circular trip back into the pockets of the masters. It was one play of the money trick which did for the working classes.[1] In 1874 there were 1,929 pubs, 384 beer houses and 272 off-licences listed in Liverpool.

I can remember in the Dingle, where Ringo came from, in

> every pub about 9.30 p.m., everybody would start singing.
> Every night of their lives these Scousers would sing . . . It is a
> fact that Celts are given to drink and song . . . it was Irish
> Country in a way.[2]

Fair enough, but when the question is asked, who were the
worst drinkers, it is always the Finns.

> All pubs had to be closed at 10 p.m., but Catholic clubs
> didn't, they could stay open.[3]

This is true. The Catholic clubs were an important source
of revenue for the Church, which was far more active in
the community than it is today. But in the early days
pubs stayed open a lot longer, as Bill Owen, born in
1900, recalled:

> Opened six o'clock in the morning till eleven at night – that's
> when they were open! That got done away with as I were in
> my schooldays. But six o'clock in the morning, if they had
> the money, they used to go into the pub and get a drop o'
> gin or whisky for three ha'pence (that's a penny ha'penny).
> And then I used to go in. They sent me with all the cans. I
> would be with the old feller [his father]. Go and get a can o'
> tea made . . . the hot water on it . . .

There were some seventy pubs in Scotland Road itself, and
another seventy in Great Homer Street. It was difficult to
avoid a drink, and pubs, still very much a male preserve
before the Second World War, were the place for a bit of
self-expression, humour and song after a frustrating day of

no work, or one of hard physical graft. It was a macho scene, as Eileen Newman recalls:

My dad was quite a character, a leader. I've been in pubs with him singing and getting a real singsong going. They didn't go anywhere else, they all knew each other in this pub, the Glass House on Vauxhall Road. There were a few other pubs that they used to go to, but they were all on Vauxhall Road.

I used to wonder why there were pubs on every corner. Was it just that everybody drank a lot, like my dad? When I was older, after visiting the Maritime Museum, I realised that these were all houses and hotels and places where people from Ireland and other countries stayed on their way to America. They had rooms where you would buy a bed for a fee. You didn't have the room and you didn't have the bed permanently, somebody else might come in.

His father was on the boats. He went off to America and didn't come back for five or six years, but by then I think the mother had become so wasted in trying to bring up six children with little or no money coming in that sometimes she turned to drink to cope. When I remember her, she seemed very old and never moved much. There were women in Liverpool who wore their long white hair up in a bun and they would have long dresses on and always this black shawl, which went over their hair and wrapped round their body and tied at the back. They were called 'Mary Ellen' for some reason, just older women. She never moved from this chair at all.

Frank Vaudrey was brought up in Walton, next to Walton Park.

My dad's locals were the Hermitage and the Crown. It's knocked down now, the Crown was a very rough pub. My granddad was cock of the pub until he was about seventy. Six foot four, he had been a stoker, chief stoker on many big ships. He had a big scar from here to here on his neck after being stabbed in a fight one night. Those days you'd see fights and some would go in the field and have a go, just the two of them.

My dad would have four pints and then sometimes he'd go outside and have a game of pitch and toss. You have two coins, you flick 'em up . . . There was always a lot of fights over 'em. Every pub had a runner, who would take the bets. He would stand by the corner; take yer bets from races that were going on the radio.

Bill Owen's memories, two generations earlier, were not dissimilar:

There used to be some tough customers. There were these coal yards by us. There used to be some rough fellows – seen battles, you know? Oh aye. I've seen them coming over the rail in Harold Street, off Maynard Street, where you go up steps. There's railings on houses above. I've seen police get knocked over them railings. Oh yeah. Oh aye. You'd be knocking about there, Saturday night like. They was drunk, Saturday night. They lived for Saturday night.

And the gambling. Oh aye, at the corner many a time I'd a ha'penny to keep douse [look-out]. If they were playing cards up the court here, I'd go at the end of the street and keep douse and wait. If I'd seen anything coming – the police or anything – I'd shout back and they'd pick the cards up. Gambling wasn't allowed then. There was no gambling allowed then in pubs, either.

Pitch and toss was on Dock Road and they used to have a belt man to keep them back, off the fellow that was tossing . . . There was a big school – all the dockers. As many as fifty people . . . There used to be a lot of money changing hands . . . Well, a lot of money in them days was if there's a few pounds knocking about.

Men, of course, had a few bob – they're in the pub, you see, and coming home drunk. Oh, aye, it was a terrible time for women. Many a time I've had to run when my old father came home drunk. Many a time he's come in of a Saturday night and said something . . . Oh, we'd be off for our lives wi' him chasing after us along Chatsworth Street! I used to finish up wi' my grandmother. She was a knocker-up.[4]

When it comes to gambling, of course, Liverpool has the great twentieth-century gambler dynasty, as Mavis O'Flaherty reminded me, although their money has underwritten Liverpool in the most enlightened way ever since:

Well, I was talking to a friend of mine, used to live at the back of me. He was a printer for John Moores. I don't know, but I think one of the brothers had the idea of starting this gambling business – you know, the coupons. And it took off in a big way, and then from there he went on to have the mail order business, then the catalogue business. They had quite a few places. I mean, there is still a lot of shopping

> through them, but just over the road here, when you're
> going along, you'll see a tower with a clock on it. That was
> their main place for the pools.

This is the *other* Liver Pool, the Littlewood's Pool, the hard reality pool that helped revive, through sponsorship of the arts, the inspirational qualities of the original Pool, as we'll see later.

John Moores was the son of a bricklayer who liked a drink and died at forty-seven. John became a messenger boy at fourteen at Manchester Post Office, studied at the Post Office School of Telegraphy and at sixteen joined the Commercial Cable Company as a junior operator. In 1922 he was stationed at Liverpool, where with two friends from his Manchester days, Colin Askham and Bill Hughes, he developed the idea of the football pool from an original idea of John Jervis Barnard, a Birmingham man who failed to make it work. They called theirs Littlewood's after Colin Askham, an orphan whose original name it was.

Each invested £50 in the company, which started up in a small office in Church Street, Moores handing out the coupons to the footballing public himself. At first the trio's version didn't work, either. When it failed, they went to Hull and tried it there. The response was even worse, and Askham and Hughes gave up. Moores might have given up too had it not been for his wife, who reportedly said, 'I would rather be married to a man who is haunted by failure than one haunted by regret.'

John Moores responded by creating a system that prevented cheating, which had apparently been the snag, and by the 1930s he was a millionaire. He turned to mail order and later to retail, founding the Littlewood's department stores. By the end of 1939 there were twenty-five stores across the UK, and over fifty by 1952. By then he was a very rich man indeed.

But gambling has a long history in Liverpool, and the gambling fraternity of the eighteenth century had a meatier predilection than filling in coupons. Gamecocks belonging to the 11th Earl of Derby, with razor sharp artificial spurs attached to their legs, displayed in the Liverpool Museum, give an idea of the lure of the local cockpits at Aintree, and in Cockspur Street, behind Tithebarn Street.[5] Anyone who keeps cocks, as I do, and knows the damage that can be dealt with natural spurs, will be startled at the barbarism of this entertainment. But, as Albert Joseph Kane, born in Liverpool in 1916, remembered:[6]

Scousers love a gamble. As a newsagent, my mother loved and understood horse racing along with the rest of the family. The family had interests in bookmaking, and had a number of street-corner runners from whom my elder brother and I would collect the clock bag at the appointed times. Attempts were made by the runners to delay giving the bags on time, hoping, of course, to push in a couple of bets for which they already had the result. This was a continual battle of wits as one trick after another was tried to beat the book. It was part of our education and helped us to become wide awake.

When it comes to a gamble, Liverpool was unique in having the lock fields. These so-called fields are the areas of land that lie between the various locks and docks. They were a Mecca for gamblers. On Sunday afternoons you could gamble on almost anything except the stock exchange. There were football matches at half a crown a man, there were bare-fist fighters, boys swimming races in the docks, card games of all types, pitch and toss, picture and blank, but best of all for the boys was the rat catcher. For a penny he would sell a live rat from his leather bag, which contained many rats. Many men had dogs on leashes, and the dogs were paired off for the purpose of killing the rat when it was released. The men formed a ring and the dogs were held at an equal distance from the centre, where the rat catcher would release the rat. The dogs would be freed, and the dog that caught the rat was the winner. Bets of course were placed on the dogs. If the boys' mothers had known, they would have skinned them. It had to be experienced, it was super entertainment.

Molly Monaghan, whom I met at the Toxteth Community Centre in Upper Mann Street, with friends Anne Clarence, Meg Whitehead, Mary Wilcox, Edith Flanagan, Pat Maloney, and the late Theresa Connolly, took this up immediately:

The dogs were more popular than the races for entertainment and betting. The men mostly used to pitch and toss, and had to run when the police come. The men were hanging round the corners because they had no work, and the bookies in the back alleys, they would run when the police come. They used to run through people's houses to get away from the police.

I remember Bill. We used to stand on the terrace and soon as we heard them, [we'd shout,] 'Watch it!' and he would run through our house and out the back door. One day he ended up in the bedroom!

At first, these women dismissed the violent aspect of the macho culture as nothing very significant.

Oh the men, the men would fight, probably through drink, I don't know. You did see that, but it was rare.

You would find that the men would fight but it would be man to man, and they would shake hands when they'd finished, or go for a drink afterwards.

No gang violence or anything, not round here. Oh there was later on, the Toxteth riots [1981]. But no gangs no, because all the kids were well behaved in those days and brought up with one another. We used to go round the back here, down in Mann Street [a dead-end alley off Brassey Street] and they used to form a ring and we would watch them two fight and then it would be finished with. We would go into school and say, 'There's a fight at four,' and we would all go down to see them fight.

While we were talking, I noticed a woman at the far end of the table keeping her own counsel, and asked her who she was.

Anne Clarence. I was born in 1918. My father was a seaman from Demerara[7] in British Guyana, South America. He came

> through [to Liverpool] and decided to stay, but he didn't last
> long. He was murdered in Dexter Street. February 1918.

Dexter Street is just south of Upper Parliament Street. I was aware that pimps made it their business in the nineteenth and early twentieth centuries to waylay foreign sailors, often lured by women decoys. The open-mouthed interest of the other ladies at the table indicated that the murder of their friend's father was news to them. I asked Anne to tell us what happened.

> I've never heard any stories [about it], but I was born in May
> and I think he was murdered in the February or March.

So you never knew him?

> No. So, you want something juicy? I'll give you another bit. I
> spoke to the man that done it, when I was about twenty-
> eight. He was a seaman. There was a club in Parliament
> Street called, I can't remember what it was called – George
> Wilkie had it – and that's where I met him. George Wilkie
> said, 'I've got someone for you to see.' And when he came
> over, the first thing he said to me, 'I owe you a big, big debt
> . . .' And I said, 'Well, pay me now.'

Anne cast us all back almost a century to dark, nineteenth-century Liver-or-your-life-pool, where, as local journalist Hugh Shimmin wrote: 'The transition from a coarse word or a ribald jest to a kick, from a poker to a knife, is made with alarming rapidity.'

On a Bank Holiday Monday, 3 August 1874, Richard

Morgan, a porter, and his young wife Alice take off across the Mersey for a day in New Ferry on the Wirral, its seaside attractions a welcome change to bare survival at 10 Court, Leeds Street, the district just north of the centre of the city that we have already visited, including Crosshall, Addison Street and Deadman's Alley. They return to the Pier Head at 9 p.m. and are met by Richard's brother, Samuel, who is their neighbour at 12 Court.

The group of three walk carelessly up Chapel Street and Tithebarn Street, one of the original seven streets of Liverpool, which lead from dockland hope to slum-land despair in the space of a few short minutes. In Chapel Street they stop at a pub for a last drink. Continuing their journey, they pass the Exchange Station and cross entries to Pall Mall, Highfield and Smithfield Streets on the north side of the street. Richard and Alice are clearly still in holiday mood. The latter darts into a tobacconist shop at 79 Tithebarn Street, run by a man with whom they'd spent time at New Ferry that afternoon. In those days, the next street to cross was Lower Milk Street, where, on the corner, a group of lads are gathered outside a beer shop.

Samuel walks past them, unaware of anything untoward, but as Richard and Alice approach, one of the lads pulls at Richard's sleeve and asks for money for a drink. Richard responds by suggesting that if he wants money for beer, he should work for it. The lad replies that indeed he does work – 'knocking down such men as you!'

Alice intervenes on Richard's behalf, and it looks for a moment as if the situation has passed – 'It's a good job you've got a woman with you,' says one. But a second later Richard is hit behind the ear and knocked out cold.

As Michael Macilwee, who reported the event with the advantage of detailed research of trial records, wrote: 'He never spoke again or uttered a single sound.'[8]

Richard's brother Samuel got stuck in and felled the attacker, but another of the lads whistled and more joined the fray, kicking Richard on the ground and kicking Alice, who was by then beside her husband, trying to help him. Samuel knocked two or three of the original assailants down, but Richard was targeted again and again, his body used as a football by these youths, who reportedly kicked him forty feet across to the other side of Tithebarn Street.

Still Alice weighed in, but was struck and deafened by a blow to her head. A crowd formed and, incredibly, no one did anything to stop the murder. It was said some even egged the assailants on, one woman reportedly shouting, 'Give him it, give him it!'

It was around twenty minutes before a policeman appeared, by which time Richard was long dead and his attackers had melted away into nearby streets. Samuel found one of them and pummelled him, but the man escaped. Later he pursued three more of them, but one threatened him with a knife and Samuel was grabbed from behind and dragged away. He survived to tell the tale.

Cornermen were a feature of life, the result of desperate unemployment and particularly of the casual employment method in the docks. Where else could young men go? They spent their time lolling on corners by a beer shop or pub, and things were bound to kick off sometimes.

But this was no normal brawl. Twelve years after the killing of Richard Morgan, a journalist claimed to have witnessed the whole episode, and said that when the police arrived, the youths shouted 'High Rip! High Rip!', a rallying call which identified them with one of Liverpool's notorious organised gangs.

In an article about executions in the *Liverpool Citizen* (16 May 1888), the 1875 hanging of two of those who attacked Richard Morgan – John McCrave and Michael Mullin – was described as 'one of the heaviest blows ever levelled at the Empire of the High Rip gang'. The murder became so infamous that it was perfectly credible for Ramsey Campbell's hero in *Creatures of the Pool* also to offer a tourist trail called 'the High-Rip Trip' along the docks.

It is possible, however, that the Victorian press was liable to lay every sort of violence at the door of the High-Rip Gang, especially as, a decade after the Tithebarn Street killing, the gang was without doubt responsible for another dockland murder, just as appalling.

Late in the evening of Sunday, 5 January 1884, two Spanish sailors – Exequiel Rodriques Nunez and Jose Jiminez – were walking along Regent Road after having spent time at the Madrid Café in Pitt Street, heart of the docker-immigrant ghetto in the centre of town.

Jiminez's ship, *Magallenes*, was docked in nearby Canada Dock. They had walked northwards out of Vauxhall towards Bootle. Regent Road runs parallel to the docks still and meets Blackstone Street opposite Bramley Moor Dock. On the corner of Blackstone Street lolled a group of five men. As Jiminez walked past, one of them punched him without warning. Jiminez ran as fast as he could, back down Regent Road in the direction of his ship, leaving his friend Nunez to the mercy of the gang.

Punched, chased, attacked with belts and kicked, Nunez

made his way only as far as adjacent Fulton Street, where one of the gang found him and shouted, 'Here he is. Knives, boys, knives!'

Again Nunez somehow managed to escape them, running up Blackstone Street under the railway arch into Boundary Street. Finally, he was captured and stabbed 'in the lower part of the neck', where it meets the collarbone.

All this was carried on in near total darkness and when a policeman arrived it was thought, despite the profuse bleeding, that Nunez was a drunk. He was loaded into a wheelbarrow, and it was only under the lights of Great Howard Street that it was seen just how badly, indeed fatally, the man was wounded.

Various members of the gang were later arrested and at their trial evidence was given by witnesses as young as ten, eleven, twelve and fourteen. It is amazing today not only that children so young gave evidence in court but that they should have been up and about in these dark and dangerous streets after 10 p.m.

Shock would be wholly out of place, however, for this is the hardest dockland area of the city, where anything goes. Two of the gang were hung in nearby Kirkdale Prison. The hangman was Bartholomew Binns from Dewsbury in Yorkshire. He arrived at the gaol on the Sunday afternoon drunk, having stopped off for a tipple on leaving the train. After being shown to his accommodation, he fell into a deep sleep. When the warders tried to wake him, he threatened to hit them. A policeman had to be called to calm him down. It wasn't the best start to an execution.

At the hanging, the heart of one of the murderers failed to stop beating for some ten minutes after his neck broke.

Binns was upbraided and, shortly afterwards, questions were raised in the House of Commons about his suitability as a hangman. Such were the gruesome, primitive pre-occupations of English law.

The gang's name, apparently, came from eighteen-year-old Thomas Gibbons, a self-employed fireman of Hopwood Street, just a stone's throw from where Nunez was done for. Gibbons, a member of a notorious local family, had already appeared in court as an accomplice of one of the Spaniard's murderers, one Michael McLean, who some say was the original founder of the High-Rip Gang. Gibbons had come off well in court because he was seen by the judge to have been under the influence of McLean. The judge made a bad mistake. Not long afterwards, Gibbons badly beat up a sailor, John Peterson, whose chest he almost crushed while hitting him repeatedly around the head. When bystanders tried to break it up, Gibbons is said to have shouted, 'We'll High Rip them!' and attacked a female witness, chasing her into her house. When he was arrested, it took five policemen to restrain Gibbons, and even when they had him, he shouted repeatedly that he would 'High Rip' any witnesses against him.

With precedent such as this, it is no surprise that there is also a history of drink-fuelled domestic violence in Liverpool. But in the twentieth century at least, if you were lucky, there was ready-made community support, as Tommy Walsh recalls of his parents' corner shop.

I now know, didn't know at the time, that my mother was a social worker as well as a shopkeeper. There wasn't such a thing, she wouldn't recognise that, but I can remember one

particular woman [who] used to come in – she was known
as May, or Auntie May to a lot of them – and she would say,
'Have you heard how Liverpool got on?' . . . if Liverpool had
lost, that woman went into hiding until the following day
because she would get battered. And then there was
another girl, Annie, who I know very well. She became a
very dear friend of mine, and her husband used to batter
her, too – on the street. Out on the street, you know,
punching her all over the place. That was fairly normal. I can
remember as a child watching this, observing this, and of
course it didn't dawn on me for years what was going on.
Annie would run into our corner shop, no word would be
exchanged. My mother would lift the flap of the counter and
Annie would run into the room at the back. Jack would
arrive with the belt in his hand. 'Have you seen Annie?' 'No,
Jack,' and he would go looking for her, and when everything
had calmed down, she would come out.

Now let me just add on to that. Jack, Annie's husband,
eventually jumped ship in New York, which was fairly
normal. As you know, the ships went between New York
and Liverpool all the time, and I was hearing regularly, from
a number of seamen, 'Saw Jack.' But Annie had no idea that
he was still alive and she was eventually declared a single
woman, and she got married, all above board. But I knew he
was in New York. This woman committed bigamy, but
natural justice now has taken over.

Not until the early 1970s did proper sanctuaries exist for
battered wives. Josie Burger was born in 1941 in Handel
Street, Liverpool 8 [Princes Park]. 'Handel Street was
named after the musician. My mother and father were both

pianists. Always had a piano in the house, a big black ebony piano.' I met Josie at her house in Granby Street, where she told me a harrowing story of domestic abuse.

Mohammed come from Sheffield. He had five shops here, and he started getting together with a couple of English fellows and started drinking very heavy. And he got very violent. 'Dr Taylor,' I said, 'if I don't get away, if you don't help me . . . I've got a knife under the pillow and I'm going to stab him when he comes in drunk again, and shaking all of us around and frightening the children. I really am!'

So he said, 'I'm going to give you these tablets. They're only very mild.' I said, 'I don't want them.' He said, 'You'll have to go into a hostel.' So I went into a hostel on Falkner Street, number 44 Falkner Street. It's still there, two houses by the women's hospital. It's changed now, the students have it. The hostel was all women. Young women, my age. I think I was about twenty-eight then. Nina was four or five, the eldest was ten, and the boy will have been six. No boys were allowed unless they were new born, so he went with my father.

You had to take a plate, spoon, tea towel, toothbrush, toothpaste, cup each. My friend Valerie helped me to take them down, sneak in the house and get them. She's dead now, cancer; her son still comes to me for a cup of tea.

Valerie went with me. The warden's name was Mrs Broom – Pat Broom – and there was a Mr Broom. I liked them from the minute I shook hands with them, and then I got in there. There was four women in that room, four women with their children. One was actually having a baby and she already had a little child. But you don't care. You're going to sleep without getting slapped in the face by a drunk. You don't care. This girl with the baby says, 'Look after your toothbrush and toothpaste, because she's handy is that one.'

I says, 'Where's my soap powder and toothpaste?' Everything gone. She was a terror, you had to look after yourself. I took her by the hair. You had to look after your children and yourself and their stuff. I was with my two girls in a big, long bedroom. They were in a single bed and I was in a single bed. Sometimes my youngest daughter got in with me.

Husbands never get told where you are. It doesn't come out in court, but somebody told on a girl called Carol Burns – I still talk to her now – and he tipped boiling fat on her head. She was a pretty little girl, but she ended up all right. Her hair grew back, but she was very, very nervous of him. She's well alive now, and he's dead! He was the only one that got in, and he got thrown down the stairs by me and another woman. Mr Broom come and he says, 'Well, there's nothing left to do here,' because we had thrown him down the stairs! He just said, 'Get out!' But if husbands did come, the police come immediately.

I was there for months, I loved it. Up early in the morning, getting the breakfast ready for the ones that worked, radio on, all the children off to school or off to nursery, and then you go back, make the beds, clean the rooms, sweep the rooms, clean the bath and clean the toilet, which was nice, don't have that now. Nice, had the music on, talking. She was very fair, Mrs Broom, very, very fair. And Mr Broom never come near you at all, only if you needed him, you know?

Eventually, Josie disentangled herself from Mohammed and married again, happily, settling in a house in Granby Street, where she lives to this day.

In a culture dominated by drink and machismo, it took some guts to opt out, but it helped if you had the character (and stature) of centenarian George Cross:

My father, he was an Evertonian and his brother was a Liverpudlian, and they nearly came to blows on a Saturday in the pub, drinking the beer, you know. I remember the eldest brother, he was telling us about me father and how me mother, she wanted to buy a quarter ham. She used to cut all the fat off and save it for me father. But he wouldn't know what he was eating, he'd come home that drunk. [Getting religion] was through a man he met. They got talking and [this man] got him to go to the mission, and me father was a changed man. He abstained and was a changed man. Yes, and we all followed suit.

I remember one time I come home and we heard a knock on the knocker, and we knew that knock. It was the minister or the missioner from the Mission. It was a scatter match – we didn't want to listen to him, you know? But this time I couldn't get out quick enough, so I got underneath the couch. I had just turned seventeen years of age, and I had to get underneath the couch. This missioner, he was a big, six-foot Irishman, and he was just in the doorway. He would enquire about all the brothers and me mother and father, and invite us to the mission hall on a Sunday, and he used to go out then. But this time he sat down on the sofa with me underneath, and what with nerves I wanted to cough – I didn't want to cough, but the cough wanted to cough! If there was a place called Purgatory I was in it until he went.

Came the day I played football for the Mission and it was a condition of playing that you had to go to the Mission on a Sunday night. I remember we went on a Sunday night, all the football team, and we would talk about who played a good game and who had likely to be dropped the following Saturday, and the only time we listened was when the choir sang (they had some lovely girls there, you know).

Then a minister from Northumberland came down to preach for a week. He was called 'the little man who could move the miners'. I remember him talking. It was the first time I listened to anyone, and he spoke about being a Christian. He said, 'If you want to live a good life, a happy life, then there is nothing like being a Christian. You can either accept Christ your Saviour, or don't. But if you do, you will find out your life will be changed.' And I thought it was a good challenge, so I raised my hand at the end of the service, indicating that I was going to become a Christian, and from that time onwards I've never looked back.

When I joined the flour mill, there was one man who used to go down with the betting slips and all that, and he offered me one. He threw the book at me with slips in and I give it him back. He said, 'They all buy them,' and I said, 'I don't, I'm a Christian,' and word went one to another, and he was going to do an awful lot to me. He wanted to challenge me to have a fight outside the firm, so I took it on, and he come to me later and said, 'We will call it.' And we became the best of friends.

Again, when I got called up for the Army, I got called up at Chester, and I remember all soldiers together. This was 1939. There was one chap, he was giving the pay out about ministers and about Sunday-school teachers, and I couldn't stick it no longer. I said, 'Hey mate, I'm one of them you're talking about,' and he shut up. A chap said to me the next morning, 'I'm glad you spoke up last night, but to be quite honest, you don't look like a Christian, you look like a thug!'

I was well broad you know. There was one time during the war, one of our chaps out of our unit, he came home drunk as a lord, and I said, 'Drunk again, Andy?' And he was swearing and called me everything. He said, 'If you think yourself clever, come out and fight.' We was in bed, and I didn't know what to do. He was quite a big chap, but I knew I could handle him if I wanted to. I thought on, 'Soft hand turneth away wrath,' so I did answer him. But in the morning when he was sober, he come over and he apologised to me, and we became the best of friends.

When I asked George whether Christianity had made things difficult for him, he replied, 'Oh aye. But I have had a wonderful life, you know.' With his massively strong physical presence, even at a hundred years of age, and impressive pragmatic spirituality, George is unusual to say the least, but not unique. It is possible to find others in the masculine world of Liverpool docklands with the nerve to unearth their feminine, spiritual or artistic side. I was attracted in particular to the story of William Herbert Bannister, born in 1890 in a pub in Lawton Street in the heart of the city. After his father died at forty-six, William and his mother moved to Benson Street, off Renshaw Street, where his mother took a boarding house.[9]

We were in the boarding house in Benson Street for a few years, and then she took a chip shop in Kensington. She had to move there because she had varicose veins badly, and she hadn't the help, and she lost most of her money from the public house – all of her money. Then we came back to the Benson Street boarding house and we were there quite a while. [In between] there was a period when my mother took a cook's job in a public house in Great Newton Street, off Pembroke Place.

I was in the pub with her. I lived there, and I was in the chip shop, too. I used to chip the potatoes. In the pub, I used to mix with the customers more than anything else. Real lads. My [new] father was always showing me off, as he could put the tip of my head on one chair and the tip of my feet on another and I would be stiff. He was quite proud of a thing like that.

[Occasionally] he would go out . . . to the Isle of Man, probably several times over the years, and be two or three months there without coming back. He was a knockout man. He'd punch you up if [there was] any trouble in the pub. Bullet head and short-cropped hair, and he didn't mind as long as he was first to hit. And his son [William's step-brother] was similar. He had a fight with his father and that was the last we saw of him.

Also, he kept pigeons, and bantam cocks and hens to fight. And we had a goat. Used to eat the pigeons. My father got hold of their heads and screwed their neck and drew them down, and then my mother would bake pigeon pie. I could choose what to eat. No notice was taken [if food was left uneaten on the plate.] Everything was free [and easy] – I could ask for a second helping. I was [not expected to hold my knife and fork in a certain way or sit in a particular place at table.] I could leave the table when I wanted to. We had no restrictions whatever. I was never checked for anything I did in the way of table manners. I just learned them myself.

My mother was a very easy person to talk to, very knowledgeable, she was. She was always attentive and looking after me, you know, but there was no loving or anything like that shown. Not a word. She had her own troubles, I think. With the bar, and the barmaids, there'd be pilfering . . . drinking the stock. It was a strain. But I never had any worries.

With my father I had no dealings at all. He just wanted to be the big head or the clever man. There was no family life really. No family life. I was well looked after, had good food, and clothes. I had plenty of bread and milk, and plenty of rice puddings and all the fruits. But I was left on my own. They had no future for me at all.

There were no books in the house. The only outings I ever had was the yearly trip to the Isle of Man with my mother only. A fortnight in a boarding house in Douglas. My father had his own devices. He went to the races a lot. He bet. He went with a party of friends who had as much, or more, money than he had.

I went to church every Sunday with my mother. Methodist. In the evening. Father never went. I went to Sunday school in Lowhill, St Jude's, by myself.

As a child, I never played games . . . I was mostly fond of female company, even as a child . . . I never had any rough games as a child. There were more girls about . . . You might get girls up to sixteen, although I was only perhaps eight or nine, joining in, for the fun of the thing . . . one was a little Chinese girl. We had a bad lad at the time and he used to – he used . . . [William stopped there.]

I went to what they called the Old Star cinema to see *Face at the Window* – this was drama, live drama. *Face at the Window* was so creepy that when I went a second time, when the cellos went hmmm, and the face came at the window with green lights, I'd do this [hides his eyes], even though I'd been to see it once. I was fifteen when I began as a choirboy in the Mission to Seamen in Hanover Street. My voice never broke at all. I was good at singing, but I hadn't the brains to commercialise on it. So it went.

I used to go to the service in the Central Hall for years . . . I went out in the evenings . . . and I'd meet one or two friends, and we used to wander the streets, singing in harmony – we all had good voices – we were all choirboys, or choirmen.

I had two sets of company [as a young man] – these and more intimate friends. We used to go to [each other's] houses and every evening through the week was a party sort of thing – a singsong. One could play the piano and then we would join in – tea and sandwiches at different homes . . . even while I was in my apprenticeship. [William was an apprentice engineer after running messages for the now defunct Lewis's Department Store when he left school.] We carried on even when some of them were married, but not as often as when we were single, unattached.

What impressed me about William's story was that he had been brought up in the heart of macho Liverpool without much obvious love from his mother or step-father, but his sensitive, loving and artistic side, with girls, with music, somehow found its way through. At first, I assumed he was gay, but he was, in fact, happily married from the age of twenty-five.

Believe it or not there was a gay Liverpool, as Unity Theatre's unique archive of the gay communities of Liverpool from the 1920s shows.

There were the main cottages at the Gorey at the Pier Head, the Island outside the East India buildings, and there was the Wheel of Fortune, Williamson Square. Most boys would go at night. They would go on a cottage crawl, some would go on a pub crawl and some would go on the cottage crawls. On the way, you would meet other people on the way back from where you were going, and they would say, 'It's not busy there tonight,' or 'It's all right tonight.' But I think that one of the reasons why this was taking place, the cause of it all, was poverty. All the people that did the sort of thing . . . were all very poor people and they came from homes where there was no entertainment, where there was no kindness, there was no free food. Life was very, very hard and people were struggling to find whatever pleasures they could get. So, whatever people feel about that, even me, what I feel about it, it's unwarranted because people do things out of necessity.[10]

CHAPTER SEVEN

Walking Free

Necessity made savage demands on the working classes in Liverpool from the eighteenth century right into the 1950s. Love was the recompense, but it was love in the hearts of hard-as-nails women, needy men and generally happy children, often made proud of their hopeless position by their mothers, while strictly disciplined both at home and school. For them, the Liverpool streets were a colourful adventure playground.

There were some sad exceptions, however, such as George Alfred Doyle, born in 1901 in Bickerton Street in the Dingle.[1] George remembered his father as a very jovial person, who used to play the mouth organ, the clappers (two bones held between two fingers and waggled about) and the accordion. He used to black his face and invite the neighbours in for a bit of a singsong. But then, as George relates, his father 'went bedfast' and his mother had to go into domestic service. George was six when his father died. His mother couldn't cope. His elder sister was put in a home in Princess Road, and his other sister went with George into the Bluecoat School, leaving the youngest, a three-year-old brother, with his mother at home.

The Bluecoat School was set up in 1708 on the profits of the slave trade, as already mentioned, and to start with was for boys only. When George and his sister entered it, there were 250 boys and 150 girls, and they weren't allowed to mix. Uniform for him was trousers, waistcoat and frock-tail coat, with a bib. The girls wore dark navy material and a big flared skirt, with 'the proper big bib'.

[We were] all in the one building, one side the boys and the other the girls. The only time we saw the girls was at meal time, when we went into the big room – meal time and at church and at Sunday school.

Punishment was a case of six of the best, as it's called. They came down heavy and your hands were bruised. They punished you for any minor details that they considered were wrong. As a matter of fact, in my estimation, as I have seen life since I left the school and the way children are treated at the present time, I've come to the conclusion that they were brutal. Any of the masters could chastise. It wasn't left to the headmaster. And if he caught you on the spur of the moment, perhaps whispering, he came round with the cuff of his hand right behind the ear, and sent you flying. You always left your feet and went over. And that's, really speaking, why I am blaming my deafness . . .

You were really on your own. They were very keen, very strict. Everything was very regimented. Up at six o'clock, dressed and out of the dormitory and straight down and get yourself washed. And I think it was seven o'clock breakfast. When you came out, the teachers went in to have their breakfast. We started school at eight. Eight till twelve, and we had an hour's break for a meal and then back to school at one o'clock till five. You had your tea and the evening was your own. In the winter, you had to go to bed at eight, in the summer it was nine. We had the big play yard. You weren't allowed to play on the sports field. If it were wet weather, you had the big play room.

The food was very poor indeed. Very poor. Insufficient for growing children. Two mornings a week breakfast was just porridge. One morning it would be a piece of bread and cheese. The meals were always insufficient. You always felt hungry. You were always ready for the next meal. The only thing I couldn't face was the porridge, because it had massive lumps like eggs in it. You had your main meal at twelve o'clock. I can remember Mondays was rice pudding only, with a small piece of bread and cheese, and nothing else. Tuesdays and Thursdays, I think it was, you had beans in tomato ketchup and nothing with it, no pudding. You got stew one day a week. I think it was on a Sunday. I can't remember ever having roast. If it had been roasted it had been put in the gravy and served from there. But we were so hungry we were glad to eat anything. You didn't get pudding every day. The rice pudding was a meal on its own. Sometimes you'd be lucky and you might be able to get a

second helping. For your evening meal you got a slice of
bread about an inch thick, the full square, with margarine,
which had been melted and poured on to it in liquid form.
Sometimes it'd be dripping. On a Sunday, you got two
thinner pieces of bread and butter, and sometimes one
would have a bit of jam on. And you'd have a small piece of
cake. That was Sunday only. For breakfast and tea you would
drink either milk or cocoa. I've no recollection of having tea.

Music saved him. Being in the Bluecoat School band meant
you went on all the outings, for boys and girls, and were
excused cleaning tasks. George was known as 'the handyman', because he played all the instruments.

I learnt them all. I started with the tenor horn, then I got to
solo tenor, and then I got on to the cornet, then to soprano.
Then I went on the euphonium and on the bass. I don't
know as I done much with the trombone, but I played the
clarinet. Father was very musically inclined. If there was
anybody short, I used to be taken off my instrument to go
and replace them.

The band was the Bluecoat's advertisement. It played on
the tram cars, at the Pier Head, and leading the school
right down to the ferry on trips out; and while the
children were on the boat, and when they got to their
destination, they played there also. It was exhausting, but
it got him out. Music was his passport to a sort of freedom.
But what really did for George was Sunday afternoon
church services.

Your mothers were allowed to sit in the gallery while you had your meal, but at the same time you weren't supposed to wave or anything. They weren't allowed to speak to you. At the service, the boys were on two sides of the chapel and the girls were in the centre, and we were placed that way for the singing of the hymns. But we could see our parents in the gallery, and all the visitors and ordinary people were down on a level with us. After the service was over, we marched out to the dining room and then these people just walked through while we were having our meal and our parents were up top, but we weren't allowed to let on. We used to try to read their lips when they were trying to say something, but you hadn't to let a teacher notice you were staring hard, otherwise that was wrong. They knew that [the mothers] were trying to say something. We were solely in their charge, and they were going to make it their business that we were going to be that way.

Holidays were a fortnight home from school twice a year. When George and his sister arrived at the Bluecoat for the start of the new term, the two children used to break down as soon as they got anywhere near the school. The contrast with the life lived by the majority of children in Liverpool at this time, and for the next fifty years, couldn't be more marked.

In those days, we were allowed to walk free in the streets, everywhere was safe.[2]

Hordes of children played in the streets and we were never short of playmates. The street was our territory. It belonged

to us and, because there were no cars, our mothers felt it
was quite safe to let us play unsupervised.[3]

To begin with, the streets looked quite different from
today, as Albert Kane points out.

Imagine streets completely devoid of the present type of
motor car, lorry, bus or coach . . . In the early days, the bulk
of the traffic was horses and carts of various shapes and
sizes, and there was also the tram car.

Horse-drawn trams became a way for the poor to earn a few
pennies, as Terry Cooke records in *Scotland Road: The Old
Neighbourhood.*[4]

There were many toffs using the trams, which ran along
Scotland Road in those days, and the lads playing truant
would dress up as clowns, paint their faces and turn
cartwheels on the pavements to amuse the 'gentlemen' on
the open top deck of the trams. The passengers were
delighted and would throw coppers to the boys . . . At
various points the local 'Mary Ellens' boarded the trams
loaded with baskets of flowers, oranges and apples, sticks of
rock and toffee apples.

When electric trams replaced the horse-drawn vehicles,
and other motorised vehicles began to appear, so interest
in them grew among Albert Kane and his friends:

One of the delights was the steam traction engine. These
were extremely powerful lorries, which usually pulled a trailer

and what seemed to be huge loads of flour or sugar. In front of the engine, between the wheels, there was a firebox. The driver would light a fire in this to heat up the water, which in turn created steam pressure. They were extremely slow but faster than horses and many times stronger. We became good friends with the traction engine drivers, who would allow us to open up the front of the firebox and stand there warming ourselves in the cold weather. Sometimes we would put potatoes in and bake them. This was popular with our mates, who were always hungry.

But even as change came, horses remained an inextricable part of people's lives. Right up to 1935, as Billy Woods records, 'there were still 4,920 horses in the city, working for the Corporation, the breweries, railways, docks and so on.' Continues Albert Kane:

To see the May Day Parade of the Liverpool carters was a spectacle. Hundreds of horses would be groomed and decorated in a most colourful manner. Their tails and manes would be combed and plaited, the carts and drays would be cleaned and painted in an attempt to win the premier award, and all the horses would have their own name on a plaque above the stable. The passing of the horse altered life a great deal.

Eric Coffey's grandfather ran a wedding and funeral service, 'white horses for weddings, black horses for funerals'. Bill Owen's dad worked for Robert Cane, the Liverpool brewers, 'where he drove a pair of horses'. The 12th Earl of Derby gave his name to the Derby horse race, which he started in 1780, after winning the toss of a coin with Lord Bunbury. Frank Vaudrey points out that, 'the Aintree Grand National was always a big event for Liverpool, biggest race in the world. Used to go there with my brother and mates. It's only two or three miles from Walton. We'd walk over, bunk in. Back of the canal, you could jump in.' Continues Albert Kane:

The fading of the horses was something we didn't like. Horses provided quite a lot of our excitement. For instance, if we boys decided to make a boxing ring, we would creep up behind a loaded wagon as it was going along the street, get under it, climb on to the rear axle and from there lean forward to the tray that hung down, where the driver kept his sheets and ropes. Then we would drop the end of a rope on to the ground until it trailed behind the wagon and climb back the way we had come. Once off the wagon, it was simple to pull the rope until you had all you needed to make a ring. It was probably a very risky thing to do but we thought nothing of it, and I did it many times.

Where there are horses, there are rats, and rats were good for sport. A favourite sport was to isolate a rat, chase it until it ran up a down spout, then smoke it out with wet straw. One of our pals would fetch his terrier and when the rat made a run for his life, we would release the dog. We thought that was great. When the stable middens were being emptied was really super. There was always about twenty rats in a midden, word would pass around that a midden was being emptied and the gang would turn up with their dogs. As the manure was being lifted out, a rat would jump out and make a run for it, the dogs were always ready, up went the rat and we all cheered. Few rats survived.

I suppose we were considered to be heartless little brats but really we had a lot of feeling. One of the things we hated was to see a horse killed. The streets were cobbled and as well as being hard-wearing the cobbles were spaced to enable the horses' shoes to get a grip, so that they could pull the heavy loads up from the docks. Many of the streets had a steep incline and it would be necessary for a lead horse to be hitched to the front to help pull the load. These were magnificent animals, shire horses of tremendous strength. It was common to see a load being pulled up a steep hill by a team of three horses. During winter the cobbles would be icy and the ground frozen. The horses would struggle to get a grip and a horse whose shoes were worn would fall to the ground bringing down the other horses. There would be chaos. The heavy loads would start to roll back, dragging the horses with them. The carter would act as quickly as he could to apply the chocks – a breaking system to halt the load. Very often a horse's sides would be skinned, but the worst was when a horse broke its leg in the fall. The poor creature would writhe on the ground, making valiant efforts to regain its footing. It was a horrible sight. Eventually, a veterinary surgeon would arrive on the scene and put the horse out of its suffering with a humane killer. The horse would be detached from the team and a cart, known as the knacker's cart, would arrive and take the dead horse away. When this sort of accident occurred, the carter would be very distressed. Liverpool carters and their horses were inseparable. The horse always came first, and no matter how late a carter worked he would always brush, clean, feed and water his horse before

he bedded it down in a clean stable. The horse was the
carter's pride.

As Clifford O'Sullivan, born in 1913, recalls: 'People used
to say that they thought more of their horses than they did
of their families.'[5]

The other great allure for children was the docks. With
poverty widespread even into the 1950s, many children, if
not actively on the scavenge, knew where to find the odd
hand-out, as Mavis O'Flaherty recalls.

As a child I would stand and watch them unloading ships,
and you would see all the bananas, and the dockers used to
say, 'All right girl, come on.' There used to be some steps
and you would go down to the docks and they would give
you a big handful of bananas, a big handful, quite a few
pounds worth.

Seventy-five years earlier, a dredging operation had begun
the job of accommodating passenger liners off the Pier
Head, and once the Princess Landing Stage was completed,
that became a particularly popular hunting ground. Behind
it, the Port of Liverpool, Royal Liver and Cunard Buildings
were completed in 1907, 1911 and 1917 respectively. A
group from Toxteth recalled:

You know, the immigrants coming in, or people going to Pier
Head to go to New York? Well, we used to go there when
we were kids, and when they came out, we would ask them
for a penny. They were poverty stricken, but we took the
penny off them. When we knew they were coming in, we

would all be down there. They would come right along the dock road.[6]

As a boy, John Burns lived in a Toxteth tenement and made Herculaneum Dock his patch.

Later on in years, my father, when he came out of the Army, went down there as a docker and we used to go down to the Herculaneum in Grafton Street and look over the railings, and you would see the coal coming on little trolleys, little trolleys. My God, in trucks, and the whole truck would be lifted up and put into the ship, you know, with the coal on it. When the Pakistani sailors came up from the dock, they'd walk along in a line, one after the other. They always used to say, 'The man in the middle has got the money!' There was a bobby on the gate – there was always a bobby on the gate. Never knew his name, I was too often running away from him.

For Bill Owen, Milner's Safe Works was one of many targets.

All the men used to come out – you know, at night when they were knocking off at six o'clock – and we used to ask, 'Any bread left mister?' and things like that. It was, 'Carry your bag, Mam?' down at the landing stage when a boat came in . . . or for the emigrants going out, 'Get a penny to carry your bag?' I once found half a sovereign in the St John's Market. We used to go down there looking for anything faded – faded oranges, faded apples. I'm sure I didn't know the difference between half a sovereign and a sovereign then, but I'm going through the market and I've seen this and picked it up. I don't say nothing. I turn around

and I run. Tha' knows St John's Market. I ran right to
Kingsley Road, where we lived. Well, off Kingsley Road –
Maynard Street. I ran all the way home. Couldn't get home
quick enough to give it to me mother. That was half a
week's wages. Oh, I'll never forget that.

None of this is a sign that money was the focus of life, or that
there was ever much of it to be found in a boy's pockets.
Shops were more for looking in than buying from, and
shopkeepers existed to be annoyed, recalled Frank Shaw.

'Any broken biscuits, Mister? . . . Well, mend 'em.' 'Any
empty boxes? . . . Well, fill thum.' You smacked the sides of
bacon hanging outside grocer's, tipped over bins, opened the
doors to make the bells ring before scarpering down a jigger,
over the dead cats and discarded mattresses.[7]

Nevertheless, for Bill Owen the reality was that a few
coppers did make a difference.

A halfpenny'd get us some sweets, and you could get a big
wet Nellie – you know, a square pudding cake . . . you could
whack it out between three or four of you. If we ever got
money, we spent it on something to eat. Always something
to eat . . .

Mostly, said Bob Tooley, everyone was as poor as the next
person.

We didn't notice, and we didn't want things. We were
bought things and our parents would think, 'Well, that's

enough.' We never asked for anything because we knew we would never get it. Today it's horrible. Everybody talks about money, money, money.[8]

Sam Perry remembers various enterprising schemes undertaken to earn a bob or two. I met Sam with his friends Jim Kennedy, George Marsden, Harry Whittaker, Jimmy Caples and Freddie Ashcroft in the archive room of the Shrewsbury House Boys Club, their *alma mater*, in Everton.

We would strip some old floorboards out of an empty house that had been damaged by the war, chop them up and sell them, or we would go down the fish market and get the boxes. They would smell terrible, you know, when you broke them up, and they would be damp. You'd try to sell them on and people would say, 'This is damp firewood,' and they would undercut you.

Freddie Ashcroft: I remember one time there was this boat, an empty boat. It was made of wood – the floor, the surface, was made of wooden blocks [setts]. The Council was removing them. Well, overnight they was left there, so me and my mates went up and filled a cart with these great big wooden tar blocks. Full of tar, they were, good for the fire, but the state of the chimneys!

Jim Kennedy: Those setts were laid in the road to quieten horses' hooves, which was all right when it was dry, but when they were wet, they were a hazard to bicycles, and absolutely lethal when they were frozen during cold winters.

Sam: You know, 1947 was a really bad winter and I can remember [my mate] Alan said to me, 'Me dad wants me to help him out tonight.' All the neighbours [were involved]. The GPO people had left three telegraph poles on the waste ground, and there must have been about twenty grown men lifting these poles up. Me and Alan, we had to go on ahead and make sure there was no police coming down, and give everybody the 'all clear' before they come up to the waste ground behind the houses. Within half an hour, those poles were sawn up and chopped into blocks, and everyone in the street had firewood!

Harry Whittaker: When the club started in 1903, you must remember, a lot of the lads weren't as fortunate as we were. A lot of them were living rough on the streets, and the club took in homeless boys.

George Marsden: Well, it was a mixture, wasn't it. There were people with bare feet, they didn't have no shoes!

Harry: More in the thirties and forties that. We used to put pieces of cardboard and paper in the shoes to stop up the holes, many a time. The top would be well polished and shiny and there was a hole in the bottom.

I expressed surprise that Harry would find it important to clean his shoes.

Harry: Without a doubt. It meant you looked tidy.

While some mothers vied for respectability, sometimes with

ridiculous strategems – Joan Gibbons remembers a Mrs Onions who wouldn't answer to her name, even when she came to collect her divvy at the Co-op, unless it was pronounced O'Nions – children were not conscious of being poor. Police clothes were, however, the great divider. They marked you out, as Eileen Newman told me.

> When my dad was little, one of a family of six, his father went off to America and just stayed there for five or six years, leaving the whole family with the mother, who then I think went on the drink. Extreme poverty. They would get police clothes – you couldn't get worse than having police clothes. They used to have a fund or something where you could get clothes. When I looked at photographs of the courts and that down at the museum, that was my dad!
>
> He told me a story of how they were living near Tate and Lyle in Vauxhall. The kids used to be out playing football and one day this great big flash car came and stopped at Tate and Lyle. My dad rushed up and opened the door for the bloke, and he sent out somebody to give my dad an orange. So then my dad did this on a regular basis and got fruit and different things for the family.[9]

A group from the Dingle recalled:

> There was a kid walking along one time. He had no shoes or socks on, only a pair of trousers and a bit of a ragged shirt or something. When he saw a policeman, he started running. I said to me dad, 'Why is he running?' He said, 'Well, if the policeman gets him, he will take him to the police station and he'll get police clothes.' Now, they wouldn't wear these

because they were like a herring bone. Do you remember
them? They'd give the kids a pair of trousers and a damn big
pair of heavy boots. But they were so distinctive, the kids
would always run for shame of wearing them. They would
sooner be in rags than wear police clothes, because
everybody would know where they got the clothes.[10]

Children identified completely with their environment.
Indeed, their environment sucked them in. For example,
many families worked the market as a unit, with Paddy's
Market the central feature of the wider Scotland Road
community, and the children watched without blinking an
eye as their mothers harangued with ear-splitting invective
an unfortunate trespasser on their territory. Frank Vaudrey:

They were tough women. I'd not like to pick a fight with
them, I tell you. Hard people, very, very tough. My Nin –
that's me mother's side, Nan's me dad's side – she had a
barrow, down Scotland Road, Paddy's Market. That's where
Paddy's Market[11] used to be – they moved it off the road. On
a Saturday I'd go outside with my cousin, we'd have a sheet
on the floor and sell second-hand clothes, shouting, 'Tanner
or a bob on the floor.' You'd pay the Council Toby the rent,
my mum or Aunty would do that. The Council got the
Charter off King John. You'd get lots of guys off the ships,
lots of ships then. Asian seamen would come down and buy
stuff – we'd shout, 'Two shillin' Johnny' and all that. Cilla
Black was next to us, her name was Cilla White actually.
They had the barber's in Scotland Road. Sometimes her
mother paid me threepence to carry her stuff down to the
market. She sold the same sort of stuff, bric a brac and all

that. But what characters, auctioneers, real characters, you know? People went down there for the patter. Saturday morning, everyone got there about half past six and set up. People started to come in about seven. Lashing down with rain, blowing in the wind, and you've gotta get a sheet out. It was like trying to get a sail up, and you had to be quite agile.[12]

Boys of the area were soon inured to anything they encountered on the street, as Frank Shaw recalled.

Once I ran home to tell my aunt I had seen 'two ladies fighting' . . . no sight should have surprised me. I saw men releasing rats from traps in a street off Islington for dogs to chase, and I remember seeing cattle being driven through the streets to the bloodstained alleys behind London Road where unhygienic slaughter went on all day. Us lads could get bladders from kindly slaughterers, which were better than a tin can or roll of paper for street footballs. Of course, we couldn't afford a full-sized ball, a 'casey' – not even a half-sized one, called a 'tanner megger' because they were only sixpence-ha'penny.[13]

George Cross worked among these unsavoury sights.

When I left school [at fourteen] I got a job going round to Carruthers Street, near Vauxhall Road, where they used to kill the horses, you know, and they used to sell the horse flesh. I worked for a little shop and I used to push a handcart from Mill Street to Vauxhall Road to collect the horse flesh – one hundred weight and a quarter, and it was only five shillings the hundred weight. Cat and dog meat we would call it. On the way back, all the juices would run down the tailboard of the handcart and you used to have the dogs coming round and licking it up.[14]

Albert Kane had mistier memories of dark winter nights, when they'd rib the lamplighter and eat hot roast chestnuts, and just sink into the spirit of the town they loved.

He used to go from lamp to lamp with a long pole. He'd push the pole into each lamp, pull a switch and the light would come on. Us kids used to follow him round and as soon as he had moved on to the next lamp, we'd climb up the one he had just lit and put it out. We thought it a great joke to see him having to return a number of times to the same lamp. Eventually, he would realise what was happening and put the police on to us, but we were always too quick to get caught.

During November, as the damp night air hung over the city, the smoke from the liners' funnels along with the smoke from the chimneys used to make really thick fog. There were times when you couldn't see across a narrow street, but the gang never used to mind. We used to like it. It gave a spooky and mysterious atmosphere.

We would gather on the street corner by the Elephant pub, where Joe Podesta used to sell roast chestnuts. Joe was an Italian immigrant who spoke pidgin English, just like on the films. We loved him and he loved us. We would gather round his handcart, which had a firebox on the top. He would roast chestnuts and potatoes, and we would laugh and joke, sing our songs.

In the summer, Joe's cart became an ice-cream cart. Cornets were half a penny and sandwiches one penny, but we were always trying to get a better bargain. One idea we had was to take a cup and ask for a pennyworth in the cup. We usually got a lot more that way and then we could share it out.

Sharing with your schoolmates was automatic. On Saturday morning, after delivering the newspapers, we would meet at about nine o'clock and set off for the school playing fields, about eight miles away. We would call for the latecomers on the way.

Mollie Connor, born in 1926 in Fulford Street, off Great Homer Street, recalls other warm, colourful scenes.[15]

Great Homer Street was full of shops, pubs, churches and businesses, and on every street corner there were women with handcarts selling fruit and vegetables. The street was always bustling and alive with people, and above the general clamour came the cries of the handcart women, selling their goods. At night the shops would be all lit up and not barricaded as they are today.

My friends and I used to go looking in the shop windows, especially Reuben's, the shoe shop, admiring the shoes we never could have . . . We also looked longingly at the sweets in Hignett's window, and the coats and suits in Charles the Tailors . . .

Nearby was Bradley's, the factory that made overalls. All the factory workers used our street to get there. Everyone walked to work then. I used to love sitting on our step watching them and listening to them laughing and talking.

There was also Flanagan's, the wireworks on Kirkdale Road, and in our street there was a builder's yard. All the workmen there used to whistle and shout after the girls on their way to and from work.

Even on a Sunday our street was very busy. Bullen's Dancing Academy was just across the road, where they used to hold afternoon tea dances. All the girls who went there used to wear long dresses and dancing shoes. I used to love watching them as they paraded past our house. I promised myself that when I grew up, I too would go to Bullen's. I did eventually get there, but it was wartime and austerity affected every area of our lives – so no tea dances and lovely dresses. It was the time of the jive and jitterbug, exciting new dances that were all the rage . . .

Frank Shaw remembers the colour and bustle with nostlagia, too.

Who would want to run home to telly then when the Negro still had a puppet show in Scotland Road with his famed butter-milk rhyme? When a happy families display of dogs, cats, monkeys all living in one large cage was to be seen? When in most streets were the ballad-singer and the sellers of sandbags to keep out the draughts? And coal-bricks mingled their cries with, 'Here you are ladies, ripe bananas, four for a bob, buy me last one an' I'll give youse six!'

The barrel-organs have almost gone. The father of a famous boxer used to let them out on hire for so much a day and had to keep changing the tunes. 'The Sheik of Araby' would have to replace 'Give Me a Little Cosy Corner' if the shopping crowds were being slow with their pennies . . .[16]

'The famous boxer' was Don Volante. He died, aged seventy-seven, in 1982. Between 1921 and 1935 he had 130 fights, winning 94, losing 25, and drawing 11. Although never a champion, he fought most of the top feather-weight boxers in the USA and Europe and is a legend of the area, honoured with a plaque on the wall of the Salisbury Boxing Club in Salisbury Street, Everton. In 1930, more than 18,000 people packed into Madison Square Garden, New York, to watch him draw with Harry Carlton in what was at the time reckoned to be the most exciting fight in history.

There was nothing soft about the streets then. Learning to fight was 'the greatest thing in the life of the British schoolboy. Fed almost exclusively in the schoolroom upon the valour of the more obvious British patriots, the greatest stigma to attach to anyone was that of coward . . .'[17]

Some boys, however, were less than keen.

I was brought up in a fairly tough area, you had to be robust to survive. I've never been keen on violence . . . Sometimes you had to stand there and literally fight your way out. I recall quite a few instances. Someone picked on you and you could either lose tremendous face and become an object of ridicule or stand up and fight it out, when you became accepted. You didn't even have to win, but you did have to fight your corner. You learned how to handle yourself. I did a bit of boxing. I'm talking maybe five or six fights. After that very little, just occasionally when a gang of youths would attack for no particular reason. In those days, it was only fists. It wasn't clubs or knives or anything. There was a religious dimension, there was a territorial dimension, there

was all sorts. If you went to a grammar school . . . secondary
modern school . . . Basically, they were Irish, always fighting.
I don't know what makes it. This helped me in the rest of my
life. You couldn't get by without standing up for yourself.[18]

Boxing and football have always been major interests of
Liverpool boys, as they vie to be accepted into the macho
culture of their fathers. I found Alan Lynch in the Solly,
which is the name by which the Salisbury Club is known.
Alan lays claim to twenty-six internationals who have all
boxed more than once for England; the club has won every
major medal in the Amateurs section. Unusually, boys
come to box here not only from the locality but from all
over Liverpool, which is what serves to ensure a mature
attitude to territorial boundaries, so often an obsession
among the young, as Alan explains:

I was born near here in 1949. The people formed a very
close-knit community. So it's like a boys club here. I've got
parents. I've got children and grandchildren of boxers who
box with me. I've got the coaches who boxed with me years
ago, and their children. Liverpool itself is a boxing city. The
first thing – we give them 'a free boxing lesson' if anyone
misbehaves, a free lesson on how to behave.[19] So discipline
is good.

I call ours a gypsy club, because they come to us from
everywhere. I could have a kid in the gym here two or three
years before they box. I allow them to come in at nine.
There's a few exceptions, where the children are relations of
boxers or coaches. We have public liability insurance that
covers that age you see. You've got to be eleven to box. In

Wales, it's ten. Years ago it was a little bit 'lacksydaisy', but that's all changed over the years.

The gym is huge, with two 20-foot (international size) rings, one of them used in the last Commonwealth Games. The walls are cluttered with trophies, gloves and mementoes of great moments in the club's history. The Church has been solidly behind Alan's efforts, facilitating the acquisition of the property.

We got a note from the Archdiocese saying there was a possibility of renting this place. It was in a fairly poor state, but the community came round, ex-boxers from the club who have got businesses or whatever came round, so we got it to a standard that was good for the kids. I think it was a fifteen-year lease at a peppercorn rent, which was good. We were really happy about that. After fifteen years was up, they turned round and said they needed the land to build new houses. So a few of us weren't happy with that situation. We are a community-based club, open to the world, and we didn't want to move outside the community. A few letters passed and I went to see Archbishop Worlock, and I actually said if nothing was going to be done, I'd set up the boxing ring in the centre of Liverpool and block all the traffic.

Anyway, we got a letter back, which is on that wall, saying what a thing it was for the community, and what followed then was dialogue between the Roman Catholic Church and meself and others, saying that the cost of the building in the state it was in now was £35,000, which I believe they thought we couldn't match, but we did. We got trustees for the club. And I have just insured the property now for £500,000, and the contents for £25,000. There are no finances coming into the gym other than what we charge – a pound for the kids. The seniors, if they are in work, we charge £5 a week. And then we go for grants. The City Council has supported us. This was only three-quarters of the size it is now. Through the City Council and Sport England we got a £260,000 grant to extend, only because of the numbers.

I asked Alan how he recognises a young boxer with potential.

I feel it's genetic, because you always find that children of parents who box are worth watching. First of all in a child you are looking for toughness, someone who can accept what is being thrown at them. You know, where's there's no fear of getting hit. I think of it like the Yellow Brick Road. You've got to have the lion's heart and the brain of the scarecrow. Even the little dog, you know, he's always biting like a little Jack Russell at the feet.

There are all combinations of a good lad, but probably five out of forty-five will ever reach any heights. You never know though. I had a young child, twelve or thirteen, come from another club that's defunct now. He'd lost thirteen out of fourteen bouts I think, and if you swore in front of him, he would go, 'Woo,' but he was a lovely lad. I never let him out of the gym. He had boxed for about two years, but he wasn't ready to my mind, and I could see where his defeats were. Anyway, after about ten, twelve months in the gym – the kid kept coming and he kept coming, and started improving, and that same child won an ABA title. He boxed for England. We turned it round, the club and the coaches turned it round.

The girls come on a Tuesday and a Thursday, and they mix with the boys. They've got their own facility for showers and changing, of course. It may sound crazy but it was a novelty at first with the lads. They were looking at the girls, showing off, but now it's part of the system. The girls' strength probably is suppleness. It's important. It's the difference between being there and being here, you know? The reactions. They don't necessarily develop differently from other girls. We've got some fairly petite young ladies here as well.

Do you class Liverpool as a violent city?

The only time I ever hear of anything is in football. It seems to be football related. We don't have a problem here in this area, though having said that, anything can flare up. Some of the kids, the Chicago Teddy Bears, come in with a tough attitude. I've seen a lot of bullies in there and realised they haven't come back once they put a pair of gloves on.

Football is more widespread, of course, and street based. There are three major teams, Everton, Liverpool, Tranmere Rovers. Anyone can surprise you with a fanatical interest in the sport, whether it's an otherwise seriously committed twenty-something female community worker who accompanies her father to Anfield Road every Saturday that Liverpool is playing at home, or an octogenarian erstwhile political activist. Tom Best came alive when discussing the school he attended, St

Sylvester's[20] in Vauxhall, solely because he sat next to Johnny Morrissey.

> Morrissey was a footballer who played for Liverpool, and Everton snaffled him, and Bill Shankly was going to resign over it. He played for many years for Everton and then Tranmere Rovers. He was a year younger than me, but God he was such a good footballer![21] He originally came from a parish called St Gerard's, but their school was bombed during the war so he had to move and he came to ours! Oh, yeah, he was quite affluent. His family owned two shops in the Scotland Road area.

The late John Peel was not exactly Liverpudlian born – he came from Heswall on the Wirral – but, like many, he undertook his visits to Anfield as if he was performing a rite.

> When I come to a match on my own, I go through this elaborate ritual. I always park the car in the same place, I always go to the same pub and I buy two pints and sit at the same table and read the *Daily Mirror*, and when I've finished my pints, I go and buy a bag of chips at the Chinese chip shop, and then I go in through the same gate at the same time and it's all very ritualised.

Football *is* a religion. Everton is the Catholic team, Liverpool the Protestant, although it's nothing like as big a deal in a political or religious sense as Celtic and Rangers in Glasgow. Nevertheless, a religion it is, as was confirmed while I was writing the book when a prescient public notice appeared asking, 'What would God do if he came to Liverpool today?' It was defaced with the response, 'Sack Rafa Benitez.' Clearly someone up there was attentive.

To tenement kids such as John Burns, football and cricket came as naturally as breathing.

There were fifty-eight families in one tenement, so I had more than one mate. I had more than two mates! We played football because there was a big open space before they built the shelters in 1939. When they built the shelters, we used to chalk the wickets for cricket on them, or failing that, we'd use a bin. We lived in a flat on the bottom, and the kids used to knock on the door, asking, 'Mrs Burns, can we borrow your bin?' And they would take the bin over to the square and put chalk on it.

You could get fined five shillings for playing football in the street – yeah, if they caught you! If you broke anybody's window, we used to have a whip round for the glass. The sergeant in those days, well, he had a night stick, a truncheon, and he used to knock on the edge of the pavement with it. A bobby about forty yards away could hear him. The sergeant would get his stick and call the constable down with it. It used to go ding, ding, and the bobby would hear it, put his fag out and know he was wanted. There couldn't be any relationship with the police really because as soon as you saw one you'd run!

Frank Vaudrey spent all his childhood 'in a pre-fab on the edge of a field next to Walton Park. We played football every day. Fantastic, yeah!'

We're all Evertonians in my family. My granddad on my dad's side played for Everton before the First World War. He was a real athlete. He didn't go out in the first team a lot, but he played for the reserves. Everton is the original team in Liverpool. Liverpool FC is derived from Everton. There was an argument over the rent for the ground with the Lord Mayor at the time, a fellow called John Houlding. Liverpool's ground was Everton's ground at that time. They split up. The Mayor helped start Liverpool FC and Everton moved to Goodison Road, which was a farm – they call it 'the farm'.[22]

Everton was actually founded out of a church in St Domingo, by a group of boys by that name, long before they were founder members of the Football League. Besides playing football for Everton, my granddad played cricket for Bootle. At that time it was a very big cricket club. And he also ran for New Brighton Harriers, which was a top athletics club. He was a cavalryman and was mustard gassed on the Somme in the Great War, which destroyed him basically. He was very lucky because he was on his horse when the Germans fired mustard gas. He fell off his horse and the horse fell on top of him into a crater, which probably saved his life.

So football and cricket are part of the social fabric, but they came along with a box-load of other games, innocently played out in the days before television and computer. The 'back-jigger' was the narrow back alleyway where children often played.

Billy Woods: The narrow back alleyways had rough uneven paving slabs, and were a wonderland of magic with side-gutters and grids. After a heavy rainfall, the gutters provided a watercourse for boat races. Matchsticks and bits of wood became racing boats, which eventually plunged 'over the rapids' down the grid into the drain.[23]

John Burns: One thing about those days, nobody complained about noise. You would be running round the landings until it got dark, you know. We used to play a game called 'Pawn Shop'. Someone would chase you and when he caught you, he told you to take an article of clothing off. The only thing he wouldn't let you do was take your trousers off, because in them days nobody wore underwear! So the only thing they would leave you with was your trousers. Every time you got caught you lost an article of clothing. Everything was bundled into a corner, so that when the game was finished, everybody had to go rooting for their clothes!

Another game was 'Can on the Line'. You would draw two lines, one about four yards away from the other. One group would stand on one line, and one group would stand on the other line, and you had to throw a flattened tin can. If it went on their line, you all had to run backwards and when they caught you – this is the good thing! – when they caught you, they had to give you a donkey ride back to the line!

In another, you had a bicycle wheel, no spokes in it, and a piece of wood. If a few of you had these, you would decide to have a race. You would keep the wheel turning with the wood, and run all the way round the outside of the tenement. If you wanted to go on a bike, it used to cost you threepence from somebody who had one.[24]

May Duke: As girls, we had the games the parents joined in
– skipping rope after tea every night in the summer, and
rounders, all in the street. 'Top and whip', 'Levo', 'Lallio',
'Kick the Can' . . . We played ghosts down in the
tenements in St Martin's buildings. Things like that. Every
minute was occupied. I remember the songs my mother
used to sing . . . 'The Sunshine of Your Smile' was one, all
those sad songs. And it was probably New Year, every
auntie had her own song and they all sang them with
their own gestures. My cousin and I were only little ones
and we'd sit on the top stair – we weren't supposed to
be up – we'd sit there listening to Auntie Jane. And I
peeped down one time and there she was with her hands
across her bosom, her eyes closed: 'On a bed a girl lay
dying, with her baby by her side', you know? We thought
it was wonderful. We went to bed in floods of tears all
over this! 'In his passion he did tempt me. It was then
I lost my name. Then he ran away and left me to bear
my sorrow and my pain.' All this was in the song! And
then another auntie would get up and sing 'Where the
River Shannon's Flowing'. And then of course my mother
always gave 'The Sunshine of Your Smile'. Every one of
them had a song.[25]

Once a year, in the Dingle, all the kids would get together
in an extraordinary re-enactment of a rite that is supposed
to have gone on for centuries. None of the children quite
knew why they were doing each part of what was done, but
they did it all the same, as members of the Dingle History
Group recalled.

Has anybody told you about Judas? This is particular to the Dingle. It was supposed to have been brought here by the Norwegians, you know from the docks, before my lifetime. What we used to do, we had one, two, three, four lofts in the tenements, and in October or September we used to go round collecting wood. In them days it was easy because the bombs had done most of it for you. We used to go to old houses, get the wood and take it back to the tenements, and we put it in the lofts. Then, about half past four, five o'clock on a Good Friday morning, you would hear somebody yell and you knew they had started. All that wood used to come out of the lofts and we used to get an effigy and put it on the fire and say it was Judas, and burn it in the middle of the tenements. That was our Judas! And then we would sit round the fire.

We had a pig's bladder at the same time. We used to buy a pig's bladder and inflate it like a large balloon and that used to be to hammer the other people. The fire would be in the middle of the road, and it would really be going. The wood had tar in it, of course, and they used to get the fire brigade out to extinguish it. And then we used to play football with the bladders afterwards.

When the firemen came to put the fire out, all the kids used to stand on the landing shouting, 'I'll waste the water!' And the firemen – they'd do things then that they wouldn't do now – they would turn the hosepipe on you, right along the landings! We would all get soaked and the kids were made up with it. They couldn't do that now, they'd get locked up! We used to love it when we see the firemen come. We all used to jump on to the second landing, but there you go, waste of water![26]

George Cross: Every street round the Dingle had their own Judas and if theirs was better than ours, we'd pinch theirs. We used to put them in a coalshed in the backyard, or in a toilet, until Good Friday. Then we would probably stay up all night, a gang of us you know, and we would meet in the early hours of Good Friday morning. We'd carry a Judas up and down the street shouting, 'Remember Judas!' And bang on the doors – and the language! 'Get Out !!!!'

We used to go to the slaughterhouse on Copperas Hill and get our own bladders. Then we would blow them up, still with pieces of fat on them and all the rest of it, and we would have a battle royal after the Judas. At the burning of Judas, the policeman used to come round and chase us. And then we would have [another] battle royal with the bladders. Everybody coming near got it There was no sides! Bang! Then we would play football after Judas's trousers had fallen off.

Pigs' bladders were about a halfpenny each, a sheep's bladder was about 2d. If you got a pig's bladder, you were well off.[27]

CHAPTER EIGHT

Mother Liverpool

———

Families were large – six, seven, eight children were common, thirteen not unheard of – and it was simply not possible for a mother to give each child the close attention that is common in much smaller families today. Now, each phase of a child's early life – nursery, school, sport, entertainment – is fiercely scrutinised and vetted, and childhood is too often spoiled because of a competitive edge that turns children into failures or celebrities before they are ten, and their mothers, caught between motherhood and a job, into depressive wrecks.

That simply didn't occur. It was foreign to working-class families anyway, where children were brought up by holistic means, with support from family, the parish, the

neighbourhood, and various other tribal and philanthropic helpers, and with love and great wisdom by robust
Mother Earth figures with their coarse aprons and shawls,
who are remembered with awesome respect to this day.
Frank Smith:

> My mother had very, very old sayings that to me were better
> than the Ten Commandments. She used to say to me 'God
> pays debts without money' and 'Don't do anything to
> anybody you wouldn't like done to yourself'. She was very
> knowledgeable. She gave me a strong sense of family.
> Nothing else bothers me, just me grandchildren, me two
> daughters, me wife. And my sister-in-law and brother-in-law
> are very clannish on my wife's side as well. My mother could
> read me like a book, I daren't step out of line. She knew, she
> could tell. I never stole or anything like that, because she
> said I'd get paid back if I did.

However, to those working-class Liverpool mothers of the
nineteenth and early twentieth centuries, enormous
pressures came from different quarters, notably the law.
From 1834,[1] the specific threat facing the poor, the
unemployed, orphans, unmarried mothers and the old was
the workhouse. It was this threat, and the less disastrous
one of 'going on the Parish', against which the Liverpool
working-class mother strived, often with no help at all,
indeed hindrance, from her man. May Duke was born in
1912:[2]

> We were considered posh because my father had a constant
> job. He was a foreman in Threlfalls Brewery [but] the

difference then to now [when he lost it] . . . There wasn't
any money around. You couldn't go and get social security
or anything like that . . . I think dole lasted only six weeks if
my memory serves me right, then he had to go on the UAB
. . . the Parish, and they would come round and say, 'You
don't need that, and you don't need that, and how many
children have you got?' So you only need so many beds. 'Sell
your bed and your piano . . .' Anything at all that they
thought you didn't really need to keep you alive, you were
told to sell.

The workhouse was the end of the line. The pauper tests,
along with the conditions of the new residential
workhouses – made awful to deter claimants – were the
demeaning 'Star Chamber' aspects of the law that caused
such a furore.

The declared purpose of the Act was to encourage
unemployed, able-bodied men to get a job, and all
employers to pay at least a subsistence wage; while the
asylum aspect would, it was felt, prevent paupers from
breeding, because once in the workhouse, a man would be
separated from his wife. Also, as shown in a report on the
West Riding of Yorkshire, it was expected that 'the
separation of husband and wife would have a beneficial
tendency in rousing the indolent to exert themselves'.
Records depict firm discipline and terrible sorrow. In
reality, the agonies of the receiving wards, where husbands
were separated from wives, and children from parents,
were devastating.

Mrs Joan Bevan's parents, Colin and Pat Roberts, were
Master and Matron of Walton Workhouse in Liverpool for

thirty years from 1915 to 1946. Joan grew up in the place. Her interview, undertaken by Chris Jackson in 1982, is in its entirety an important document, but its special value is that thirty-six years later, she clearly had difficulty in reconciling her feelings of loyalty to her father and what the law, which it was her father's job to put into effect, had done to the wretches who fell foul of it.

What had been overlooked by the law was that the unemployed and vagrants were not all shirkers, that unmarried mothers were not all prostitutes, that orphans were not a lower order, and that if you lived into your sixties, you could easily become destitute because there were no state pensions in those days. All these classes of people had effectively been criminalised by the Act. Adding to their burden, workhouses were made to take in 'lunatics', mentally defective children and the physically sick. Guardians displayed their patronising attitude by lumping their charges – 'idiots and lunatics, bastards, venereals, the idle and dissolute' – together. Segregation was by gender and age only, which, of course, split families asunder.

The law was a milestone in a series of Acts designed to relieve poverty, but it turned on the principle that relief should not be so benevolent as to encourage people not to work. 'Every penny bestowed that tends to render the condition of the pauper more eligible than that of the independent labourer is a bounty on indolence and vice,' argued the commissioners. What of the needy?

Fear of the workhouse was palpable, fear of the stark reality and the smell of death with which the workhouse was indelibly associated. Poverty was for the first time a stigma, by law, and largely it was up to Mother Liverpool to balance the books. In her interview,[3] Joan Bevan says:

> The inmates were treated as well as could be possible with such huge numbers. When my mother and father went to Walton, March 18th 1915, there were over a thousand inmates in the place. There was a small hospital of about seventy-five beds and there was a Superintendent Nurse. Mother was the matron. Father, at thirty-one, was in charge. If anything went wrong, he would be responsible to the Board of Guardians.

Asked how a person ended up in the workhouse, she continued:

> It was poverty, and not being wanted. There were huge families and they had no place to go. They had what was called a Liberty Day once a month when they could go out, but an awful lot of them hadn't anybody or anywhere to go. Some of the brighter ones did. They were given a shilling and they went out for the day. Some of them got drunk, of course, but how you could get drunk on a shilling I don't know!
>
> I always felt that the able-bodied, younger woman was the hardest done by. She invariably had an illegitimate child and was chucked out at home into the workhouse.

Doris Windsor, born in 1917, spelt out the problem for the young women of Liverpool.[4]

> [My parents] went on to have eleven children . . . Mother

had the last baby when I was nineteen. I was not even aware that she was pregnant. These things were never spoken of and I was very naïve. 'Sex' was what coal was delivered in to Blundellsands households – that was the local joke.

In the 1920s and thirties there was no sex education in schools, and parents rarely told their children about the 'facts of life' – the subject was taboo . . . Our meagre knowledge was gained from sleazy remarks . . . Sex was dirty and sinful and only to be enjoyed by the male sex. Men 'sowed their wild oats' and were not quite men until they had done so. Women were 'sluts' if they did, although they were the ones who bore the full consequence of their 'sins'. Some were incarcerated in mental homes, or convents, and were considered 'not quite nice' if they had a baby and were not married.

It has to be said that there were a few birth control clinics around. The first one was opened in Clarence Street and another in Linacre Mission, Litherland, but very few women used them. It would have been far too embarrassing [and] for many women, birth control was against their religious beliefs.

Women were raped, children sexually abused, but it was all kept under wraps. Such crimes were not reported. The word 'paedophile' was not used, they were just 'bad men' in our day.

Joan Bevan observed that the unmarried mother consigned to the workhouse was kept busy.

There were miles of corridor and wooden floors to be scrubbed and so on. She would feed the baby and then when the baby was weaned, the baby would go down to the blocks, five or six separate buildings. There would be wee babies in one and perhaps infectious diseases in another, and so on. Then these girls would be sent to a home other than Walton, [from] where they would ultimately be employed as servants in hotels, houses, you know?

The able-bodied woman never saw her children, did she Mrs Bevan?

The babies, of course, when they were old enough, were sent to the Cottage Homes at Fazakerley, where they were educated, and then prior to fifteen, the boys were very often sent to the Colonies, to farms and so on. Some of them have done awfully well and some of them have never been heard of again . . . My father really was a remarkable man, he just loved people, you know?

How many inmates were there at Walton Workhouse?

2,100 odd inmates, and the staff was 74 or 73, something like that.

It must have been a hard life, when you look back?

It was a lovely life for me. I was only a child. I mean we lived there and it was huge, it was like a ship, it was self-contained. It really was a great life for us. All the wards, even in the hospital part, had coal fires. The lighting was all gas . . . and then after 1930, after it was taken over by the Corporation, it was converted to electricity . . .

Prior to 1915 there would be beer served at breakfast because it was cheaper and then . . . they had what the paupers called skilley, which was a thin type of porridge. The main meal was at lunchtime. There was meat or stew or something, fish on a Friday because there were so many Catholics. It was quicker for them all to have fish, you know. I don't mean quicker, it was easier to all have the same.

At Christmas they had Christmas pudding and bags of oranges and apples and thick twist tobacco. Tobacco pressed – you cut it off with a little machine. The old men all had tobacco and the women had snuff if they wanted it. That was the Christmas treat. Oh, and they had bun loaf, which was a sort of current bread. This was extra. And a piano was brought in and somebody obliged . . .

If there was nobody to bury them, they were buried by what they call 'under Parish'. Now, at the back of Walton, there is an orchard over the railway where there are several hundred people buried . . . but there is no mark . . . The bodies I don't think have ever been removed.

Were other inmates allowed to attend the funeral?

If they wanted to, but they weren't very friendly, you know? Not like that sort of friendship. They kept themselves to themselves. You see, they were quiet. This was all before you had psychiatrists. It was the psychiatrists that made people talk. They kept themselves to themselves, they rather resented probing, a lot of them. Quite a few of them resented bathing when they came in. They didn't have baths in their own houses . . .

Where were these people to go? That was the whole

thing. They were what you would describe as like 'Alice in Wonderland'. You could give them money, they didn't know how to use it. And Mother made the remark to me once that as long as they were fed, watered and warm, some of the older, little bit normal cases, they were quite content. It doesn't sound very nice, but you see there was such poverty, there was no social security, there was no money given to them. They just didn't have enough, and if they weren't within a family, if they were lonely and unwanted . . .

Tommy Walsh recalls vividly the workhouse in the centre of town. The Roman Catholic Metropolitan Cathedral, consecrated in 1967, now occupies part of the site.

It was enormous. I mean it was the entire block running along Mount Pleasant down Brownlow Hill. It was a collection of very big buildings. One of them was knocked down only a few years ago, and you know it's funny, this morning I passed the building that's in its place and I thought isn't that a heap of rubbish! They pulled it down about five years ago, the last building of the workhouse.

Marie Francis, whom I met at the League of Welldoers in Limekiln Lane, recalled the threat of it when her father, a ship's plater,[5] had an accident and was off work for a while, and that the workhouse wasn't the only institution to fear when there was no work to be had.

Well, they didn't get money then, they got a piece of paper to go for food. Written on it was what they could have. The shop they took it to would give them the food, say the Co-op. Then the shop would get the money from the Council or wherever. That's how it worked. That was known as going on the Parish. People were still in the workhouse and worked there and earned a few bob.

Copperas Hill was where they put children. Then there was a place, not far from Scotland Road, I can't remember the name, for people who went a bit mad. I knew one lady, in fact it was my mother's sister, her name was Winnifred. She had a child before she was wed, you see, and in them days it was a wicked thing. It was wicked! She had this child before she was married, then she met a man and he married her, and then she had a daughter with him. She had gone in because she had the milk fever, and then it must have turned her head a bit, because she wouldn't come out. She was there for a long, long time. My mother and my father tried like hell to get her out, I know that. As a child I took everything in.

Her family and relations wanted to bring her home, but she had no confidence to come out. They couldn't get her to come out, just once a year on Armistice Day. She used to give us half a crown out of her bag. She had some money because in the end they made her become a cleaner. A certain amount of money was kept for her some place by the Council. Now, when she did come out of this place, she was put into an old people's home. My sister and I and my niece, we used to visit her. When we approached that place [the old people's home] we were told, 'She's got no relatives.' Nobody had gone to see her. I told the lady nicely, 'Well, we are her nieces, and this is her great niece.'

So, for Mother Liverpool, the pressure was on. The home was her domain. The rent and any tick or bills that had to be paid were her responsibility, whether or not her husband had returned from the pub at the weekend with the wages to cover them. Eileen Newman's father began life in extreme poverty, and he liked a drink. She remembers it being tough, even in the middle of the twentieth century.

My mum would always have, on the window ledge, all the amounts that would have to be paid out, like the milk money. We would know what each was. When the men came round, we would pay them. The fact that you don't have to pay the milk until the end of the week . . . There is a scene in *Blood Brothers*[6] that was just so [true] and I felt so moved by it. You know, my mum at the end of the week had his wages, and she could pay off the things. No one would ever dream of touching any of it.

Did she ever borrow money?

No, that was one of the big things that Mum never did.

Would she get tick at the local shop?

No. My best friend down the road, her mum did, and I know my brother-in-law's family got into dire trouble with that. Since he has been married to my sister, he has always been terrified of being in debt because of the humiliation and stuff that he went through.

With no National Health Service, healthcare was an added area of expense, while overcrowding was the friend of infection, as Lil Otty, born in Everton in 1919, recalled:

> Like all my contemporaries, I caught many childhood diseases. At seven I had rheumatic fever, and at fourteen, scarlet fever, both very serious illnesses at the time. I lost count of the number of times I had tonsillitis, but, with good nursing from my mother, I survived them all.

Like Lil, Vera Jeffers[7] depended on time-honoured natural cures, rather than paid-for medicine.

> Often when we were sick with some childish ailment, we would lie on Gran's old horsehair sofa, wrapped up in her black shawl in front of the fire. Many a toothache was eased with a clove to bite on, or an earache soothed with warm olive oil. A sore throat was treated with a drop of Friar's Balsam on a cube of sugar, which we were given to suck . . .

If you had whooping cough, you would be taken down to the nearest 'cocky watchman's' hut and held over his hot tar bucket to breathe in the fumes. But on occasion, you simply had to stump up for treatment. Not all illnesses were susceptible to home cures, and killer diseases, including polio and diphtheria (there was a serious outbreak in 1935), were far more common than they are today, terrifying young sufferers as they were carted off to the fever hospital.

For Molly Huggins, born in the Dingle in 1916, one particular doctor's bill caused her no end of anguish.

Money was very, very tight. It was awful really. You had to pay for doctors, didn't you, and everything. I can remember my eldest brother. I would be very young. He was only a little boy and he had to be taken for an operation to Dr Marmian. Apparently, people from round there owed him a lot of money, but we never did. He said, 'I've done my work, I want my money,' and of course my father couldn't pay him for this operation – hernia I think it was. He was only a little boy. He did the operation on a table in his surgery.

With lack of funds, a mother's ingenuity knew no bounds. After the First War, Anne Clarence's mother arranged to provide food for better-off people so that she could feed her family on left over crumbs.

Yes, I had two brothers and a sister. My mother was working, cleaning you know, cleaning a bar. She would get up early in the morning to get us ready for school. She'd go down to the market and buy a whole load of stuff that would be about a shilling at the time. Then go into Coopers. Do you remember Coopers? A high-class shop. You would go there and buy buns – lovely shop – and home-made bread. Then she would have us all at the table and we would have to put it in little piles, and so that we could eat she would say, 'That's for so and so, tell her she owes me sixpence, and take that to so and so, and tell her she owes me sixpence.' We would get our meal out of that. Every day she went, every morning.

A friend of Anne's chipped in:

We were all in the same boat at that time. Some people would open up the cellar and sell potatoes, cabbage and shank at 4d a meal. People would just go to the market.

So there would be like a secondary sale? You would buy wholesale almost.

A woman who couldn't afford a meal for her husband coming in, she would go there and get one of those dinners for him, make sure he was all right. You had to make sure that the man was fed, because he went to work.

If there was no man, as was the case for a period for Anne, there was no money. What would the women do then?

You would take in washing or something. When there was a man, you always made sure he was fed.

Later, I was talking to a group of twenty or more with long memories of the Dingle. What did they eat, what was their favourite meal in those terrible days of want? They responded as one: 'Scouse, that was the main one.' George Lund had earlier described the origin of the dish.

There was a large Irish settlement in Liverpool. That's where scouse came from. The actual stew came from Nowegian sailors. They called it 'lob scouse' – you know, lob everything in the pan. In them days it was mutton and veg and potatoes. That saved a lot of families, really, because it was cheap you see – potatoes, veg and very thick, like a broth.

But here in the Dingle, mutton was off . . .

Well, when we were little it was blind scouse, with no meat in it. It wasn't like a stew, it was thicker than a stew. Everything was put in the pan and boiled together. You would have it two or three days. I can remember Mother going down the road with what was left of the scouse in the pan to a family who couldn't afford to buy it, and they would eat what we had left.

Besides playing the food game, Mother Liverpool had to have her wits about her in the pawn shop. Pat Maloney and then Marie Francis:

First thing Monday morning, whatever you wore on a Sunday, you would take to the pawn shop, and some people would get it out on the Friday. Say you got a shilling for a bundle, you would receive 10d, and when you went back, you had to pay another 2d to get it out. It cost so much to redeem that parcel, and if you didn't redeem it in that time, he could do what he liked with it. More often than not he sold it. You've got the same now with the jewellery.

What women would do then, they would go down to Woollies and get a cheap ring, put it on and pawn the wedding ring! Oh they were up to all those sorts of tricks. I know me mother used to pawn dad's suit, and when she had pawned it, he wasn't supposed to know. So what she used to do, she used to have his braces dangling with his shirt over it and he thought his suit was there and it was only the braces!

As a child you knew that was going on, but we couldn't

do nothing about it. You were afraid that she wouldn't be able to get it out! It happened. Me mother pawned me boots, didn't she? And she sent me brother to get them out for me on the Saturday. They had to. More tricks than a monkey![8]

My mother was very ingenious in the face of poverty. She used to get dress patterns and make them up with the linings of old coats from second-hand shops. Those dresses were in the pawn shop the next day, hanging outside to be sold. Think about it, she made these dresses out of old linings of coats that she bought in second-hand shops. Some of the coats were rotten, but . . . the lining was all right. First time I saw our dresses outside, we'd only worn them once, and I am only a child and I am thinking why has she put them up there? I didn't realise then what a wonderful woman![9]

As a lad, Frank Vaudrey worked for a while at Cookson's, the well-known pawnbroker on Scotland Road, and observed the skills of these women firsthand.

Old Cookson himself owned many shops in Liverpool at one time. He lived in Caldy on the Wirral, a very posh part of Merseyside. There was a fellow at the Pier Head with a taxi. I'd have to wait outside the shop with an umbrella and with the taxi fare of 7/6 [about 38p]. I'd have to pay the taxi and get him in the shop. He was always there dead on nine o'clock. Sometimes he would go for a walk. He wore a trilby hat and carried a stick. He'd walk down Scotland Road, and he'd say, 'Always walk on the sunny side of the street, young

Vaudrey; you never know when it's going to rain.' The women would be washing their doorsteps and it'd be, 'Hello Mr Cookson.' He'd know all the names, you know. A character. I was only sixteen. Once I got kidded when two women came in. They had low-cut dresses on, flopped their breasts on the counter, and said, 'We'll want to look at the sets of rings.' Next thing, a couple of the rings are gone. I got a right bollocking for that. It was a learning curve.

Mother Liverpool's tactics were the art and science of her success. But they would never have been enough to ensure her and her family's survival on their own. What saved her was the tribal culture, a series of concentric circles, in the centre of which was the family circle. The next circle included the neighbours, then the wider local community, the parish (the religious circle), and possibly a cultural circle, like the Irish Centre, and of course the circle that encompassed 'the working class'. There were all kinds of levels in 'working class', which bonded together and vied for supremacy with the next. Finally, came the Liverpool circle to which everyone belonged. This was really the most supportive of all psychologically, because it was the face shown to the world. It was the identity to which everyone laid claim. Liverpool against the world.

Very often, survival depended on a woman's success in maintaining contact with each of these circles in turn, in particular her neighbours closest to her. How did she do that? Bill Owen:

[Mother] never went out. Sat on her steps and talked. That's

the way they used to get to know the ins and outs of
everything, sitting on the steps.[10]

Joan Gibbons: I used to listen, because in those days women
used to congregate. They didn't go out to work – well,
women didn't in those days – they used to congregate and
jabber, jabber, jabber.[11]

The wash-house was another place for Mother Liverpool to
jabber, as we have seen, and the corner shop. Tommy
Walsh's little shop in Blundell Street, where sanctuary was
offered to battered wives and where seamen shopped for
'blue mottled soap, long bars roughly three inches long by
three inches deep, that looked just like Gorgonzola cheese',
became something of a linchpin of the local community.

Yeah, yeah, yeah. I knew more about my customers than
they knew about themselves. I mean, I will tell you now, the
women would get a coupon for extra milk when they were
pregnant – we are talking about food rationing days. They
would come in to me and they would pass it over like that
[surreptitiously], and I would say, 'Yes, yes,' and it was like,
'Jimmy doesn't know yet.' Her husband didn't know! OK, I
would just make sure they got their extra milk and never say
a word. My lips were sealed.

At the centre lay the family home, rented of course. Even
when Mary Smith was living in Sedgemoor Residential
Home, where this interview was conducted, in her heart
and mind she never left it.

I loved living in that house, and still do. My happiest times were when we had a crowd in it. It was a crowded house. My brother and his wife died, leaving seven children, so we took in two of them, aged one-and-a-half and two-and-a-half. The happiest times were when we were all together. We enjoyed ourselves amongst ourselves. We didn't have parties with outsiders. Dad used to sing after a drink. He only ever knew the choruses. By degrees my brothers and sisters left Liverpool. We used to cry our eyes out when one of them left. It was very sad but we got used to it. Then eventually it was just me left. Years ago I knew everyone in the street. Now I know about five people . . . Eventually, my brother bought the house, and my nephew and niece handed it over to me. 'It's yours while you're alive.' We first moved in there just before the war. I wouldn't change it for the world but there might be a time when I've got to go.[12]

Don't let the nostalgia of old age mislead you. These women were strong, physically and emotionally. Mother Liverpool exuded a muscular femininity. Take washday, for example. May Duke remembers:

Mother had to be up at six o'clock to light the old brick boiler out in the kitchen – it was called a back kitchen then – and you had to light a fire underneath the boiler, see. When the copper was boiling, the whites went in, and the coloureds got done when the whites were finished . . . They had dolly pegs, wooden dolly pegs, which they used to use as a posser – a round stool with about six legs and a long stem in the middle and a handle. You just [pounded] that inside the boiler and that did the rough work for you. It lasted all day, because the afternoon was spent in blueing and starching . . . To get the water out of the washing we had a mangle – two huge rollers and a big iron wheel. No wonder they all had good muscles, you know? To get the soapy water out they had to go in cold water [first] in the old tin bath, which we all got bathed in on a Saturday night. To get the clothes dry, they were hung out in the street. There were lines strung out across the street and they had an arrangement between the families who would be using the lines and how many hours on a certain day. It was a rota system. When the ironing was done the clothes got put up on a wooden rack hoisted up to the ceiling. So anybody who came into the house could see everything that you wore and everything your father wore and his long-johns and everything, you know? She was always in a bad temper on washing day.

Emotional strength flowed from having to handle tragedy, infant death or accident, since childhood:

Saturday night was bath night, and it was always a nightmare. Because there were no fridges in those days, and we had little money, Mother, like lots of other housewives, went shopping on a Saturday night when the food was sold off more cheaply, rather than it be kept in the shops over the weekend to go bad. As a consequence, I was left in the house with six children to bath, whose ages ranged from three weeks to ten years, when I was a tiny twelve-year-old.

I had to fill the boiler from the kitchen tap and light a fire under it using paper, wood chips and coal. In order to keep the water warm enough for the children to be bathed, I had to supplement the hot water from the boiler with kettles and pans of hot water, which I heated on the hob in the other room. The next job was to drag the heavy zinc bath in from its nail in the yard. The bath then had to be filled from the boiler, which entailed putting in cold water first, then topping it up with hot. I had to make sure the children were bathed in order, with the youngest child being first, so he could be put to bed first.

On one particular night all was going well until the baby started crying, and I had to attend to him. My brother, Ivor, the next eldest, at ten years old, asked if he could help. As the water in the kettle had mostly been used up, I asked him to refill it. He removed the lid from the kettle before he reached the tap and the escaping steam burned his hand. With a yelp of pain he dropped the kettle. The boiling water that it still contained spilled down his bare legs and feet, badly scalding him, and he cried out even more loudly. The other children started to scream as well. I was terrified . . . All I could think of was to send for an adult to help and I sent the next eldest child, Phyllis, aged about eight, to fetch a neighbour, but they were all out shopping for cheap food as well. In desperation, I emptied the flour bag on the burn, because I thought this was clean and dry. I can still hear his screams, and he bears the scars to this day.[13]

For girls, especially older daughters of large families, childhood was an apprenticeship for what was to follow.

Joan Gibbons: You meet someone, you get married, you have children and that's it. There were no high aspirations, there was no education, but some clever people lived up our way. I've heard since they have done very, very well. The brain ability was always there, the initial education was never there, it just was not there.[14]

Mother Liverpool and her daughters were not without their champions through this time, however. Eleanor Rathbone was a leading campaigner for women, and the biggest demo in favour of women being given the right to vote took place in 1910. Hundreds were arrested and taken to Walton Prison for two weeks hard labour. Jane Warton, a young seamstress, was one of them. She went on hunger strike and had to suffer the horrors of forced feeding. The press were uninterested in her story until it emerged that, in fact, she was Lady Constance Bulwer-Lytton, the influential British suffragette activist and campaigner, in disguise. The ensuing furore led to suffragettes being categorised as political prisoners and getting slightly better treatment as a result. By 1914 there were no less than nine suffragette organisations functioning on Merseyside.

Eleanor Rathbone, born in 1872, was the daughter of William Rathbone, older brother of the aforementioned Hannah Mary Rathbone, and described by the *Liverpool Daily Post* in 1902 as 'one of the grandest old men whom Liverpool has ever claimed as a son'. The Rathbones were quite a family, probably as wealthy, relatively, as the philanthropic Moores family today and highly influential in the city's early history. Eleanor worked throughout her life to improve pay and working conditions for Liverpool women, and was the principal mover behind the Family Allowance. She was the founder of many organisations, among them the 1918 Club, an exclusive women's only discussion forum, which still meets twice a month at the famous Adelphi Hotel in Ranelagh Place[15] by Lime Street. Recently, they approached Ken Dodd to speak, holding out little hope that he would accept. Dodd, a Freeman of the City, is among Liverpool's most loyal celebrities and leads anything but a celebrity life. Aware of the significance of the invitation, he agreed and immediately waived his fee, treating the relatively small membership today (which fact bothered him not at all) to a special rendition of his signature song, 'Happiness'.

Although most Liverpool mothers didn't have a job outside the home, some, of necessity, did. Frank Smith's mother was orphaned at two years of age, and was widowed when Frank, born in 1934, was a child. So she had to work. Tragedy seemed to shadow Mrs Smith from the day she was born.

> My mother's date of birth was the day, the minute, the hour the *Titanic* sunk, 15 April 1912. It was significant. She read everything she could about it. Also it was the same [date in April] the Liverpudlians got crushed at Hillsborough.[16] She was born in Netherfield Road. She worked for the British American Tobacco Company as a young girl and then, when the war started, she worked as a milk-rounds woman, pulling a handcart. Then she wasn't strong enough to pull the handcart, so she went and worked for the Co-op on the bacon counter, groceries and stuff like that. She retired when she was seventy-two. I learnt everything from my mum.

For all her privations, Mother Liverpool held a position in

the family and in the community that reflected her special qualities, her power certainly, as Tommy Walsh recalls:

> The wife was always more powerful than the husband, in the sense that she managed, she made all the decisions. I still see that around me now. I know couples and the fellows are all, you know, 'big talk'. But for the little woman, would they have a roof over their heads?[17]

Her fecundity was recognised, too, and also her intuitive side, what you might call her wisdom, which perhaps fewer women replicate in society today, now that the extended family is no more.

The extended family was the first and principal connection in the tribal network, the collective well on which a mother could draw, not only for practical help. Eileen Devaney's father, a miner from the West Coast of Ireland, met her mother, again of Irish descent but born in Liverpool, in the 1940s. As soon as they were married, the couple became part of a multi-generational family community.

> What happened, me mum has got lots of sisters and they all lived in a rented house in Everton Brow. This house that we stayed in, my grandfather, my mother's father, had rented it when he was a full-time officer for the Transport and General Workers Union.
>
> It was big. It had a basement, ground floor, first floor. And so, what would happen, as a sister married, she and her husband would take the front parlour, as we called it, and a bedroom up at the top, and a little pantry at the back for

cooking. Then, once they got their own place, they would move out. For example, my auntie Eileen, she lived in the living room, bedroom and that until she got this little two-up two-down farther up in Everton. Then there was two brothers, but one was very seriously damaged from the Second World War, mentally and physically, and he never married, and the other one, Uncle Ted, he was very young compared to the aunties we lived with. Downstairs, well, there was Granda and me uncle James, and there was Auntie Lilly, who had been married – she was one of those who had a terrible marriage – and Auntie Nelly, Auntie Sheila and Auntie Frances. Auntie Sheila and Auntie Frances were very much into opera and I remember being given the old gramophone that you wound up. Mario Lanza. We would have all that.

This was normal. Next door to us there was a family who rented a house the same size. There were about four families, five families, and us, who were all in a similar situation. I was born in 1951 and me mum had to have three jobs. Me dad was down the mines, but she would be cleaning in a solicitor's office at 5 a.m., then she would be somewhere else cleaning. So how she did it I really don't know, it was just so difficult. She would tell you she was lucky because she had her sisters to support her as well, and neighbours. Everyone was in each other's houses, and if someone was going to go to the park with the children, they would say to us, 'Do you want to come along?' Give us a bottle of water and a couple of biscuits, you know, that kind of thing.

The extended family supported the mother in her

children's moral education too, as Peggy Tully, aged ninety-five, whom I met in Limekiln Lane, observed:

> My mother, my father and all the relatives were responsible
> for how I was brought up. It was strict, but within reason.
> We knew where to stop. Our children were brought up right.
> But they've deviated and their children have had more
> freedom. These days they don't know where to stop. Look at
> these youngsters with knives. How can you condone that?

Peggy's experience of the extended family was crucial, as we shall see later. So often childhood memories of a grandma or a grandpa or of some other member of the extended family is the most significant, because of course there is wisdom and experience in the older generation, and seasoned love, as Joan Gibbons discovered when still a child:

> We didn't have much money, but me granny and
> grandfather were lovely and I clung to them. They were
> lovely people. Now, my grandfather was a docker, a lovely
> big Irish man, quiet as a mouse. He was lovely. In Liverpool
> we chose the strongest men, and the men who were
> workers. Well, you had to go out to work each morning and
> stand in the Pen, and the boss would come along and pick
> out. Oh yeah. They always picked my grandfather. He was a
> coal heaver. They called them stevedores. But the coal got on
> his chest and he died when he was my age now, when he
> was seventy-two.
>   Me grandfather was so quiet he hardly spoke at all. He
> would come in and just say, 'Hello child.' He adored children,
> adored them, and the only time he ever raised his voice was

if a child was out in the street crying. He'd say, 'What do you think is ailing that child?'

'I don't know, Grandfather.'

He would go and find out. He would stand by the door and ask, 'What's your child crying for?'

'Oh well, she's had a fight.'

'Go and comfort your child, don't let the child cry.'

And always the neighbours would say, 'Oh, if Martin Walsh is in, don't let your child cry, or he'll be out!' I used to think, isn't my grandfather soft, but I realise now he was wonderful, he cared about children so, so much.

But anyway, I will tell you this tale. This is one of the saddest tales I have ever heard. The rate of infant mortality was high, and me granny and grandfather had their last little child, Catherine. They called her Kitty, and she was ten months old when she died. She got pneumonia. Well, of course, no antibiotics then, no antibiotics and she died. Me granny used to tell me, 'Joan, when Kitty died, I wanted to die too, and I used to go to bed early every night to be on my own and just cry, cry and cry. Your grandfather used to come up to bed and I was still crying, and he'd say, "You've got to stop it, you've got to stop it," and I'd say, "I can't."' She couldn't stop crying for however long. Me gran was ill with depression, but they didn't know such a word then. Anyway, she said, 'Martin, you don't understand, you're a man, you don't understand.'

Decades later, when me grandfather died, me granny said, 'Child, gather up your grandfather's stuff.' And I said, 'Granny, he keeps his donkey jacket in the hallway. Do you want that?' She was blind, couldn't see a thing, and she said, 'Yes, bring it all in.' She said, 'Search the pockets,' and I looked in the pockets and I said, 'Oh, there's a little thing in here, it's a baby's shoe.' Me gran said, 'Joan, describe the baby's shoe.' I said, 'Well, it's brown,' and she said, 'That's right, a light brown.' I said, 'Yeah,' and she said, 'And it's got a strap across.' I said, 'Yeah,' and she said, 'A little buckle with a brown button on the end,' and I said, 'Yeah, Granny, how did you know?' And she started to cry, 'Oh, God,' and I said, 'Granny, what's the matter?' And she said, 'Joan, it's Kitty's shoe.' I said, 'What? The little baby who died all those years ago?' And she said, 'Is it very soft?' I said, 'Oh yeah,' and she took hold of it and she cried and cried and cried.

And when she stopped crying, she said, 'Joan, do you remember I told you men don't understand, and I'd said, "You're only a man, you don't understand"? Well, not only had he understood, he cared more about that baby than what I did.' Well, he did, didn't he? God knows how many jackets he'd had since Kitty died. He had that shoe and he kept it.[18]

Critically, in moral and practical terms, the extended family fostered a sense of duty, which was often exercised beyond the home, in the community. Saturday morning for Josie Burger in Handel Street meant 'steps cleaned, steps scrubbed, then all the messages, my mother's messages and two grandmas' messages'. Neither 'grandma' was a direct relation.

There were eleven children, so by the time Jacob and George and Karl were born, Edward [Teddy], my eldest brother, lived with Grandma Besantie. I looked after Grandma Besantie with the messages.

Teddy used to run from school, knock and shout through her letter box and take me to put my hand through to get the key and get in. He'd run up the stairs and I would have to help her to get up then. I had to sit in front of her on the stairs and come down, like so. She sat on each stair, I was in front so that she didn't go forward until we come to the bend, where there was a big post. And there's fifteen minutes gone! I washed her, I combed her hair. She couldn't walk, only round, like, from one piece of furniture to the next.

Every Saturday night I went up to the Boundary public house at the top of Lodge Lane, got a cab, the proper cab with the shed on like a baby's pram, a hansom cab. I would have said that was about 1954 I was doing that. I was born in 1941. I would hail it. Every taxi driver knew me and they knew they had to come down and get my grandmother. Then they would help her in, because she was big. They would push her in, and I would sit the other side of her and they would take her to Mulberry Street, where the old Children's Hospital was. It's the University now. There's a little pub there, where her sons were waiting for her. It was a little corner pub, it was lovely. They were all steel erectors and she was in for the night.

She had seven sons, one of them married my father's sister, that's how she became Grandma. Every son come [to see her] every night before they went home to their wives. So I used to have to get a quarter of boiled ham, a quarter of brawn, a quarter of chopped pork.

Now, Grandma Besantie was a bit of a moneylender. She was very busy. She had a pocket on. Under her pinny there was another pinny and an underskirt, and under that there was a big pocket. It was nothing to do with me, I was too young. You had to go out of the room [when business was being conducted].

Knock at the door. 'Who is it?' she would say. And I would say, 'Mrs so-and-so.' 'OK, come on in. You go down and see if your mother needs you.' Those were the words so you knew not to be there.

I remember the morning she died. It was a Saturday morning. The landlord was collecting the rent in the street and he said to my mother, 'Oh, isn't it a shame and sad about Mrs Besantie.' 'What's the matter with Mrs Besantie?' And the landlord told her she had died. I think I was thirteen.

Her grandson came last year. He was looking for me in St Bernard's church. He went to Mass and asked, 'Does Josie Burger still come to Mass?' And they said, 'Well, we'll take you to her.' They didn't even ask who he was! And he was here. He gave me the picture I have of her. We called him Binty, I don't know why. I said, 'Oh Binty, come on in, stay for your dinner, have your dinner.' He'd been all around here, into the church and everywhere where he was courting his wife. She'd just died, so he'd come back to look at it all. I thought, isn't that lovely!

After Grandma Besantie died, all the attention fell on the other grandma in the Kingsley Road. Her name was Granny Forsyth. She lived in a very big house. I used to go at four o'clock to her. She was, I think, Welsh. Not related at all. How did it begin? One day she called me up the step. She couldn't walk and I was going to school. She said, 'Come girl,' and you had to go in, didn't you?

I was interested to learn that Grandma Besantie had been a moneylender, also that she'd had seven sons who doted on her. The arrangement sounded similar to one that I'd heard about in the East End of London, where the matriarch of the family, holder of the purse strings, entered into the money-lending business and relied upon her sons to chase up bad debts. Had there been any splitting of heads, cracking of bones in the Besantie household? Josie claimed to have been too young to know 'the ins and outs'. Later, however, I came upon a case that shows quite clearly that Mother Liverpool was equal to anything for which Violet Kray could claim credit. Veronica Blyth grew up in the 1930s in Edge Lane.[19]

My mother was a moneylender, my father a bookmaker. She had to go to court once a year to get a licence. I think you paid £10 for a licence in those days, and then people called at the house and borrowed money. They used to pay back weekly what they owed her. They had a little book and she'd sign it, how much they paid each week . . . I think there was a lot of poverty, an awful lot of poverty around, because otherwise people wouldn't have wanted to borrow money, would they? There was knocking on the door all the time. It must have been very hard for people [in the thirties]. I don't think there was much work at the time, really.

We had everything. We had a cellar full of food, and I don't think we were rationing anything. My mother wasn't anyway. She didn't seem to be. We had big hams hanging down there . . . I think it used to come from the docks. We had so many people to the door all the time that you wouldn't know who was coming in, but there was food taken down to the cellar. So we were never short of anything, and as I say, I'm sure it was black market. I think it must have gone on quite widely.

My mother used to buy coupons from people who came to the door . . . food coupons and clothes coupons. I think buying coupons was pretty illegal, too. I think she would have been put in jail. She'd have had a bloody good fight, I'm sure, if they'd taken her! Oh God, she had a terrible temper!

We had the best of everything . . . I remember my mum and dad having a row, it's funny this. My dad had done something. I don't know what it was, but there was a big row going on. And my mother had a nice fruit bowl, middle of the table, and she picked it up and hit him with it. Then she looked at the price underneath and put it down again! Very dominant woman. They say I'm like her, you know. I'm not at all happy about that. I suppose you can't help your nature, can you? My father was a very placid man. Used to take us to the cemetery every Sunday. 'Want to have a good time? Let's go to the cemetery!' We used to go to Ford's Cemetery on the bus to look at the graves, the big families that had died. We'd walk around and then go back home for dinner . . . He used to love cemeteries. Got to quite like them myself.

When I mentioned all this to Freddie Ashcroft at the Shrewsbury House Boys Club in Everton, he could only give me the economics:

Our local moneylender was Polly Shaw. She was the richest woman in the area. She lived in the same street as us and if you borrowed £1 off her, you had to pay 2/6 [about 13p]. So

if you borrowed £1, the following week you paid £1 2s 6d
[£1.13p], and if you missed, it went to £1 10s [£1.50p].

It was a good rate of interest. The next circle of support was
the Church. The parish circle was significant – baptism,
confession, absolution, marriage, funeral, and of course
new arrivals to the area. A pair of sisters I met in Wavertree
told me about their experience in the 1950s, which
although far removed in time, was strikingly similar to that
of the famine migrants in 1850.

Sisters Lol and Vera from Wavertree were two of many
women I spoke to who came to Liverpool for love. It all
began when they met a group of Liverpool lads over in
Mosney, 25 miles outside Dublin, at Butlin's Holiday Camp.

> There were five of them. We were just dancing with them all
> week, larking around. We had other fellows as well! What
> happened was, when we all split up for going home, they
> said they were having a day in Dublin. They didn't go until
> that night, you see, and they asked us, could we spend the
> day with them? We went home to Mother and asked her,
> and she said, 'Yes, just look after yourselves,' and we went
> all around Dublin with them, spent the day . . .

The boys stayed in touch, and the two girls decided to give
it a go in Liverpool. I wondered how their mother had
taken it?

> Well, we fell out with Mother, bit of a row. What was
> happening was Vera was going to go first. I was in Mother's
> business, you see – baby linen manufacturing. It was just a

small business. I said to Vera, 'I won't come until August.'
She was to go that April. It was a bit of a shock to my
mother, the two of us going. We had a huge row and
Mother said to me, 'You're sly. You've got your tickets and
you're slying away on Friday!' And I hadn't! I was that hurt, I
said, 'Right now! I will go!'

So we came over and the first thing we did was to go to
the Church, to St Patrick's on Mount Pleasant. And the priest
said, 'OK, I know a hotel where you will be safe,' and we
went to the Vernon. You had to have an address to get a job
then. So we got on the bus and we said we would go
somewhere where it was nice. We saw Sefton Park and
thought that looked nice. It reminded us of where we had
come from, the greenery and the open fields and all that. So
we got off the bus there and we went to St Clare's, Arundel
Avenue. The parish priest brought us in to where the ladies
were, and the confraternity,[20] and we got the flat through
them. We went into a factory to work. Then Vera married
John, the fellow she met at Butlin's. I didn't marry mine. I
just wasn't keen on him, although he was a very nice lad. I
got my husband later through a blind date in Liverpool. He
was a blind date through Vera's John.

'So that worked out to be very romantic,' I said to Vera.

Oh it was lovely. He was a hosiery knitter at Bear Bran
in Woolton.

So the Church had an important role in the community,
but as I have already suggested, at a price. Joan Gibbons:

The priest came round not so much because you were one of the flock, but for money. He would go round every Friday night, and Father Fitz, our priest, said to me, 'Joan, would you come round every Friday with me? Ask your mum and dad if you can.' Father Fitz said, 'Go in front of me, three houses in front, and say, "Father Fitzpatrick's on his way."' I did that, and I asked my mother, 'Can I do this every Friday with Father Fitz?' And she said, 'Oh yeah, you can do that.' I said, 'Isn't it nice, Mum, that he wants me to go in front of him so they've time to tidy up before the priest comes?' God, I was naïve! Me mam said, 'No, they're not tidying up before the priest comes, they're getting the money together.' I suppose scratching around for money. The priest had a canvas bag and he would come in and say, 'God rest all in the house.' Everybody would stand up. 'Is everybody all right? How are things? Yeah, good, good,' and – it was so degrading – hand the canvas bag out and you would put your money in and that was the Church revenue. It was the only revenue apart from the Catholic clubs.[21]

Sometimes this got comically out of hand, as May Duke recalled.

The area I lived in was very, very Irish Catholic . . . churches on practically every corner . . . and there was a lot of rivalry among these churches, too. Every Sunday without fail the priest would come round collecting, but the priest from our parish would go and collect in St Anthony's and the priest from St Anthony's would collect in our parish as well, you see? Then sometimes a priest from All Soul's, and there was St Bridget's, St Mary of the Angels, all these. A knock would come at the door – 'Father Swarbrick!' And there'd be a dive to hide the *News of the World*, because it was forbidden!

One might imagine that births and deaths assumed less significance in the community because instances of them were so much more frequent, but in fact they were celebrated in the office of one of the key persons in the community, who delivered the newborn and dressed and 'laid out' the dead, a figure whose unheralded appearance held a strange, rather primitive significance. Being so important, she was of course a woman, not a man. This was something a priest couldn't possibly do, as Bill Owen describes.

We didn't have midwives. The community had what they called a helper, a handywoman, and they allus had a shawl around them, you know? Well, as kids we used to know when there was a birth, we used to see her going into the houses. Births, deaths, marriages, that's all the women lived for in them days. An' of course, they'd have a few gills when they come back [from a funeral], you know? They put the coffin in the house. Oh, if it were a youngster, all kinds of schoolchildren would be comin' in and that. Oh aye, yes.

Well, of course, we were Protestants, but my mother was a Catholic, and the real Catholic families used to have wakes. They were all right, them wakes. Our best 'do' before we got married was a wake. Oh we used to have some fun at a wake. Some of 'em might have it going on for two or three days. Well, the day before the funeral, they have all sorts of things in the house – you know, eats and that, and then all kinds of bevy. And they'd be singing. Many a time they used to dress the corpse up while they were having these wakes. Oh aye, put 'em in their best clothes. [The body would be there in the room.] Some of them slept in the same room, if there were a lot of kids. Oh aye. Just lay the body out . . . Oh aye . . . The wakes.

We had how many died! I think we had a death every year – one of the children. There was thirteen. There was about eight died between me and my sister that's living now. She's seventy odd. About six or seven births and about eight deaths. Nearly every year there was something, you know? What did they die of? Mostly of convulsions. Underfed.

Occasionally, the community stepped in at a humanitarian level that simply amazes us today. Mavis O'Flaherty was born Mavis Cubbin in the Toxteth Park neighbourhood of the early 1940s, when the community culture was rich enough to defy any law so low as to penalise unmarried mothers.

My mother had me before she was married. It was the war years – I'm sixty-seven years of age – and she came out of the local hospital just down the road from here, which was Sefton General, and her sister and my uncle said she couldn't go back with them because they already had some children and another one on the way, and it was overcrowded. So this neighbour said, 'I'll look after your baby for you,' and the neighbour looked after me for twenty-seven years, and she didn't have a husband behind her. I don't know my father. I was brought up by a lady who lived in the same street as my family.

It was just by Princes Park, not far from the docks [Herculaneum], the area where that TV series, Bread, was filmed – Malwood Street [between Cockburn Street and Grafton Street]. I grew up in a two-up two-down, where everybody knew everything about everybody else.

She had never been married. She had five children of her own, two brothers and three sisters, three I think with Chinese . . . I think it was the same father, I think it was a Chinaman. I never met him and when I was growing up you would never ask. There was never a man living in the house when I was a child. The other two children were English. Their father I did meet. He was a musician. At one stage he played with the Liverpool Philharmonic Orchestra. As I was growing up, they had these (well they still have them) industrial concerts, and when it came round to my birthday in May, he always invited us, sent us two tickets to go to a concert. We would meet him in St John's Gardens behind St George's Hall. I can always remember, we had a box of Quality Street! He was 'Uncle George' and he was English, but I don't know anything else about him.

I struggled to take in what Mavis was saying. Was the surrogate being paid by Mavis's natural mother? What was the situation? Mavis knew only that she had been 'the most amazing person', and, of course, she served the whole community as this mythical figure we met earlier.

Well, she helped everybody. She was the person in the street who would go along and lay a person out after they died. She used to say it was the greatest honour. The youngest next to me when she took me over was seventeen. I was the baby, so that's why I was fussed over.

So when you were growing up, there was probably just you and this woman?

> That's right, yes. We were very, very close. She influenced me to treat everybody the same. Be cautious about people, but try and help people in your life and you will always be rewarded. That was her way. She was a lady who never had very much in the way of money, clothes or anything else, and I vowed to myself that when I left school, I would look after her, which I did.

Beyond the local community was sometimes a cultural centre, which was the Irish Centre for most families in the Scotland Road area. In 1960, Tommy Walsh decided that 'the only way we could have events as we wanted them was by having our own Centre'.

> I wanted to have the sort of social attitude that my father had. I wanted the awareness of Irish culture and history that he had . . . I became very conscious that the Irish community in Liverpool had no home of its own, nowhere to have functions and so on and so forth. So, in 1960, we formed the Irish Centre Building Fund Committee, and in 1964 we bought the premises in Mount Pleasant. I think of the next twenty-five years as the golden age of the Irish community in Liverpool – 1965 to 1990. If we didn't retain our own dancing, music, language, then we would have nothing to give to the community in which we live, and we would sink without trace, and that's not integration. Integration is leaving your mark by adding your cultural activities to the society in which you live.

It was this organisation that helped keep the Liverpool Irish community in touch with its cultural roots – Irish music, dancing, Gaelic football, which Tommy refereed – and suddenly life began to revolve around all the Irish traditions. They were valued again, and those values could be passed on from one generation to the next.

> There were three Irish families all living next door to each other in our street, the McDermots, the Dylans and me mum and dad. When we were children, there would be Irish music playing in the streets at midnight, because we didn't go out when we were young. Me mum and dad would stay at home and we would have a party with the Irish music and everything in the street. We had the community at home.[22]

Breege McDaid came over from Ireland in the mid-1980s, another chasing love, as it happens. She has since married her quarry and is now coordinator for Irish Community Care on Merseyside.

> I'm one of the new arrivals in Liverpool. I wasn't part of that lovely big strong community, campaigning to get the Irish Centre together, or in the days when the Irish Centre was buzzing. I wasn't part of that, but people tell you all their memories and you think, wow, that must have been fantastic. Children of the Irish communities of the fifties and sixties have done particularly well. That became clear in the film, *Craic*, that the Irish Centre produced, when they were saying, 'Now, my children are doctors.' Lots of second generation Irish people have done well, and probably will continue to do so.

Half a century earlier, a few philanthropic organisations were started not by the community, nor by the Church, but by some well doer. I choose the term advisedly. The League of Welldoers, based in Limekiln Lane, off Scotland Road, saw a clear advantage in not being attached to any church or tribal group of any sort. Lesley Black, who helps run the League today, told me about it:

> The Vauxhall area is predominantly very parochial. There were lots of churches, but people who belonged to this parish wouldn't cross that invisible boundary to go to that parish, so everybody stayed within their area.
>
> We actually started life in 1893 as the Liverpool Food Association, and are known locally as 'the Lee Jones' because our founder was Herbert Lee Jackson Jones, who was born in 1868. When he was twenty-five, he was at a loss with himself. He didn't really have as much confidence in himself as others did. He thought that he wasn't clever enough to go into business, and he actually considered going into the Church. He had started his studies, but for some reason decided not to go ahead with it. He found himself in this area of Liverpool, the Vauxhall area, and he was just appalled at the conditions that the children were living in, so he decided to do something about it. His intention was to set up a school meals service. He found an empty cotton warehouse, which was on this site, set up a big kitchen and got in touch with the great and the good to ask could they send money to help him buy the produce. This is a heavily Catholic area, but the money didn't come from the Church. He stood alone and said it didn't matter what faith you were, and it didn't matter what colour you

were. Very unusual. It went against the grain for an awful lot of people. Lots of youngsters would come here, not just to have school meals. We used to have a big party, with long trestle tables and benches, and they would come for soup and that kind of thing.

On a Monday morning in the local schools, the priests would go into the classrooms and bless all the children and ask them, 'Did anyone go to Mass on Sunday?' All that kind of thing, and the very last question would be, 'And who went to the Lee Jones?' Lulled into a false sense of security, the honest ones among them would put up their hands, and they had to do a penance, because it was so totally against the Catholic church at the time to go to an organisation that wasn't religious. We actually have two nuns as members now. I think that's lovely.

Next to the warehouse are what people here call 'cottages', but I'm not talking pretty thatched roofs – very, very small houses, all on top of one another, where large families would live. And in the family immediately next door was a dad who had been injured during the First World War and was never able to maintain a full-time job. Well, Lee Jones would knock on his door and say, 'Can you come and do this little job for me?' So this man became a DIY man on an ad hoc basis for the League, and his eldest daughter, Peggy Tully, is one of our members still. She is in her mid-nineties, and she remembers coming in with her dad.

When I met her, Peggy, whose observation on the moral influence of the extended family was mentioned earlier, remembered her childhood spent here as if it was yesterday.

I was born in 1914. We lived next door. Now, when all's said and done, Lee Jones had taken over that part of the building, so I was part of this place. It was my life! I used to play in his garage when I was a toddler. You know those old-fashioned carriages they used to have? The horses used to stand in there.

My family was very poor. My father had been injured in the 1914 war, mentally injured, and he couldn't get a job. He was in the hold of a ship that was torpedoed. He was a stoker and there was no way out. He just got hold of this relic, which he always wore round his neck, and prayed, 'Dear God, help me.' And in the distance he saw a blue light just forming into a square, and he went for it, and that's how he got out the last time.

He never worked after that. He did bits and pieces here. Lee Jones asked him to do odd jobs. And the ladies who helped Lee Jones often used to give us food parcels and things like that, or when they had clothing from people, they used to give us slip-offs.

For us it was hard, but there was always hope. There was always somebody there to help you. There was light at the end of the day, sort of thing. Without Lee Jones we wouldn't have survived, and that's all there is to it.

What do I remember about the man? He was a very, very good man. Goodness oozed from him. When he was coming towards you, you knew he was a good man. It seems impossible that anybody could have done what that man did for the children and the people.

We had a men's shelter here at one stage. Years ago, there was an old mill here and they took it over and made it into bedrooms. Lee Jones [did that] himself. They had about twenty rooms. The men used to come in, turned up the other side of Limekiln Lane, and they went up so many at a time. You got a supper, a good bath and an entertainment, and then you went to bed. I was only ten or twelve. I'm ninety-five this year, so this was in the 1930s. I was only a youngster.

Then he used to take us to the beach at New Brighton.[23] There'd be a little parcel and a drink. We used to walk down to the Pier Head with about four helpers watching over us. When we got there, we'd make castles in the sand, see who could build the best. Then a naughty one'd come along and kick them all down, and then there would be tears. But you'd build a castle again.

At Christmas time he had a big party in a big hall. [There'd be a] great big tree, and every child got a present. But before you went out to play you had chores. You had to wash the dishes and I always had to wash the floors. I had to look after the children, too, so wherever I went I always had a little one with me. I had five brothers and four sisters. Lee Jones was part of my life. Then in my teens you had to go out to work, so you weren't as close as you were.

I spent fifty years in London when I got married. Lambeth. My kiddies were born in London, near Lambeth Palace. But I could never leave Liverpool, though Liverpool today, pardon me saying it, is not the Liverpool I knew. It's completely different – different houses, different buildings, changed roads, and the names of them. But, inside, the Liverpudlians are the same.

Liverpudlians are known all over the world. They have travelled the world and they know how to welcome people.

They are freehanded. They don't hide behind a cloak. What
you see is what you get.

This was the ultimate support for Mother Liverpool, the
sense Peggy had of belonging, carried with her even
through fifty years away in London.

CHAPTER NINE

Solidarity

This sense of belonging found expression in political terms as 'solidarity'. Whether it was solidarity over race politics, religious, union or class politics, it was bred in the lap of Mother Liverpool and the extended family, as the following seven witnesses tell so forcefully:

Eric Lynch: I come from a political family. My mother was very political. Within our house there were always meetings taking place. When I was little my mother used to say to me, 'Come here, keep quiet,' and she would put me on her knee and she would say, 'Listen, you might learn something . . .' So, yes, I grew up with this political background, although we were poor, working-class people.[1]

Eileen Devaney: I think my politics goes down to me grandfather, because he was so determined that they would get everything that life could give them. He fought tooth and nail with the Labour Party over nationalisation, and he really had a lot of time for my father. Me dad and me granda really were very close. They were both avid socialists, totally committed. Me grandfather was the full-time officer for the Transport and General Workers Union for Liverpool City Transport. He was a union man. He had been on the Council, one of the very few early Labour councillors . . . so this is where a lot of it comes from. I mean, in our family everyone was in the Labour Party. The front parlour that we lived in was always the committee rooms when it was the elections, and that was always an exciting time for us. It was just great. We would be out on the loud hailers long before people said it was disgusting to bring children into politics. It was just wonderful for us.[2]

Joan Gibbons: Everybody, always, always, everybody, everywhere always voted Labour. There was no such thing as Tories, not at all.[3]

Anne Thompson: It is sort of instilled in you. Everything other than Labour is a swear word basically. Me Nan was a lifelong member of the Labour Party. She went on rallies down in London. She was really active in the Labour Party.[4]

Tommy Walsh: We had one of the few radios and I thought that the radio was Athlone. I didn't know you could get other stations. Athlone was the original name of Radio Eireann. Much later, I realised there were other stations, too, but my father only had Athlone, and he would only have the *Irish Press* in the house. We would get it in the local shop, and if they didn't have the *Irish Press*, he wouldn't allow the *Irish Independent* in the house. I have seen strangers, guests, visitors coming to the house and he would say, would you leave that outside please! The point about this, you've got to understand, is really very simple. The *Irish Independent* called for the execution of the 1916 leaders, but it went much deeper than that with my father. William Martin Murphy was the owner of the *Irish Independent* and he was the leader of the bosses in Dublin who locked out the workers in 1913 and caused dreadful hardship. Liverpool dockers brought kids over to be looked after by dockers' families here during the lock-out.[5] Still today, every time I buy an *Irish Independent* I feel guilty.[6]

(Member of the Irish Centre): My mother was born in Liverpool, but her parents were from Dundalk and she spent most of the summer holidays in Ireland with her relatives there. The Irish Volunteers were formed about 1914 to defend Ireland, mainly against the Germans because the First World War had broken out then. Now, attached to the Volunteers was an organisation called Cumann na mBan [an Irish republican women's paramilitary organisation]. My mother joined this organisation in Liverpool. Then in 1915 she went over to Ireland to the funeral of a well-known Irish Fenian[7] and she was part of the honour guard . . . so she had a thorough knowledge and background of Irish politics and history. She also took part in the Easter Rising in 1916.[8] She was actively in the Post Office with another four or five ladies. They went over for the Thursday night and took part

on the Easter Monday in the rioting in the GPO.[9] She was helping a guy called Captain Turner, who was in charge of the defence of Hopkins and Hopkins, a jewellery store opposite the Post Office in O'Connell Street. She was also involved in the 1940s when they started up the anti-partition of Ireland. About 1948 she joined that and I joined that with her.[10]

(Anonymous female): I remember me dad going to union meetings when I was about eight or nine. It's a strong memory that the meetings were important. So I was informed really young about politics. There were the rich and the poor, though in retrospect we lived quite well. But it was about where he was from and his inheritance. He was a working-class man, with a real low-skilled job. He was a lorry driver from Bootle. I got involved at fourteen or fifteen, when me sister worked at the Tax Office in Bootle. She was in the union there and they used to meet at a pub called the Jawbone. I used to go down and meet her. I'd not say much, but I'd have a laugh with these people, and they were all talking politics. That's what we'd talk about from fourteen years of age. So, the next thing, I was out in the streets, campaigning for the Militants when I was sixteen, knocking on doors.[11]

There is a political attitude deep in the heart of the Liverpudlian, a bit of an anarchic streak, which finds expression more light-heartedly in the humour, as one incomer found:

The first time I drove into Liverpool I came at night in my old van with Lucy, my daughter, who was two, and my lights

muel Walters' 'The Port of Liverpool, 1836', and *(inset)* Antony Gormley's 'Another ace, 1997', on permanent exhibition on Crosby beach. Both evince the call the sea made so many Liverpudlian seamen, and pay homage to the goddess who controls its tides.

e city's essential femininity ught by Arthur Dooley's iss Liverpool, 1969'.

Famously, the psychiatrist Carl Jung found himself in Liverpool, albeit in a dream.

Liverpool's heart of darkness, an African slave breaks free of his bonds (19th century).

Above: The famous Royal Liver, Cunard and Port of Liverpool Buildings.

Left: Mann Island, 1890s, showing th Docker's Umbrella, the world's first electrically operated overhead railwa

Bottom left: 'We used to go down to the Pier Head and ask them comir off the boats for a penny.'

Bottom right: 'We didn't notice we were poor, and we didn't want things. Today it's different.'

Right: There have been markets in Liverpool since the 13th century. 'This is life in the raw as hawkers try to make a few pennies.'

Middle right: Mrs Emma Hayes serves tea to some of the Shrewsbury House Club's youngest members.

Bottom left: Poverty was rife, starvation a reality. Lee Jones started the League of Welldoers in 1893. 'Lee Jones often used to give us food parcels. Without Lee Jones we wouldn't have survived, and that's all there is to it.'

Bottom right: When the Shrewsbury House Boys Club in Everton opened in 1903 'numerous groups of suspicious and unkempt boys poured in from the street'. Boxing was one of the disciplines. You had to be robust to survive.

BLUECOAT PRESS

SHREWSBURY HOUSE

SHREWSBURY HOUSE BOYS CLUB

'Merseyside at War'. Britain declared war on Germany at 11.15 a.m. on Sunday, 3 September 1939. In Liverpool, young men who had been at boys camp (*below*) only a few years earlier were now drafted to the front line. *Bottom left to right:* Jimmy Mackay, Bill Foulkes, Joe Rimmer and Private Bill Reece were among the first old boys of Shrewsbury House Boys Club to be called up. Secretary Barr Adams (*far right*) organised a Club of War, a book of all the letters from the front of serving old boys, to ensure that none would be forgotten.

ght: Coronation street party, 1953, in
ndel Street, Liverpool 8, where Josie
rger (*centre, looking up at camera*) was
rn in 1941.

ow left: Scotland Road, 1969.

ow right: The old world sat
ebrating in uneasy alliance with the
w. Nothing would ever be quite the
ne again.

tom left: Bill Harrison (*with guitar*)
d other Cunard Yanks, Liverpool
rchant seamen who brought the new
rld from America.

tom right: The Beatles surround Little
hard. It is a sobering thought that,
d it not been for the Liverpool slave
de, white rock and roll might not
e been.

JOSIE BURGER

BLUECOAT PRESS

PETER LEESON

BILL HARRISON

PETER KAYE PHOTOGRAPHY

Above: Joan Gibbons grew up in Kirkdale. 'We didn't have much mo[re] but my granny and grandfather wer[e] lovely and I clung to them.'

Middle left: Frank Vaudrey (*far right i[n] family group in 1966*) was brought up in a pre-fab next to Walton Park and at 16 went to work at Cookson's the pawnbroker in Scotland Road.

Top left: Eileen Newman (*far left with her cousin and sisters*) dressed for Mass in the 1950s. 'At Grammar School I was beginning to learn middle-class ways of being able to mix.'

Bottom left: George Lund (1960) in the back seat of his sister's boyfriend's 1958 Vauxhall Victor. 'I used to polish it for sixpence. In the late sixties we used to go to the GI camp at Burtonwood, to Base, the club there, because of course the music was up to the minute.'

Bottom right: Josie Burger has been p[art] of the Liverpool 8 scene all her life. black fellas that we mixed with then, had lovely parties and carnivals. Stee[l] bands – fabulous! Motown, jazz – lov[e] Dinah Washington, Brook Benton. Lovely, lovely era, that time.'

orror writer Ramsey
mpbell (and wife Jenny),
no took me down among
e creatures of the Pool,
fore the swamp alongside
og Lane had been
ained.

Eric Lynch, who was born
in Liverpool in 1932, and
has run a Slave Tour of the
city for thirty years. 'When
I was little my mother used
to say to me, "Come here,
keep quiet," and she would
put me on her knee and
she would say, "Listen, you
might learn something…"'

Phil Key, sometime Arts
Editor of the *Liverpool Daily
Post*, arrived in the city more
than forty years ago. 'On
every street corner there
was a musician, and then on
every street corner there was
a playwright. They went from
music to writing plays and
there was an embarrassment
of riches.'

ll and Wendy Harpe started the Blackie in Great George
reet in 1967 and took what was going on in the arts into
e black community. 'Allen Ginsberg came to Liverpool,
- had people who had been at the Paris riots, Tom Wolfe
.s around, and so on. We were part of an international
ene.'

Alan Dossor, who gave the
Everyman Theatre its golden
years, with his wife Dinah
in Ossie Clark dress (1968).
'I think one of the reasons
[the arts explosion] was able
to happen in Liverpool was
the huge energy that went
into local grass-roots activity.
You could feel it. You
could smell it. This wasn't
happening in other places.'

While the artistic transformation was proceeding in Liverpool's Bohemia, the area to the north of town was undergoing wholesale demolition. Joe Lundon (*above*) in Sylvester Street, Vauxhall, in 1970, as the neighbourhood crumbled about him.

Right: Toxteth boys on the move – a common problem during the cleansing of working class Liverpool was a feeling of exile, but children didn't notice the loss as much as their parents.

Below right: Sculptor Arthur Dooley in his workshop, a Liverpudlian first and an artist whose work relays the spirit of Liverpool for all ages.

Bottom left: Liverpool today, the spectacular 42-acre 'Paradise Found' development in Liverpool One, where retail is the relentless focus.

Bottom right: Dooley's 'Madonna', the inspirational feminine principle, which he found at the heart of Liverpool.

Peter Leeson discovered while making his film, *Us and Them*, that even as the new high rises went up and the old terraces came dow the removal man still used a horse and cart.

failed. I thought, 'Oh my God, I'm going to get arrested for driving in the dark with no lights.' So, the first policeman I saw, I stopped and said, 'What shall I do? My lights have failed and I've got to get into Liverpool.' I was in the outskirts. 'Oh,' he said, 'you'll be all right. If anybody stops you, just tell them, "Ernie says it's all right".' And I thought, 'I'm going to love this city, because it's sardonic.' It was anarchistic in a way that, at that time, felt quite safe to me.[12]

But early on in Liverpool's history, the anarchic was not as evident in the political forum as one might think. Liverpool was not initially a hotbed of militancy. The reason given is that 'the dockers, right up to the 1930s, still saw politics as an extension of the Fenian/Orange struggles over the water'.[13] There is strong evidence for this, as we shall see, but it may not be the whole story.

The first recorded strike in Liverpool was by shoe-makers in 1756. Then, in 1775, when the war with America, Liverpool's main customer in the lucrative slave trade, depressed seamen's wages from 30 to 20 shillings a month, a group of them took to the streets under a red flag and with red ribbons in their hair and stormed the Town Hall, brandishing guns. Tragically, troops brought in from Manchester turned bigger guns on them and there were a number of fatalities.

The Chartists' rallying calls came in 1838 and 1850. They might have been expected to get things moving in Liverpool, what with the dock industry now sizeable and the notorious 'casual' system of employment biting. But when, in 1840, Liverpool Chartist William Jones spoke in the area of Queen Square, a mere seven or eight thousand turned up, a poor showing compared with the hundreds of thousands the movement attracted elsewhere.

A group of skilled workers were the first to form a Trades Council (1848), followed by the city's Elementary Teachers in 1870, which nineteen years later became the National Union of Teachers.

The first real action occurred in 1889, when the tram workers, initially in Birkenhead, then in Liverpool, took matters in hand with amazing courage, bringing the city to a halt. Wages were at the heart of it, but also long hours and child exploitation. Young boys operating the tram points could expect to work a sixteen to eighteen hour day. The strike continued into 1890, when men were driven back to work by the threat of starvation.

The tram strike created awareness, and by the 1890s St George's Plateau was being used by demonstrators connected with Labour and the Left. Then, in 1892, the first meeting was held of the Liverpool branch of the Independent Labour Party (ILP), an organisation with a socialist constitution, albeit not as radical as the Social Democratic Federation, which had had its first meeting in Britain in 1881 and become the first Marxist political group in the country.

This was progress, however. Docker James Larkin was a leading member of the new party. His magnetic personality, gift of oratory and deep commitment to socialism attracted thousands to the cause, and he is commemorated still with a mural in Newz Bar in Water Street. Even so, Larkin found more to get his teeth into in Ireland, and he is better known for his resistance to the 1913 Dublin lockout than for anything he accomplished in Liverpool. But he was an important and heroic figurehead, a kind of Liverpool equivalent of the Glasgow Red Clydesiders, James Moxton, William Gallacher and John Maclean of this era, the latter appointed by Lenin himself as the first Bolshevik Consul for Scotland.

The critical notion of worker solidarity was first realised in Liverpool in the transport strike of 1911, which brought union leaders up from London, including one Thomas Mann, who was convinced that the city could become the centre of an international fight.

There arose a complicated and tremendous movement which convulsed Merseyside for at least seventy-two days . . . an interwoven complex of several strikes involving at one time or another every section of transport workers in the port and culminating in a general strike of all sections; a movement which was at the same time part of a national, and even international, upheaval of mounting proportions, only cut short by world war. The Liverpool strikes were also part of the national seamen's strike . . . and of the national railway strike; and separate local strikes of carters, tramwaymen, dockers, tugmen, barge-men, coal-heavers and others broke out in many parts of Britain throughout the period . . . Liverpool was spearheading a national movement.[14]

Bloody Sunday ensued on 13 August 1911. In the midst of a demonstration by twenty to thirty thousand workers, a scuffle broke out when a man refused to come down from a window ledge of the Station Hotel in Lime Street when ordered to by the police. The fight spread and became a battle, guerrilla warfare in the adjoining streets. Fighting continued for several days. Police were called in from Leeds and Birmingham. The Earl of Derby sent a telegram to Home Secretary Winston Churchill: 'Revolution has broken out in my city.' Troops were sent and a gunboat anchored in the Mersey, just in front of the Liver Building. Fighting and rioting continued, often around food transportation and lorries taking prisoners out of the city. An ambush of prison vans on nearby Vauxhall Road led to two people being killed on Tuesday, 15 August. Meanwhile, with the voices of great orators, including Tom Mann, ringing in their ears, thousands of workers flocked to join organisations such as the National Union of Dock Workers.

The Liverpool carters, one of the earliest groups of Liverpool workers to be fully unionised, now organised. Frequent ambushes were undertaken on police convoys of wagons carrying essential goods and foodstuffs, particularly in Church Street, one of the main thoroughfares through which the police convoys passed. Bill Owen's father was one of the strikers.

> They used to go out in the morning . . . on these picket things. Right, they got no money, there's no Parish. Nothing. And me and my mother lived on a halfpenny barm-cake. That's what we lived on all day. He was out all the while. And no fire unless she went and borrowed, got a penny off the woman next door, and I went for a halfpenny block of salt . . . put paraffin oil onto the block of salt, then go and cadge a match somewhere . . . cos it was all cadging. That kept us warm . . . it'd be glowing for about a couple of hours many a time, that salt would – with paraffin oil on it – keep pouring paraffin oil. They gave us paraffin oil then. I

think it was about a penny a pint, or something like that.
Well, that 1911 strike was my worst. It was absolutely
starvation. We were going around begging. And those
strikers, them poor buggers had nothing either, and they
were getting battered down . . . Churchill fetched the
Birmingham police here – mounted police – to quell the
strike . . . and they battered them down. As soon as we see
'em we run. We had to run.

Only months before this seminal battle was waged on the
streets of Liverpool, one of the great exponents of
socialism, Robert Tressell, who has since become an
adopted son of the city, lay dying in a local hospital, the
manuscript of his famous novel *The Ragged Trousered
Philanthropists* as yet unread among his effects in his
daughter Kathleen's keeping.

Tressell's story is a good one. He was born in 1870 in
Dublin, the illegitimate son of Samuel Croker, a senior
member of the Royal Irish Constabulary. His mother
married and Robert had a decent education, but aged
sixteen he rebelled, finding grist in a political aversion to
his stepfather's capitalist tendencies. (His stepfather was an
absentee landlord.) Two years later, Robert left for Cape
Town, South Africa, taking his mother's maiden name,
Noonan, to distance himself from his stepfather.

In Cape Town, he entered the milieu of the novel,
becoming a painter and decorator, and over the ensuing
years he no doubt met many of the men later to be
immortalised in his story as Sloggit, Crass, Sweater, Misery,
Slyme, Grinder, and so on.

In 1889, he helped form the Irish Brigade, an anti-

Imperialist (anti-British) force that fought alongside the Boers in the Second Boer War. It is unclear what then precipitated his return to England, but around the turn of the century he ended up in Hastings, Sussex, where he worked as a sign writer until a dispute with his employer led to the loss of his job. Unemployed, his health began to deteriorate and he developed TB. Unable to remain politically active, he started writing, something he hoped would earn enough money to keep him from the work-house. He wrote with honesty and great insight.

Frank Owen is the author's 'voice' in *The Ragged Trousered Philanthropists*. The book converted millions to socialism from its first publication in 1914 and continues to do so today. An adaptation for the stage by Howard Brenton is playing at the Liverpool Everyman as I write. Tressell, aware of its explosive content perhaps, adopted his name as a pun on the trestle table, an important part of a painter and decorator's kit. He completed the work in 1910, but the 1,600-page, hand-written manuscript was rejected by three publishing houses, which depressed him severely, and his daughter had to save the manuscript from being burnt. It was placed for safekeeping in a metal box underneath her bed.

Unhappy with his life in Britain, Robert decided that he and Kathleen should emigrate to Canada. With that in mind, they travelled to Liverpool, the first and last time he was in the city. Falling ill, he was admitted to the Royal Liverpool Infirmary Workhouse, where he died of phthisis pulmonalis – a wasting away of the lungs. He was buried in a mass grave with twelve other paupers opposite Walton Hospital. The location of the grave was not discovered until

1970. 'It was Eric Heffer who found his grave,' Tom Best told me. 'He was MP for Walton at the time. Building-site workers and whatnot, when they pop their clogs, they get their ashes put up there.' The plot is marked at a cemetery at the same location, which now goes by the name of Rice Lane City Farm. A nearby road is named Noonan Close in Tressell's honour.

Fortunately, Kathleen mentioned her father's novel to a friend of hers, the poet and journalist Jessie Pope, who recommended it to her publisher. In April 1914, the publisher bought the rights to the book for £25, but a full unexpurgated version, available today, did not appear until 1955.

If it had been read widely in Liverpool in the early years of the twentieth century, the entire history of the city might have taken a different course, for Tressell argues for nothing short of a complete overthrow of the capitalist system. His message is that money is the cause of poverty. Owen's friends revile him for his stupidity – '"I always thought it was the want of it!" said the man with the patches on the seat of his trousers as he passed out of the door.' But calmly Tressell explains 'the money trick', how the system is designed to ensure that money will ultimately always pass the working man by. His argument runs like this:

With the wealth he had already accrued, or inherited, the capitalist employer buys raw materials and machinery and hires workers to produce 'the necessaries of life'. But the necessaries of life are then owned by the employer and his workers have to buy them back with some of the money they have been paid to produce them.

Tressell works out that each worker has to buy back one

third of the produce of his labour. The employer keeps twice as much of the necessaries of life as the workers and increases his capital by selling elsewhere what he himself doesn't need. Whereupon he begins the whole round again, with the workers as pliable as ever, because they are back where they started financially, possibly worse off, and there is no way out of this vicious circle for them.

The employer's power over the worker extends further. For, in effect, the necessaries of life can only be produced if an employer believes that he can make a profit out of producing them. So, it is quite possible for a worker to stand idle and starve by the side of mountains of raw materials, which he is forbidden to touch.

Money, wrote Tressell, has caused people to lose sight of the true purpose of labour, 'the production of the things we need'. Society can only function fairly, he argues, if work increases the benefits of civilisation and supplies everyone with the necessaries of life.

He was especially worried about the growing numbers of people who worked very hard doing unnecessary work, i.e. work which was neither to the benefit of civilisation nor productive of the necessaries of life but which oiled the wheels of the money-trick system.

He numbered among these salesmen, publicity people, insurance agents, the greater number of shop assistants, designers, advertisers, etc. He was writing half a century before consumerism took off, but he could see where things were leading.

'If you want some butter,' he wrote in 1907, 'it doesn't matter whether you buy it from Brown or Jones or Robinson . . . If you go down town you will see half a dozen drapers' shops within a stone's throw of each other – often even next door to each other – all selling the same things. You can't possibly think all those shops are really necessary? One of them would serve the purpose for which they are all intended – to store and serve as a centre for the distribution of the things that are made by work. If you will admit that five out of the six shops are not really necessary, you must also admit that the men who built them, and the salesmen and women or other assistants engaged in them, and the men who design and write and print their advertisements are all doing unnecessary work; all really wasting their time and labour, time and labour that might be employed in helping to produce these things that we are at present short of. You must admit that none of these people are engaged in producing either the necessaries of life or the benefits of civilisation. They buy them, and sell them, and handle them, and haggle over them, and display them, in the plate-glass windows of "Stores" and "Emporiums" and make profit out of them, and use them, but these people themselves produce nothing that is necessary to life or happiness, and the things that some of them do produce are only necessary to the present imbecile system.'

'This is a lot of bloody rot!' exclaimed Crass impatiently.

'It all helps people to get a livin'!' cried Harlow.

But Frank Owen, who is Tressell, was unmoved: 'The only rational labour is that which is directed to the creation of the things necessary for the life and happiness of mankind.'

The concept of working-class solidarity gained increasing credibility with the advent of the Russian Revolution in

1917, and after the First War, politics and want bound Liverpool workers together as never before.

In 1921, unemployment and the rising cost of living triggered the formation of the National Union of Unemployed Workers, and Bob Lissyman and Jack Hayes, ex-policemen sacked from the force for their part in a police strike, which had led to a city-wide crime wave two years earlier, took over the Town Hall. During the following decades, Islington Square became the starting point for many demonstrations against horrendous unemployment, many led by Leo McGree, a communist who, at one stage, chained himself to the Town Hall railings.

The first hunger march was organised in the winter of 1922, and found the unemployed with barely enough cash to organise it. The money collected at each stopping place was sufficient to pay for an occasional sandwich, first-aid requisites and bundles of boot leather. Jack Brotheridge's father was there:

> The hunger marches started up in the north-east. As men marched to London to face the Prime Minister (Stanley Baldwin), they gathered strength on the way south until there were thousands, mainly ex-servicemen from the First World War. They pawned their medals and even their false teeth for a few shillings. The pawn-shop windows were full of them. The Welsh miners, from the South Wales coal mines, with their wives and children, walked in the gutter, singing and passing a hat around for a few pence, or anything. They had to walk in the gutter because the police would tell them they must not, by law, obstruct the pavements. What a mess!

Born in 1920, Jack remembers in particular 'one of the coldest winters on record, 1928–29'.

[It was] very bad . . . many children ran to school in their bare feet. When they put their feet on the school's hot pipes, they suffered chilblains and frostbite.

I remember that year, snow and ice started early, before Christmas. I would say from November to March the canal was frozen, and big lumps of ice could be seen coming down the Mersey. A flu epidemic killed many. The local paper, the *Echo*, had nearly every page covered with recorded deaths. I, as a child, had pneumonia, and the boy next door, William Knowles, died.

The docks had some casual work, and men would queue for hours to get half a day. If you weren't well in, you had little chance of it. The foremen, it was said, had to have a backhander if you were picked out. As time progressed, my dad would get short trips on a caster ship trading to Belgium or France. The seamen had to feed themselves, buying in food as they went. It was four hours on, four hours off, giving very little time for sleep, washing clothes, cooking . . . The crew would be very sparse, very often only six men in all. He also had to supply his own straw mattress, a donkey's breakfast it was called. He would be away four or five weeks, leaving my mother 20 shillings a week. He would come home with what he went away with, nothing. You had to have six months' work to get dole money, which only lasted six months. People were literally in rags – clothes were patched, and [you'd hear] the thump of men nailing home-made leather soles on the family's footwear, as they drove the nails in and clenched them over inside . . . They would use an old mangle roller with a 'last' stuck on the top. The leather was usually old belting leather, discarded by factories that [had machinery] driven by belts. The saying would be, 'He's walking on the Blacken.' That was the polish they used in those days to keep looking respectable . . . A 'front' was often used instead of a shirt. It looped over a man's head – just a short front, no back or sleeves, and a collar put on with studs, front and back.

Things got so bad that politics at last meant militancy. Ordinary people became passionate, political animals. Support for a new workers' democracy was brewing nationally. In 1925, after a dispute between coal miners and mine owners over a reduction in wages, the General Council of the Trades Union Congress (TUC) threatened widespread worker support in other industries. The government responded, apparently benignly, by making available a subsidy to restore wage levels for a period of nine months, during which time a Royal Commission would investigate the problems of the mining industry.

When the report was published, however, it recommended a reduction in wages. Around the same time, mine owners projected further adjustments to wages and hours. That was the inflammatory situation that led to the General Strike in 1926.

The TUC brought dockers out on strike in sympathy with the miners, along with railwaymen, transport workers, printers, builders, iron and steel workers – some three million men. Engineers and shipyard workers would follow, if their terms were still not met.

A conference of the Trades Union Congress was convened on 1 May, at which it was decided that the strike would begin two days later. Tensions ran high. However, it was all rather short-lived. Only days into the strike, the chairman of the Royal Commission, whose report on the mining industry had caused all the problems, got in a huddle with the TUC and together they hammered out a set of proposals – a National Wages Board with an independent chairman, a minimum wage, etc., etc. The proposals were accepted by the TUC negotiating committee, who on 12 May called off the General Strike. It had lasted nine days in all.

The men went back to work, and only then were the proposals rejected by the Miners' Federation, and by the government, who even introduced a Bill into the House of Commons that permitted the mine owners to announce new terms of employment based on an eight-hour working day, which had earlier been reduced to seven.

The miners had been cheated, sold down the river. They held out on strike on their own until December, when hardship forced them to drift back to work.

The following year, the Conservative government passed the Trade Disputes and Trade Union Act, which made coming out on strike in sympathy with another industry illegal. The General Strike had been an unmitigated disaster.

It later emerged just how duplicitous Stanley Baldwin's government had been – even the wages subsidy granted in 1925 had been designed simply to give them time to prepare to smash the unions. The government justified its tactics on the basis of the threat worker power posed to national security.

Following the disastrous culmination of the strike, many workers lost their jobs, and employers, with the tacit approval of government, often refused to reinstate trade unionists, choosing the moment to break union power within their workforces.

Docker Bill Smathers remembers how it was in Liverpool:

In 1926, the General Strike was on, right? But quite a few men still worked at the docks. Course, they got the name of scabs. Out on strike, we got £1 to live on and we were out for three weeks. When we came back, we had to work a damn sight harder and make up for it. To survive, you pawned everything you had.

In the thirties, you had every tradesman in the city coming down trying to get a job in the Liverpool docks . . . they tried to take the place of the dockers, and a lot of them did. You had every class of tradesman coming down. It did cause a lot of bitterness, but what could you do about it? Work was so scarce. They used to call it 'the hungry thirties'. Ask your dad about it, he'll tell you. If the boss had a friend, 'Come down, I'll give you a job.' Couldn't do nothing about it . . . Some of the cowboys used to come there about nine o'clock. Well, the union got notified . . . We used to call it 'back-biting' . . . They used to get a job . . . They would not employ the proper docker because he was in the union. The union used to do their best to stop it.

In October, 1929, Wall Street crashed. By 1931 nearly six million were out of work in Germany, by 1933 the figure was twelve million in America. Following President Hoover's decision to raise tariff barriers, world trade had fallen by two thirds in three years and we were on an unstoppable course to war.

Inevitably, the crisis brought a woman to the rescue. Although Bessie Braddock was not elected as an MP until 1945, she became a councillor for St Anne's Ward in 1930. Born in Liverpool in 1899, and originally a member of the Communist Party, she had joined Labour in 1922. There was complete empathy between Bessie Braddock and the hard-pressed people of Liverpool, whom she represented with heart and soul. Famously, she once took a megaphone into the Council chamber to force action over Liverpool's slums, speaking of the soup lines from personal experience:

> I remember the faces of the unemployed when the soup ran out. I remember their dull eyes and their thin blue lips. I remember blank, hopeless stares, day after day, week after week . . .

Even in death, in November 1970, her influence was felt. Alan Dossor's first season of plays at the Everyman Theatre in Hope Street included Stephen Fagan's *The Braddocks' Time*, a history and mythology of Bessie Braddock, who was no more nor less than Mother Liverpool writ large. A bronze statue of her by Tom Murphy now stands in Lime Street Station. It is a striking sculpture, and not the first time that an artist has characterised the spirit of Liverpool in this way.

CHAPTER TEN

War

────────

Britain declared war on Germany at 11.15 a.m. on Sunday, 3 September 1939. In Liverpool, preparations had long been in progress. A Civil Defence Committee had been set up,[1] and Garnet Chaplain, Master of Belmont Hospital – who had come up from Sussex and been in Liverpool for just a couple of years – had organised the Civil Defence Ambulance Service:

> On that Sunday morning, the 3rd of September 1939, when the balloon did go up, there was one service at least in the country, and certainly in Liverpool, [that] was ready, willing and able to do its job for the citizens of Liverpool, because on that day, there were over four hundred vehicles at my

headquarters at Belmont, manned, ready to go out . . . In
Liverpool, we were talking about a possible casualty list of
about a million people.

There had also been a programme of training on what to
do in an air raid. Bobby Blues of the Warden Service was all
keyed up:

We were well prepared in that we knew people in every
street in the city, wardens who had already been enrolled.
Their primary function was working a stirrup pump up and
down, which was very simple, and [they'd been told] how
not to get near certain types of bombs, which was also quite
an easy matter. If there were one or two incendiary bombs
dropped, they would know what to do.

Gordon Murray, principal ARP adviser with the Liverpool
City Council, knew that war was about to be enjoined.

On the Friday, 1st September, we received, as all other
authorities did, the code telegram, which to us meant that
we must establish our emergency committee, in Liverpool's
case a committee of three: Sir Sydney Jones, the Lord Mayor,
Alfred Shannon, the leader of the Conservative Party, and
Luke Hogan, the leader of the Labour Party. The emergency
committee went up to the Town Hall on that evening as a
result of the telegram. We started moving into the Town Hall
with office equipment, and the committee had its first
meeting that evening.

On Saturday, 2 September, the Walker Art Gallery closed

till further notice, and the city's main stores shut their doors early. The shadow of war was falling over the city. The *Echo* warned people to use their gas masks properly and described 'how to tackle a fire bomb'. At sunset, the blackout came into force: 'All lights inside buildings must be obscured, and outside lights put out. Motorists must ensure that their lights do not exceed 7 watts and car lamps must be masked.'

There was a run on blackout curtains and black paper. Trams ran without lights and conductors collected fares by torchlight. On the ferries, the blackout was so effective that the passengers couldn't see each other's faces, and they had to grope their way along the gang planks. Cinemas and theatres were closed. Then came the instruction to get the children away and the evacuation started.

On the first day, 56,000 children, parents and teachers were evacuated from Liverpool in seventy trains. Streets were left strangely silent as lines of children formed on the station platforms. It was a day out with a difference – gas masks and sandwiches, identity cards and sweets. Eddie Braburn remembers that morning:

We lived down the Dingle and were surrounded by oil tanks, so they had to get us out. We were vulnerable, it was dangerous. I can remember hundreds of us standing in Dingle Lane with labels on our coats – 'This side up and use no hooks' – waiting for buses to take us to the station. We went by bus to Lime Street Station and then we got the train – the longest journey I had ever made – all the way to Bangor. And then we got another little train and we went to a big tin hut. Then you had to wait while all the ladies of the

village came round and had a look at what they had to take
in. They picked out the children they would best like to have
live with them, you know? I don't know why, but I was the
last! There was only me left in the hut with Geoffrey, and we
were there until about two o'clock in the morning. So this
very kind lady, Mrs Hughes, she took us in. I don't know
how she is now, poor lady. I think we gave her a bad time.

For some children, such as Mavis Harrison, the evacuation
went well.

I was evacuated during the war to a farm in Burscough,
between Southport and Ormskirk. My main memories of it
are feelings of security, safety and sadness. We grew
potatoes, carrots, turnips and string beans, and we had
chickens and cows . . . From Burscough we could see the
bombs in the distance being dropped on Liverpool.

For others, including Dorothy Curl, life would never be the
same again.

Along with three sisters and a brother, I was taken on a very
long journey from Edge Hill railway station, which was in
sight of our home. Mother had provided us with a pillow
case each, containing a change of clothes and a few other
belongings. Off we went with our gas masks slung over our
shoulders, a few sandwiches and tears in our eyes.
    To our dismay, we were separated at an early stage of the
journey. Edith, who was five, was taken with the infant
department of our school. John, who was ten, was taken
with the boys – girls and boys were separated in those days

at junior level. The other three girls, including myself, stayed together. The journey seemed never ending and we had not been given any information about where we were being taken. Finally, late on Sunday evening, we arrived in a village called Llanberis, at the bottom of a steep pass, several miles from Caernarfon in North Wales.

The school hall was crammed with unfamiliar faces milling around. I remember feeling utterly devastated, lost and lonely. Then we learned with alarm that there was no available billet for three children; we were to be separated, that is, until a dear lady, obviously noticing our distress, agreed to take all three of us into her home. This was to be a happy time for us, but at first we longed to find Edith and John.

All evacuees were issued with a postcard on which to write their new address. Edith was about three miles away from us, and our brother John was about sixteen miles away. We found out much later that he was having a very unhappy time – his temporary foster parents were unkind and gave him little food. When our parents eventually visited and realised the situation, they applied to have him moved to the same village as Edith. He was then billeted on a farm where he was expected to work very hard – up at 5.30, milking the cows, followed by many other unpleasant tasks on the farm. He remembers many a morning falling asleep while milking and toppling off his milking stool.

Not only were we far away from our city home, this was actually another country, with its own strange, sing-song language that we had never heard before and couldn't understand. But we had our school friends around us and this helped to keep the tears away. The mountain scenery around Llanberis was breathtakingly beautiful and we spent many hours exploring the countryside. School was attended on a part-time basis only, sharing the classrooms with the Welsh children, so we had plenty of leisure time . . . Our foster parents, whom we referred to as Auntie Blodwen and Uncle Tom, were very kind and thoughtful people.

Within a few weeks, some of our friends returned home to their families. The air raids that had been expected didn't happen.

However, Dorothy's parents did not turn up for her.

So we remained in Wales with a feeling of desertion by our own family and increasingly heavy hearts, even though my mother wrote regularly and sent us pocket money. It was usually a one-shilling postal order that we cashed at the Post Office in the village . . .

The months dragged on and we received news from home of the birth of a new baby sister on 23 April 1940, my mother's tenth child. Mother, father, little brother and new baby finally came to visit us in the late summer of 1940, a very happy occasion, as one would expect. I accompanied them back to Liverpool with very little confidence, to earn my own living. Leaving my sisters behind was a terrible wrench, which brought much heartache.

Dorothy stayed in touch with 'Aunt Blodwen and Uncle Tom' until 1984, when Blodwen died, spending many happy holidays with them over the years and introducing them to her own children. But, as Dorothy confides, 'life was never to be the same again' with her parents in the Liverpool household, 'as we grew apart during our separation. Life in the country had been a totally different experience for us evacuees, and inevitably coloured our view of the world from then on.'[2]

Back in the city, immediately war had been declared people had struggled to cope, but at the time they could feel optimistic, particularly if they listened to comedian Billy Russell speaking on behalf of the working classes at the Argyle Theatre, Birkenhead:[3]

> Groping around in these blackouts, you never know where you'll get to. I found meself in me own house two nights last week. And to make matters worse, that RIP man (ARP) come again last Saturday night, banging on the door. I said, 'Now don't tell me, there's no light shining through the windows.' He said, 'I know. There's a light shining under your door.' I said, 'Well, blimey, you don't expect they're coming on their hands and knees!'

At Shrewsbury House, the boys club in Everton, there was special concern for the old boys, who were already in training for the fight, and Secretary Barr Adams organised a heroic strategy to ensure that none of them felt he had been forgotten, as Jim Kennedy relates:

> In 1935, Barr had started to produce a newsletter, so that there would be topics for discussion when the old boys met up in the evenings. Eventually, when the war started, and all the people in the forces sent letters to him, he collated the

information and sent out a weekly report from all the other soldiers. In the end, there were about fifty correspondents, and Barr did all this at his own expense. Eventually, he started to compose a book called *Club of War*.

The thoughts and feelings of the boys in training and at the front, and the things that happened to them, make unique reading. The record begins with Barr's own thoughts, as war approached:

In August 1939, the club was closed as usual for the three weeks following camp. It was due to reopen on the evening of Sunday, September 3rd. At eleven o'clock on the same morning, Great Britain declared war on Germany. But the struggle had really begun two days before when in the early hours of Friday, September 1st, the German army invaded Poland. On that same afternoon, the eleven from the Liverpool Welsh, following Government instructions, had reported to their barracks at Low Hill. The country awoke next morning to find the Germans still advancing into the heart of Poland, but neither England nor France had yet made any move. Everyone knew, though, that war could no longer be avoided. It was a perfect day, calm, warm and cloudless. Never, indeed, can Man and Nature have been more at variance. Yet the bright weather seemed somehow to intensify by contrast the gloom and foreboding that settled down on everyone. There should have been a football match for the Old Boys that afternoon – the first of the season, but it soon became known that trenches were being dug in Walton Hall Park and that all games there were cancelled . . .

Next day, Sunday, from eleven in the morning England was at war. In the evening, the club officially reopened. It was the first time we had had our soldiers in uniform in chapel, and the service that fine autumn night was one of the great occasions in the club's history. There was a distinction about it, which could be felt better than it can be described, and no one who was there is soon likely to forget it . . .

One thought filled every mind – the war. One section of our Association claimed all our attention – the soldiers, eleven from the Liverpool Welsh, and Stanley Grounds from the Royal Engineers. Looking back now, it is easy to see just what those twelve soldiers meant to us that evening. The world was tumbling about our ears. No one knew what came next. Each one of us looked into the future uncertain, each one, that is, except the twelve soldiers. Three days ago our jobs and our own interests had been the centre of our lives. Now the soldiers were the only ones whose jobs and interests seemed to have any place in the scheme of things at all. If it had not been for those twelve there in uniform, how lost, how aimless and how hopeless we as an Association would have felt. The challenge had come and instead of staring helplessly round and wondering what to do, we were able to look it in the face. For in our midst we had the answer to it. Germany wanted war. We had the people there ready to see that she got it. Rather a young way of looking at the thing perhaps. But let that be. It was the spirit of the hour.

Besides those boys already in the forces as regulars, new

recruits found it hard just being away from home and club in training camps. Wrote Mike Finnegan:

> If ever I missed being away from home, I have done here to-day. Although we have had a great time, it seems funny somehow, as though everyone was forcing themselves to be gay. The Canadians are staying here and had Christmas dinner with us. I have never seen so much food, and we could hardly move after it. Aldershot is full of Canadian artillerymen. They are never sober as they nearly all drink whisky instead of beer.

This was from Stanley Grounds at Lancaster, written before the war was a week old.

> I don't know where we are going from here. The training is interesting, so the time does not drag. Tell the Old Boys I miss them, and if an air raid comes, tell Paddy Nugent to look after them. It is funny, you never realise what a grand place the club is till you are separated from it!

A few weeks later, from Stanley, a grim sense of the waste, and first thrill, of war:

> We have been on mining the coast and making it pretty hot for any Germans who may try to land. Two REs were killed by a mine. One of them trod on one and they found just a piece of flesh of one and the other went altogether. A woman found the remains and she thought it was a steak. Eleven Jerries were brought down here in one day, and quite a few are said to have been brought down previously.

The AA is very good round here. They bag one almost
every day . . .

I had a thrilling experience on Thursday. We were on the
shore and the sky went black with a threatening storm.
Suddenly, out to sea, a dozen or so Jerry planes appeared
out of the mist and attacked two very small cargo boats.
What a sight! Bombs all around the ships but not a hit. A
motor torpedo boat was soon out on the spot and it seemed
to draw the attention of the planes, for every plane dropped
a bomb near it, but what a cheer went up when we saw the
three ships still afloat and still going strong! The enemy
seemed a bunch of novices led by one good flier, for one of
their planes did everything except stand in mid air.

Incredibly, information of an apparently sensitive nature
seems to have been allowed through to the club. In early
December 1940, Albert Ash and Harry Scott of the 7th
Armoured Division share their experience of the victorious
capture of Sidi Barrani in Egypt from the Italian army. Ash
admits to being 'somewhat shocked by some of the sights I
have seen . . . I do not propose to go into the gory details
about the state of some of the poor devils'. Instead, the
boys prefer to raise a smile in the club with details of the
booty of war:

At the moment, I am wearing Italian boots and pullover, and
very good garments they appear to be, too. By gum, these
Italian officers must be a pack of cissies. Among the officer's
kit, which our duties compelled us to search (ahem!), we
found such things as shampoos, hair pomades, bottles of
scent and toilet powder. They must smell like a lot of chorus

girls by the time they have applied all these potions. And this in the middle of the desert, too!

By the way, I have acquired a very great liking for macaroni and spaghetti . . . a very welcome addition to our staple diet of bully beef and biscuits.

We had some very nice Chianti wine the other night and this together with some tinned octopus was the means of a good time being had by all.

Eventually, inevitably, news arrives of the first Shrewsbury House casualty. Early in May 1941, Albert Ash wrote his mother a postcard: 'Some Germans came along not long ago and gave us some shooting practice. I was a bit unlucky as I got a packet, but I am all right again now and I am having a fortnight's rest.'

Shortly afterwards, an undated letter from Harry Scott arrived. He told the club that he was now off the desert after a spell of ten months there. He wrote again a fortnight later to say that things were still going easily with him and he remarked that their only real worry was caused by the reports they received – not often very accurate – of the damage done by the air raids at home.

This extraordinary file of correspondence gives not only a privileged view of war, but of what Shrewsbury House meant to Liverpool boys fortunate enough to be members, and of the character that the club had built, and continues to build, in its membership. But Harry Scott was right to be concerned about what was going on at home, for the bombs had started dropping in what would be the country's worst Blitz outside of London.

The first bombs fell on 9 August 1940, at Prenton,

Birkenhead. The next day, Wallasey was the target. On 17 August, it was Liverpool's turn, and the overhead railway was damaged. Two days later, bombs fell on Walton gaol and twenty-two prisoners were killed. On 5 September, the Anglican cathedral was damaged. On 6 September, the children's convalescent home in Birkenhead was hit. And so it went on. By 23 October, the Merseyside air-raid count had reached two hundred.

At the start of 1941, there was bad weather, which diminished the number of strikes. In March, however, normal service was resumed in nightmarish style, especially over Wallasey, where 174 died. April would be looked at as the lull before the storm, for in the May Blitz, 1,741 Merseysiders would be killed and 114 seriously injured in the first week of the month alone . . .

The spirit of everyone was amazing. For all the horrors, it seems there could have been no better excuse for a laugh – not cheap laughs, mind you. There is a deep seam of colour and character in May Duke's reminiscence:

> I was living in Orwell Road on a landing – a tenement. It was only half a tenement, three storeys high – ground floor and two above. Of course, every night you prepared yourself, got all your stuff ready, and most of the people collected their penny policies for when they died. You know, the burial policies? They were only a penny . . . As if you'd need them! You'd just get shovelled up like they do with the junkies in Manhattan. But every night you got ready. And we had double summer time to stretch out the light nights, you know?
>
> As soon as the siren went, you got ready to go down

into the tannery shelter, which was just twenty yards farther on from our building. The local pub was adjoining it practically, and there was the Kirkdale Library and Kirkdale Park – they were all together. You went down three wide steps, sort of underneath the tannery. There were no lights. A couple of wardens would bring lamps in. I think it may have been a store room before it was a shelter. But there was only one little narrow doorway to go in. That was where the danger lay . . . and these barrels in the yard as you went down – what they cured the hides in or something – they were the things that would catch fire.

I was with all the other neighbours. As the sirens went, all the doors in the tenement seemed to open simultaneously. Everybody trooped out. Going down our flight of steps we met the people from the landing below and then the people from the ground floor, and we started trudging our way towards the shelter. In the blackout you couldn't see the pub, but you could smell it. The aroma of the beer was pretty strong, and it was becoming scarce then. And this poor old fellow who lived down below . . . Well, he had a false leg. He was always telling people how he had left it behind in France in the First World War, and he always wore his war medals. He was very proud of them – 'I gave my leg for King and Country!' He was always saying that. Well, a lot of the people were musical and they brought their mouth organs with them. This man, old Sammy, he brought this little squeeze box – a concertina – and he used to entertain us with it night after night.

Anyway, we went along with it when somebody whispered something to somebody else among the men, and then we saw them all nod, the men all nodding their heads.

And they got us all into the shelter, all the women and kids, and then flew back to the pub! The smell of the beer, it proved too much for them. Go for a quick one!

Well, it seemed no time till a warden came to the door of the shelter and said, 'Now look, there's an unexploded bomb.' She put it this way. Incendiaries had set the tannery on fire, and the pub, the library, the park . . . 'I'd like you all to come out. It won't go off. It may never go off.' This was to allay the panic, you see. Of course, when the men in the pub realised what was happening, they were going hysterical. They were screaming, 'Get those women and children out!' Yet they all had their pints in their hands.

All we could see was this archway of flames . . . The wardens were good, though. They were calming everybody, shepherding them out in the street. Course, when the people got in the street, that's when it really hit them . . . and hysteria took over then. Funnily enough, all those who had babies – and I was one – none of those babies woke up! The noise was horrendous, it really was – all around.

Between the bombs all you could hear was droning [of the planes] and poor old Sam – 'Oh, it's one of ours!' All night that was the chorus from Sam: 'It's one of ours.' And, of course, in between shelters and in between raids, naturally [the Germans] had to go back for replacements. Then there would be a lull, [and] Sam'd give his repertoire of all the songs from the First World War, 'Pack Up Your Troubles', all those songs, mixing them up with the songs from this war, 'Hang Out the Washing on the Siegfried Line'. It was pathetic, I think, when you look back . . . he'd be shouting after each song, 'Are we downhearted?' And everyone would shout, 'No!' But as the night wore on, the

'Nos' got fainter and fainter, because spirits were waning
by then.

Lots began to say prayers. Somebody started the rosary
off. It happened we had to make a quick exit [at one stage]
and we ended up eventually in a church mission hall in
Churnet Street, and it was there that the all clear went. And
it was at the all clear that all sorts of little incidents
occurred . . .

When we were going into the shelter, the old lady – I
forget her name now – she turned round and looked, as
best she could in the blackout, towards the tenement, and
she says, 'Oh God, please let our houses be standing when
we come out.' So now, the first thing everybody did as we
came along Churnet Street and turned into Orwell Road
was to ask, 'Is our hotel still there?' [That's Liverpool
humour, calling half a tenement 'our hotel' – you must be
awful poor to live in a tenement, so you go to the other
extreme. You learn something every day!] Well, everybody
gave a cheer. Some were crying, some people burst into
tears. A lot of them gave a cheer when we saw it was
apparently unharmed. But one of the ground-floor flats had
had its front door blown off – God knows where the door
had landed. Nobody asked questions in those days . . . there
were no windows in it and there was no door on it, but the
window frame was there. And as one of the ladies went to
step into her hall, these two cows were standing there. They
had such mournful eyes . . . The poor things needed milking
as well – of course, the dairy had been burnt down. How
they wandered there, nobody knew, and nobody cared at
the time, either. But one old fellow, one of the fellows at
the back, he said, 'Oh good God. They must have run out

of bombs! Look what they're dropping now!' And of course there was a general titter – they were laughing and crying together.

What we didn't know was that all the bodies had been taken to the forecourt of Stanley Hospital, which was at the bottom of Orwell Road, between Orwell and Fountains Road, and they had all the bodies laid out there. The people, later on in the day, had to come and identify them, you see.

Everywhere you looked there were fires. There was sand buckets . . . no water. As we were coming down, there was a crowd – two wardens were trying to pull a blazing couch out of one of the bigger houses, out of the hallway, and two other wardens were trying the hydrants – they were dry. So the next performance . . . and I'm being polite . . . urine donors, that's what he wanted! You can imagine what he was saying. I'm too ladylike to say what he was saying, but he was holding out his . . . and an old battered enamel bucket . . . and those who could, obliged, and they were just throwing it on the flames! Well, it was only with hindsight that we saw the funny side of it. We just accepted this at the time as part and parcel of that night, sort of thing.

And old Sam, he was well away. He'd demolished a bottle of whisky and he was still on cloud nine there, singing . . . talking about 'Sugar in the morning, sugar in the evening . . .' singing his head off, and then he's looking at the empty bottle of whisky and shaking his fist at the sky, you know? 'How dare they!'

There is a memorial to those killed in the Blitz in the ruin of St Luke's church on Berry Street, a peaceful spot close to Liverpool's Bohemia and the gateway to Liverpool 8.

In January 1942, when finally the bombing was over, people wondered why Hitler's bombers stayed away when they hadn't yet disabled the docks. Why stop now? One theory began to emerge, as Tommy Walsh remembers:

Alois Hitler, Adolf Hitler's half-brother [they shared the same father], married an Irish woman, Bridget Dowling, in 1910 and they lived in a flat at 102 Upper Stanhope Street, Liverpool 8, just to the south of the Anglican cathedral. I'm told that they had several children, all of whom went to America and all of whom promised one another they would never have children and none of them did. Now, this bit of the story is unconfirmed. Half-brother Adolf Hitler came to stay with them, probably to dodge conscription in Austria.

Now, the first bombs on Liverpool fell in Caryl Gardens, down by the old Southern Hospital, and – fact – the very last bombs fell on Upper Stanhope Street and several people were killed. Judge for yourself, what would Hitler have done when he was told Upper Stanhope Street had been bombed? Would he give the order, 'Don't bomb Liverpool again'?

Fact – Upper Stanhope Street was the last street in Liverpool to be bombed.

It sounds like a scenario for Willy Russell to explore. There are certainly humorous aspects, and interesting ones, like the fact that Bridget Dowling's memoirs do indeed claim that Adolf Hitler lived with Alois, herself and their son, William Patrick (born in Upper Stanhope Street in 1911), from 1912 to 1913, while he was on the run for dodging the draft in his native Austria-Hungary.

Another interesting fact is that the house in question, No. 102, was certainly one of the houses destroyed in the raid. Nothing remained of it, nor of those that surrounded it. The area was eventually cleared and grassed over. Finally, the day Upper Stanhope Street was blitzed – 10 January 1942 – was the last day of the Liverpool Blitz. Unaccountably, no German bomber did return.

Could the reason really be Adolf's grief over the loss of Alois and his family? Certainly not. Alois had left Liverpool a long time earlier and returned to Germany on his own to establish himself in the safety razor business, and Bridget had moved away. Alois married another woman, Hedwig Heiderman, and was subsequently prosecuted for bigamy, but acquitted due to Bridget's Liverpudlian kind heart. She intervened on her rat of a husband's behalf.

The door is, nevertheless, still ajar to credibility in this matter of Adolf's moment of compassion for the citizens of Liverpool. If he had spent time at the house and felt safe there from prosecution, and heard that his bombers had wiped out his sanctuary, something with as personal a reference as that just might have wakened this paranoid madman's otherwise dormant conscience . . . mightn't it?

Soon after the war, Clem Attlee's Labour Government (1945–51) promised the New Welfare State – a national insurance system that meant pensions for all, free medical care, family allowances and means-tested national assistance. But could the Government afford to deliver?

Soldiers were reunited with their families, but money and day-to-day goods remained in short supply. Rationing continued until long after the war ended. Queues were commonplace even for essentials. While nobody went hungry, supplies were pretty basic. Bread rationing was introduced in July 1946 and lasted for two years; potatoes were rationed in 1946–47; a major fuel shortage due to declining productivity, inadequate transport and the bleak winter of 1947 closed factories across Britain and left houses without electricity for five hours a day.

Britain went cap in hand to America, trading on the sacrifice the country had made for world peace, but the US felt they had won the war, and were not impressed. The deal Britain came away with was not enough and tied the country to America as a poor relation. Then America awoke to the wisdom of a speech by Winston Churchill about the danger of Joseph Stalin, who had succeeded Vladimir Lenin in the Soviet Union on his death in 1924 and whose power was spreading into Eastern Europe. Billions of dollars came flooding into Britain to ensure that we would be on the right side, many Americans viewing the rise of socialism in Britain as tantamount to communism, and regarding the politics of Glasgow and East London with special concern.

This money underwrote the Welfare State and the fabulous fifties – the era of television, ventures into space and Tory Prime Minister Harold Macmillan (1957–63), when apparently we'd never had it so good.

CHAPTER ELEVEN

Sixties Transformation

Jean Roberts: All of a sudden the generation gap appeared between our generation and our parents' generation. We thought differently, because we were different people. I know young people today think they created it, but they did not. My daughter and myself have not got that difference.

In the forties and fifties . . . we had nothing . . . but no one had anything. So we were all in the same boat. But then, you can imagine – sweets coming into the shops! It was like, exciting! You didn't know what was going to happen from day to day. A new thing was coming . . .

I was born in 1939. For the first six years of your life it was just war. After that, it took ages before they could start manufacturing, getting things together again. Fifties, it was just starting to happen. It was like Christmas every day really. We didn't have money, but we had something different, something exciting, like a Mars bar come into the shop and it was something you hadn't seen and all of a sudden you had a sweet shop full of sweets.[1]

For many born earlier, the change was just as striking. In the twenties and thirties, entertainment had boiled down to the men's club/Catholic club, occasional theatre, music hall or cinema, football, and walking, walking, walking.

Peggy Tully: Courting, well you just met and walked around anywhere. I used to walk in the Dunlop shoe factory, walked down to the Pier Head. Never went to the pictures. Always walking, walking. Even now I can walk Liverpool blindfolded, but I can't tell you all the names of the streets. Liverpool was a lot smaller in those days, more compact.[2]

There were plenty of cinemas to choose from in the city, around forty in the 1920s, a figure that had more than doubled three decades later. Local to Scotland Road were the Derby and the Gaiety, the Gem in Vescock Street, the Roscommon in Roscommon Street, the Homer in Great Homer Street and the Popular in Netherfield Road. Local theatres included the Rotunda (Roundy) at the junction of Stanley Road and Scotland Road (destroyed during the Blitz), the Electric in London Road and the Adelphi (the Delly) in Christian Street, where as likely as not it was a Saturday matinee (film) that attracted a crowd.

In Toxteth, famously, it was the Pavilion Theatre[3] on Lodge Lane.

We called it the Pivvy. We would go with Mum and Dad and sometimes there was a big fat local singer on called Florrie Ford. She used to sing all the old songs on a Saturday night and her voice was very loud. There was a fish and chip shop down the side of the theatre and our parents would take us there while they went to the pub for a drink. The chip shop was spotlessly clean and we would have fish, chips and peas and lemonade. Mum and Dad would come and pick us up later.[4]

Mavis O'Flaherty: I remember going to see George Formby at the Pivvy, and people like Ken Dodd. All the up and coming people appeared at the Pivvy. As you know, there were a lot of entertainers in Liverpool. There was Robb Wilton,[5] he was a famous comedian and he was from the area as well, from Hartington Road [two streets away from Lodge Lane], and Arthur Askey and people like that.[6]

Angelo Vaccarello: Lita Rosa, she was a singer at the Pavilion. It's not there no more, it's a Bingo hall now. In them days it was a theatre for second-class artists. You had to go to the Royal Court for the first-class acts, for the good acts. Empire was big.[7]

The Pivvy was refurbished in 1933 and again in 1960 when the stage was extended. George Robey, Marie Lloyd and Little Titch graced it in the old days of music hall. Ken Dodd's first panto was there in 1954; he was Wishy Washy in *Aladdin*. The theatre's electrician was Freddie Trinder, brother of Tommy Trinder, so it had quite a showbiz family feel, certainly better than 'second class'. The Liverpool

Empire and theatres such as the Playhouse and the Royal Court in the centre of town, were in a class of their own at the time, but there were local theatres all over, many old ones, such as the Royal Muncaster in Bootle, moving with the times from live entertainment to films in the 1920s.

There was also an important development in workers theatre, with the people of Liverpool inspiring and participating in the production, acting, and writing of plays, as well as coming to watch them. Merseyside Left Theatre was formed in the 1930s and became part of a national theatre movement of some 250 amateur groups that nominated theatre as a political instrument as well as entertainment. The Left Theatre became Merseyside Unity Theatre in 1944, one of fifty branches within the national Unity Theatre Society, the most famous of which were the only professional Unity theatres, in London and Glasgow. People in Liverpool still remember the relatively recent impact of the 7:84 Theatre Group, a touring socialist group which brought plays written by such as John McGrath, founder of 7:84 and author of *A Good Night Out*, the bible of alternative theatre. The theatre's name derived from a statistic revealed in the *Economist*, that 7 per cent of Britain's people own 84 per cent of the country's wealth. The current Unity Theatre on Hope Place in Liverpool is a development of Merseyside Unity Theatre, which itself ceased operations in the early 1980s.

Among dance halls before the war, the Grafton in West Derby Road was universally popular, as Lil Cameron and Edie Crew recall.

I remember getting a dress from the pawn shop for a works

'do'. I used to put on a bit of make-up, a bit of rouge – a bit more than usual. Well, I was out to get a boyfriend without being cheap and nasty. The evening dances ran from half-seven to half-nine. There were also tea dances in the afternoon. The well-known band conductor was Mrs Wilf Hammer, and a lot of sailors used to come. My favourite dance was the tango. That was our social life. I didn't let men walk me home – I didn't want that. I didn't like to drink alcohol and not know what I was doing – I didn't want that.[8]

My parents weren't frightened about my going there . . . I was with friends, my gang. I was brought up with all the boys who went there, and I couldn't see any harm in them. I was known as Little Mac. The Grafton was my life! It used to be full every night. I used to go there from about the age of twelve. We didn't have any money, but I was dance-mad.[9]

There were also dances in local church halls, with music supplied by local bands.

When I was courting, in about 1945, I went to the Grafton, Locarno, I went to the Rialto. I was a natural dancer. My mother was a pianist and she used to play in the dark when we didn't have a penny for the gas. Well, when you went to work you got about half a crown pocket money. Out of that half a crown you saved a shilling for the hops, the dances – Sunday night, church halls mostly.

There would be a band. My brother used to play the piano in one of those in our local hall in 1942. He was a very good pianist. He used to play for five shillings. Mixture of dances. The quickstep. We only danced with one another, didn't we? We only danced with one another. I think the first new one was the jitterbug. And then the jive. They more or less came out at the end of the war. The Yanks brought them over.

Automatically, you would dance with your friend. You wouldn't see fellas but you would see girls. We used to, say, get half a crown and we would make sure we had a shilling for the hop. You still had to keep some money. You needed threepence for your leg tan. We used to go to the chemist. You had to tan your legs because you had no stockings, and you would put a line down the back of your leg with a pencil, and you could get a threepenny bottle of leg tan.[10]

For many, a party in the parlour with the neighbours was the thing, with beer from the pub taken out in bottles and demijohns. There might be a gramophone and food provided, or a cluster around a piano on 'pound nights', when guests would bring a pound of this, a pound of that in straitened times.[11] Frank Shaw:

It was a disgrace not to have plenty of beer . . . A credit to the do-giver was for a guest to tell friends next day: 'It was a gear do, the wuz beer for dogs.'[12]

Angelo Vaccarello was a young Italian in Liverpool after the war, courting his future wife.

Liverpool in the late forties, early fifties, was not the place it is today. I met my wife when she was working in a shop. We'd go to the pictures. Them days there were cinemas everywhere. Like a Sunday afternoon, if the weather was

good, we would go to the park, Sefton Park. A band, a
boating lake. Really, in the fifties in Liverpool there was not
much music, not many clubs. All we had was one called the
Mardi Gras[13] in Mount Pleasant. It's not there any more. In
the early fifties it was like a new wave of music come across
from America. First it was country and western, then it was
the Italian/American, like Frankie Lane, Dean Martin, Frank
Sinatra. Then was coming rock and roll. At the start, about
'52, '53, was Chuck Berry, all things like that.

In them days, everybody had radios, and at eleven
o'clock at night on a Saturday, or it may have been Sunday,
everybody had to go home after the pictures to listen to the
radio, to the Top 20. We would listen to the Top 20, and if
there was any song we liked, we would go to the shop, ask
for the record and they would get it from America.

The record shops were not like they are now, because
now they have a stack. In them days, you had to ask in the
shops, 'When do they arrive?' After Chuck Berry, Little
Richard and Elvis, then started the Mersey sound. It was not
just the Beatles. It was Billy Fury, there was quite a few. As
the Beatles started making their name, anybody who had a
guitar would buy a suit, get a contract and hope they make
the grade.

Frankie Vaughan come on tour. I don't know if you
remember he made a film in Liverpool called *These
Dangerous Years* [1957]. Maybe some scene was in the
Grafton and some scene was set in the Dingle. Everybody
went to the Grafton. It was a nice story, all lads from
Liverpool. So already people living in Liverpool felt that they
were in the centre of things.

Song and dance man Frankie Vaughan was a mover and shaker in the Boys Clubs of Great Britain, and was active in other cities, too, helping Glasgow to tame the worst excesses of the notorious area of Easterhouse. *These Dangerous Years* didn't exactly extol the virtues of the night life in Liverpool. It was about a teenaged Liverpudlian, conscripted into the Army, who goes on the run after wounding a bully.

But it is true, people did feel they were in the centre of things in Liverpool, long before the Beatles broke, and music was much more in their veins than I ever encountered in the writing of my oral histories of London's East End and Glasgow. There were more dance halls in Glasgow, where you took your life into your own hands, but there wasn't the music in the soul of 'everyman', which there was, and is, in Liverpool. Frank Shaw:

> Unless you realise that we are all minstrel boys or girls in the 'Pool, you cannot understand us . . . To the world, the Beatles may have seemed a unique phenomenon. Not to us. It's the Irish and Welsh in us. We are all singers in Liverpool. Even if we can't sing.[14]

In Liverpool, live music was always preferred to the gramophone, with the folk scene finding its way romantically down into the roots of Liverpool life, with songs such as 'Johnny Todd', originally a Liverpool skipping song about a seaman who loses his love when he goes to sea, and 'Maggie May', about a Lime Street prostitute who robs a sailor.

The latter should not be confused with Rod Stewart's song of the same name, which has nothing to do with the

Liverpool folk song. Others have realised its importance, however. In 1964 Lionel Bart used it in a musical called *Maggie May*, set against the backdrop of the Liverpool docks. In 1970, the Beatles included a track, 'Maggie May', on their *Let It Be* album.

The late Pete McGovern's 'In My Liverpool Home' is a more modern folk classic. 'I wrote it in 1961,' McGovern said, 'but a lot of people have said to me, "You didn't write that. It was written in 1848"' – sign of a great folk song. The Spinners, who made it popular, opened a famous folk club at Sampson and Barlow's restaurant in Liverpool's London Road, and McGovern had a club – the Wash House – in the same building, opening on different nights.

Immediately preceding the great sixties musical explosion in Liverpool, jazz was the thing. Jean Roberts introduces us to an early fifties Bohemian, almost beatnik scene, reminiscent of Soho in post-war London, or the Left Bank in Paris, the cafés of St Germain.

The Basement in Mount Pleasant was a coffee place for a few years and then got a licence. I thought getting a licence ruined it, because at closing time people came from the pubs and the atmosphere changed. But it was a good place then. It really was. Everybody would always pass through. The sculptor Arthur Dooley would go there . . . Jimmy Tarbuck used to go down there, all the footballers. You see, there wasn't that many places to go. There was the Basement, then you'd find these little ones – the Jacaranda [opened by Alan Williams, the original Beatles manager] and the Kinky Jew. The Mardi Gras was the in-place, big nightclub there. Then there were all these little coffee places that opened up around the streets. Brian Gilbertson, I think, had the Black Cat. Then he had the Latin Quarter in North Street. To me, being young, that was fantastic! It wouldn't be allowed today for health and safety reasons. None of them would be allowed. The Latin Quarter was an old warehouse. You went down holding on to a rope. But when you got down, all the lights were there. It was the first time I'd been anywhere with those lights, you know, the ones that were white and made everything stand out and gave you like a tan. They'd have a steel band on. I thought I was in fairyland. It was fantastic. You'd find the same people would go the round.

I loved the music. It wasn't pop, and you didn't go to these cafés to get drunk. You would have Juliet Greco playing, Edith Piaf. From the Basement days I always loved Edith Piaf's voice. All this cha-cha music was up then, so you would be up dancing. I used to go with my feet burning. When I think about it, it was all quite innocent fun. It was a good way of meeting people. You had all different kinds of people there, a good, overall [mix] . . . People now seem to stick to their own. Students, the Greek boys whose fathers were ship owners, they were a good crowd . . . Then the Jewish crowd. They were all lovely people. I can't remember any nasty people. Ray Adams was on the door. He was a really handsome guy when he was young. He used to get all the girls' hearts fluttering, y'know?

The Cavern had started at that time, but we were soon told to move out. We were there for the jazz. I was never really into the Beatles. Never really been a Beatles fan. Jazz clubs. The Blue Magnolia. The Merseysippi[15] were around then. They used to play at the Temple. They are still going! I used to listen to them at sixteen!

The Cavern in Mathew Street was opened as a jazz club in 1957 by Alan Sytner. Two years later, Ray McFall, Sytner's accountant, took it over, and featured jazz and blues artists. The scene was changing, and the drift was from jazz to blues to rock and roll. The Beatles first appeared at the Cavern, or 'the Cave' as it was known, in March 1961.[16]

When the great change came it was associated naturally with the siren lure of the ocean, the magnetic pull of her moon-directed tides. For what rooted Liverpool in rock and roll, came from across the sea, a slave lament out of Liverpool's heart of darkness, the blues.

It sounds ironic that the victims of Liverpool's slave trade in the 1760s should supply the sound that enabled the great transformation of the city in the 1960s. No irony, it was as Jung had predicted, time for a resolution of the imbalances deep down in the city's collective unconscious. Suffering there had been enough, among the black slaves certainly and not a little among Liverpool's working classes, for well over a hundred years. When the transformation came, it occurred with such incredible energy and vitality that you could be forgiven for thinking that the Pool itself had erupted like a volcano, as it had always promised to do, its magma purging and at the same time ingesting slave city's deepest, darkest unconscious drives.

Merchant seamen, known as Cunard Yanks, were instrumental in this huge sea change.

They worked, often as cooks, stewards and waiters, on the Cunard line out of Liverpool to New York. There were around 25,000 of them, according to Bill Harrison,[17] who was one of those who brought the new sound back that would make the modern world.

These working-class Liverpool seamen brought not only records but also clothes, fridges and, later, washing machines, cameras, reel-to-reel tape recorders, but always the latest 45s, which no one in Britain had yet heard. On one occasion Bill even brought back a juke box stacked with records, which ended up in the Amber Club in Hanover Street.

Bill Harrison describes his arrival in New York as 'like leaving black and white and going into Technicolor'. For ever and a day the young had grown up wearing what their parents wore, working-class lads adopting the grey, hard-wearing materials of their fathers, which never changed from one week to the next, until lost to the pawnbroker. In New York there was style off the peg. 'You could get a shirt for a dollar and I think we were on $3.50 to the pound then,' said Bill. It was this modern Technicolor world that the Cunard Yanks brought to Britain, first stop Liverpool.

A few years ago, when Bill's nephew Stephen Higginson remembered his uncle's trips to and from America in the forties and fifties and the gifts he brought home, he had the idea for a film which was made as *Cunard Yanks* by Dave Cotterill of Souled Out Films.

In an interview with National Museums Liverpool (Museum of Liverpool – eight hundred lives project), Bill Harrison describes how the siren call first took him to sea. He was fifteen, working as an apprentice engineer:

One day, having a day off from my apprenticeship, I heard some music coming out of a window at the bottom of Sheppard Avenue, Bowring Park, where we were living at the time. I had never heard anything like it before in my life.

255

I sat on the wall and listened, and eventually went in to the football field to play football. The next day I did the same thing, stopped, sat on the wall and this time a chap came out. I thought, 'This guy's a film star.'

He wore a midnight blue suit, white socks and Oxblood slip-on shoes and a tie the likes of which I had never seen before. And he said, 'What are you doing?' I said, 'Listening to the music. I've never heard anything like it.' He said, 'It's Hank Williams.' And the song was 'Jambalaya'. Another was 'Settin' the Woods on Fire'.

'Fabulous, I've never heard of him.' He said, 'Well, I'm a seaman. I've brought them home with me from Galveston.'

As Angelo Vaccarello recalled, country and western came first, followed by the Italian/Americans. Only then came the blues, which charged rock and roll – 'Chuck Berry, all things like that', as he put it.

Bill's new friend's name was Ronnie Porter, and the next day Bill called in sick and went with Ronnie into the city centre.

He took me to the Sailor's House, which had a snooker table and coffee bars. It was another world. He said, 'If you want to go away to sea, I'll get you a form and you can get your mam to sign it.' So a couple of days later, he brings the form up. No problem with my mother but my father says, 'Oh, he's got an apprenticeship.' But I'd got the bug then. I wanted to see the world.

I was taken down to the Shipping Federation at Canning Place and the superintendent Mr Brown, he said, 'How old are you?' I said, 'Fifteen and a half.' He said, 'You're too young.' But as I was going, he said, 'Wait a minute, take this note up to Cornhill off Park Road. If you join the Royal Navy as a boy, you can come out in a couple of years and join the Merchant Navy.'

Nothing had changed in a thousand years. Once the moon goddess has you, there is no retreat. She took Bill into the heart of waterfront culture on the other side, which of course he recognised immediately as home from home. Here he is in Hoboken, New Jersey, across the Hudson from New York, with a group of guys who are having a drink in a little docksider, after discharging a consignment of hogsheads of tobacco from their cargo passenger ship moored nearby:

I had a glass of their local brew and a group of guys came in with lights on tripods. I found out later they were called dollies. The lights had wheels on. They said, 'You lot, out! Or turn around and face the bar.' Didn't know what was going on, but at the back of the bar was a massive mirror and we could all see what was happening. A couple of guys came in and there was an argument and a fight and they were filming all this. It was only about two or three years later that we realised we were in the scene with Marlon Brando and Lee J. Cobb when they were fighting in *On The Waterfront*. I have seen it since – our backs in the film!

Eventually, these Cunard Yanks caught a sniff of the hard stuff. Bill's friend and fellow Cunard Yank Ritchie Barton describes finding himself in Philadelphia listening to the sound of rhythm and blues for the first time. Was it 'Crying in the Chapel' that first took him down? He isn't sure, but he knows that straightaway he hurried to a record store. 'No, sir, we don't sell it.' He went to a second store – 'No, sir' – and a third. 'These are *coloured* records, sir,' he was told. 'Try a smaller store.'

'Coloured' meant black. You couldn't say 'black' then, although you could say 'white'. It is possible that 'Crying in the Chapel' was not the record Ritchie heard, as other sources suggest that it was written by Artie Glenn in 1953 and charted nationally the same year. But the point made is a good one, for the irony was that black records were poorly distributed in America, such was apartheid in those days. Only when R & B broke big in Britain did the floodgates open, earning the gratitude of many black artists there. Chuck Berry said, 'I spent years hacking out this stuff, but no one would buy it until these Liverpool guys showed up in America doing the same thing!'[18] Before that, generally, only white artists' cover versions were distributed nationally.

There were similar curbs in Britain, where a policy of banning American musicians initiated by the British Musicians Union made the smuggling of black records into the country all the more significant.

It is often the case that negatives lead to positives, although it is a sobering thought that had it not been for the slave trade, if the old triangular trade had not so firmly established the line drawn by Cunard between Liverpool and New York, Liverpool would not have been the importer of the sound, nor yet ever have been singing the blues. Indeed, the blues, the lament of African slaves from the plantations of the southern states of America, might not have existed.

There would have been no Big Bill Broonzy, who reached deep into the past through his adaptation of traditional blues; no Muddy Waters, the major inspiration for the British blues explosion in the 1960s; no Willie Dixon, whose blues standards include 'Little Red Rooster', recorded by Howlin' Wolf in 1961 and covered by the Stones in '64, and were an important link with white rock and roll; no Little Walter, who played with Muddy Waters and put the harmonica in British blues; and no Howlin' Wolf himself, who, according to musician and critic Cub Koda, 'No one could match for the singular ability to rock the house down to the foundation, while simultaneously scaring its patrons out of their wits.'

These were just a few of the artists who bridged African American slave blues and rock and roll, and whose records were changing hands in Liverpool dockland pubs in the forties and fifties when the Beatles were still at school – ingredients of a diet on which everyone in the city, musician and rocker alike, came to sup from the mid-1950s on.

Bill Harrison told me that Liverpool girls were as ever the catalyst. 'Girls would get hold of a copy of the *Shipping News*, which gave all the arrivals and sailings, and they'd see what ships were coming in, and go down to the Locarno for the dance.' The new sounds arrived with the seamen and immediately became part of the culture. The chronology of the development of the Liverpool club scene reflected the significance of the black sound. 'The black clubs came first, in the late forties, fifties, and the white clubs followed, with names like the Amber, Dutch Eddie's in Stanhope Street, the 69 Club in Park Road, the Bar One in Dock

Road, the Iron Door, the Maracell, and the Bird Cage, which was owned by another Cunard Yank, John Hibbert, who was in the film.'

Gradually, there was a gelling of different black styles in white music, with black soul fusing R & B, gospel and blues styles in groups such as the Isley Brothers, whose 'Twist and Shout' appeared on the Beatles first album, *Please Please Me*, a year after the Isleys recorded it. Prem Willis-Pitts points to Bobby Freeman, Ray Charles and, above all, Little Richard as other important influences, on the 'super-powerful R & B rock'.[19] Sugar Deen, an important black singer in Liverpool in the late fifties and sixties, whose work on harmonies was especially influential, makes a similar point:[20]

> The Beatles weren't doing harmonies as I recall. They were doing coverings, mostly soul and R & B stuff. The Beatles were doing things by the Chiffons and Shirelles and Chuck Berry, the Coasters, all that kind of stuff . . . Little Richard was like blowing everybody away and that was Paul McCartney's idol basically, and the Beatles', mine also and Derry Wilkie's.

Derry Wilkie was a black singer of significance, because his was the first Liverpool group to make a record, and the first to go to Hamburg in Germany, where the Beatles learned to '*mach schau*'[21] and the clubs had such an important role in hardening off Merseysound.

> Derry actually had this performance like Little Richard, and he had a similar kind of voice, and so did McCartney, sort of high voice. That's where the Beatles got the high 'Oooooh'

from, they got that from Little Richard. Little Richard put that on most of his songs, didn't he. They sang a lot of Little Richard, so I found that Paul McCartney and Derry always competed with one another to sound like Richard, and even to the present day, when you hear McCartney sing, he has got Little Richard phrasings in the songs that he does. He has never lost that, so that was one of his main influences.

This is unassailably true. Songs that Little Richard made his own, such as 'Long Tall Sally' and 'Good Golly Miss Molly', became standard Beatles fare. In the early days in the Cavern, Paul would like to end the set with 'Long Tall Sally', after wooing the girls with 'Till There Was You'. In 1962, Don Arden backed Little Richard for a tour of England, with the Beatles as the opening act. Mass hysteria ensued.

One night in August last year I found myself drinking at the Old Roan in Aintree, and at the British Legion Club opposite, discovered the Merseycats holding their regular Thursday sixties nostalgia night.[22] While most old folk elsewhere opt for Bingo and the like, Liverpool's older generation prefers bands. Indeed, they play in bands, with names like Tempest, Del Renas, Shooter, Cosmics and Lackies. It is an amazing scene. The riffs played by some of the leathery-faced guitarists, musicians from name groups in the early days in Liverpool, were unbelievable. Clearly, you never lose it. I met the Merseycats' organiser and chairman (they are a children's charity), Wally Shepard, who plays with Tempest – 'I play the bass, but stringed upside down. No left-hand guitar in the sixties, or you had to pay a lot of money for them' – and asked him how it all began.

At school, at fourteen, we got to know where all the dolls used to go – the school gals, the good-looking ones. They used to hang out on a particular street. I asked my friend Lance, 'What's so good about that street?' He said, 'There's a guy called Rory Storm[23] and he plays on the doorstep of his house. And there's maybe a dozen dolls gathering round.' We went down and talked. Rory suggested why don't we form a band of our own. So we did, and in time we got some gigs. The band was called Johnny Tempest and the Tornadoes.

The Cavern, the Blue Angel, the Jacaranda, the place was just bursting. Liverpool then was a bit like being in a fairground for the first time. The city is unique for its live band scene. Americans would say, 'You must have two bands in every street.' We more or less did. Bob Wooller [DJ at the Cavern[24]] did a count – 350 bands!

Partly I put it down to the mix of Liverpool people – 60 per cent Irish, 20 per cent Scottish, 20 per cent Welsh. Very musical city. There was music everywhere. My wife used to go home to Ireland for a holiday and it was one big music scene on the boat over – the music of the Irish, the engineering skills of the Scottish, and the Welsh ear. We never thought of people coming in as imports.

Then, in the late 1950s, 1960, our band was influenced by the skiffle scene, Lonnie Donnegan. And a big local influence at the time were the American GIs at Burtonwood. They'd come into town, the white GIs to the white clubs, the blacks to the black clubs . . .

Burtonwood, on the eastern fringe of Liverpool, was, for over fifty years, the largest American air base in Europe.

The black soldiers were segregated on the base. They were not allowed to go to the white American soldiers' dances, so they would come to the black area in Liverpool to the clubs where blacks and whites mixed.

George Lund was 'a bit of a decoy for a couple of my sisters', who used to go to Base, the club at Burtonwood, because they had 'boyfriends, you know, of a different cultural heritage. We went to the Timepiece Soul Club in Liverpool too. Afterwards, they dropped us off, but not where we actually lived because my Dad was more discriminatory. Then there came a time when they discovered where we lived and like the three wise men with the Bourbon whisky and the southern fried chicken and the King Edward cigars, my Dad welcomed them in! One of my sisters actually married a GI, she lives in Phoenix, Arizona. So that was a happy story.'

Other Soul clubs were Stanley House on Parliament Street, the Bedford and the Mona Club on Berkley Street. Sugar Deen mentioned 'the likes of Somali club on Parliament Street, and facing that was the Tudor club, which was a well-known club at that time. Then you had the Gladray, which is known worldwide. I've been in Germany and people have asked me, "Do you ever go to the Gladray?"'

Wrote Prem Willis-Pitts:

Blacks seemed so cool. As teenagers, we wanted to be like them, to walk, talk and dance like them. But some of their hip blackness did seep in by osmosis.[25]

Osmosis is a good way to describe what was going on. Cultures, notably the black culture, were being assimilated. The cultures of the different tribes were merging to enhance the whole. To see it as plagiarism is to miss the point. That it happened so fast was to do with the intensity of the moment. Everyone was learning fast, trading with each other what they knew. As Wally Shepard recalled, 'People exchanged musical styles and sounds. Everybody was doing it.' Everyone had their major influence. Gerry Marsden said, 'For me it was Chuck Berry – he was my inspiration – and Ray Charles' keyboard playing, which I converted to the guitar.'[26]

Willis-Pitts notes that ganja came along as part of the cultural assimilation, with 'all the other regalia, linguistic and otherwise, of hip "blackness", including cool jazz, Milt Jackson, Roland Kirk and Miles Davis. Either cool jazz or soul music . . .' Sugar Deen does not agree. He puts the ganja down to merchant seamen bringing it in.

Wendy Harpe, who ran a community project in the 1960s, a youth club and arts centre called the Blackie in Great George Street, was clear in her appraisal that Burtonwood was a very important influence, but one of many that in a few short years created a scene of international significance.

Burtonwood brought black power and Motown to the Liverpool black community. The Blackie ran a soul disco based on American imported records. The Beatles, as with many groups in the sixties, owed a lot to black music. I don't think any of us involved at that time saw Liverpool as being so isolated – I think we were all very conscious of what was

happening in London, America, France. Allen Ginsberg came
to Liverpool, we had people who had been at the Paris riots,
Tom Wolfe was around, and so on. So I think we were part
of a national/international scene.

At the same time as music, other art forms, including
poetry, rose to prominence and contributed to the great
sea change. Said Roger McGough:[27]

The kids didn't see this poetry with a capital 'P'. They
understood it as modern entertainment, as part of the
pop movement.

Eileen Devaney, who was at school in Mount Pleasant at the
time, bears this out.

We just started going into town. We had this nun who was
an art teacher, Sister Bernard, and she was quite different
from the rest of the Notre Dame nuns. Close to our school
was Hardman Street, where all the life was going on – the
Sink, the Rumblin' Tum, all these sixties mods and rockers
type clubs, and a club called O'Connor's Tavern. Upstairs
would be poetry readings by Scaffold. Roger McGough and
John Gorman would do poetry readings. The only time I ever
went to the Cavern was at the lunchtime sessions. I was
always too young for when it was the big time, so me friends
and I used to go to the lunchtime sessions. We used to turn
our jumpers round backwards so the V-neck was round there
and we looked as if we were like mods, you know. And then
we'd leg it back, because we had an hour and a half at lunch
and we weren't supposed to be out of school.

Of course, we girls had no money whatsoever, so we'd go out at night and all pool what we had, and in those days it was nothing you know – pint of Black Velvet was two and a halfpenny [about 10p] for God's sake. But we started mixing with a lot of the mixed race young men at the time, African/white, West Indian/white, yeah. We used to go to this pub on Berry Street – it's called the Cosmopolitan now, it used to be called the Masonic – and all the bands used to play there. We just thought we were the business.

To get to the bottom of what was happening in the city we need to go back to 1964, the year after *Please Please Me* topped the British charts and Beatlemania went national, when Peter James, Terry Hands and Martin Jenkins, who had met during a National Student Drama Festival and decided to form a theatre company together, enlisted the help of a tough solicitor in the city, Harry Livermore. He took their idea to heart and copped £5,000 from the Council to convert Hope Hall in Hope Street into the Everyman Theatre.

Hope Street runs between the city's two cathedrals – the Catholic Metropolitan Cathedral at the top, the Anglican Cathedral at the bottom. Previously, Hope Hall was a cinema, and before that a chapel. Actor Jonathan Pryce, who was at the Everyman in the 1970s, remembers Hope Hall as being a music venue, too.

[As a teenager I used to] take the ferry from Birkenhead, lunch at Lewis's, then the teatime session at the Cavern before going on to Hope Hall, which stayed open late. I just missed the Beatles. But I did see Sonny Boy Williamson and the Swinging Blue Jeans.[28]

James, Hands and Jenkins cranked up the Everyman on a diet of 'Theatre in Education' with local schools and, in the evening, either Shakespeare (keeping to set texts as near as possible, to ensure an audience) or modern playwrights, such as Pinter, Beckett and the French absurdists. It was all very hand to mouth but, as Peter James recalls, 'That didn't stop the "House Full" notices going up.' This, apparently, was not so much due to the quality of the theatre as to the doorman, Les.

> Les, who came with the building, belonged to a union and was actually being paid more money than any of us at one stage. He became a kind of doorman. He got himself a peaked hat from some store somewhere, and he would stand in the front and was a bit of a character.

Merseyside Radio's Roger Phillips,[29] another who was an actor with the Everyman in the 1970s – 'at that time, two theatres in the country mattered, the Everyman and the Citizens Theatre in Glasgow' – takes up the story.

> The audiences loved Les. He used to work at the Pivvy, the Pavilion on Lodge Lane, used to be a doorman there. It's where he picked up his techniques. You'd have an empty house. Les would be outside, having manipulated a queue . . . Such a character. He used to tell me the same joke every single day, which was, 'How do you get a parrot to speak?' Answer: 'Put him on the 42 bus.'[30] He used to think that was hilarious.

How Les enticed people into the theatre on difficult nights remained a mystery until Peter James happened by early one evening.

> Terry [Hands] had done a production of *Arabelle*, an immensely obscure play, and nobody was coming to see us very much. I came back from some terrible meeting about whether we could survive another week or not, and outside was the 'House Full' notice. So I went in, and there was Les. I said incredulously, 'Is the house full?' and he said, 'No.' His idea was that if anybody came late, they'd say, 'Is the house full?' and he'd say [as if offering a special favour], 'I'll get you a ticket,' and they'd give him half a crown.

Roger Phillips remembers the Everyman as full of characters, naturally including a Mother Liverpool figure:

> Winnie Owens, one of a variety of cleaners, but she was the outstanding one, she ran them. She absolutely adored the theatre, came to all the shows, kept every programme. She mothered the actors and actresses. Like Les, she is an important part of why it happened. She carried that theatre through her life. And at a very simplistic level . . . she taught the actors how to speak Scouse. But it was a lot more than that with her. She embodied the theatre in a person.

Just as interesting was what was going on down in the basement, the Bistro, as Peter James recalled:

> The poets were down there on a Tuesday evening, and some

nights we would do improvisation there after the show –
improvisation was very fashionable as an entertainment.

Principal among the poets were Adrian Henri, who formed
a poetry band called the Liverpool Scene, which grew out
of *The Incredible New Liverpool Scene*, a record of Henri and
Roger McGough reading their poetry. Said Phil Key:

Adrian Henri wrote a lot about love. He and Roger McGough
and another poet, Brian Patten, were three very distinct
personalities. Adrian Henri liked his music, so you find a lot
of jazz references in his work. He was also an artist, so [there
are] references to popular culture, pop art, you know? Roger
McGough was the comedian, always looking for a pun and a
twist and a bit of a joke, though some of his poetry can be
poignant; and Brian Patten always thought he was on a
different plane from the other two, 'poet's poetry', if you
know what I mean, not as easy to get into as the other two.
They got together in this place down below the Everyman
and did lots of poetry readings. But there were various places
dotted round the city where poetry readings were going on,
little enclaves of poetry very popular at the time.

Bohemian was better than a fair description of the Bistro at
this stage. The legend survives that if someone ordered a
steak, they'd take the order and then slip out the back and
buy one. 'Well, yes, it was true,' says Peter James, 'and you
were lucky if it was steak! Not until Paddy [Byrne] came was
it a proper concern.'

Soon it was adopted by the art college crowd, the cool
descendants of John Lennon and Stuart Sutcliffe, of

course. The college had become a magnet for Bohemian beat poets and musicians, as well as producing some good artists, Adrian Henri and lecturer Maurice Cockrill among them.

The poets and improvisation in the Bistro were the start of something new – not poetry, not music, not theatre, but all three art forms mixed up with attitude, challenge, humour, anarchy. There was a spontaneous breaking down of boundaries of all sorts (sexual inhibition included).

Peter James maintains that what was going on in the Everyman above the Bistro was not to do with traditional theatre, either, and that the audiences understood this:

> I am not sure they ever thought we were proper actors, because proper actors had suits and were on at the Playhouse and we were mixed up with Mersey poets and part of another sort of scene – the whole semi kind of pop culture that was going on in the city at the time, which made the Playhouse look kind of old-fashioned. Fur coat, bald head; fur coat, bald head; if you go up the top and look down.

It was here, too, that the famous sixties 'happenings' were first produced. The Everyman had a wonderful one called *The Dead Dog Incident*, which they took out into the streets of the city:

> It was a dog twitching in its last throes. We'd put it by a kerb and we had this thing to make it twitch, and we would watch people's reactions and film them. Then we did

Plattform One. George Platt invented the firelighter and very
cleverly sold out to the Gas Board for millions. Now George
was a voyeuristic sort of person, and he knew that in
experimental drama girls took their clothes off. He quite
liked that, so he gave us some money and we did *Plattform
One*, experimental theatre in which Pip Simmons[31] and all
that lot came up and did things for a week. The People's
Show wrapped the audience up in wool, and having
wrapped them up, they let twenty-four mice out of a
suitcase – we didn't tell them we had a bunch of big ones of
our own . . . It was before the Royal Court did *Come
Together*, which was exactly the same thing, but in London

Happenings had been pioneered in the late 1950s in
America by avant-garde artists such as Allan Kaprow and
Jim Dine, post Jackson Pollock and the Abstract
Expressionists, and musician John Cage. The Shed
Experience, which had Stephen Ray in it, and the People's
Show, which was formed in 1966 in the basement of Better
Books in London's Charing Cross Road and is still going
today, represented English experimental theatre, alongside
Ed Berman's Almost Free Theatre and Noel Greig and
Jenny Harris's Brighton Combination. Again, there was an
American genesis – Living Theatre (the first, founded as
early as 1946), Café La Mama, Open Theatre, Bread
and Puppet Theatre, and Joseph Papp's New York
Shakespeare Festival Public Theatre. Interestingly,
American experimental theatre took off in Europe – above
all in France – more readily than it did in its home country,
as Peter James recalls:

La Mama had been across and a lot of people took the cue from there. Very operative from that time was a man called Ritsaert ten Cate who ran an experimental place in Amsterdam, which was, later on, called the Mickery Theatre. Earlier he ran it from his family's farm, which was called Loenisloot. He was wealthy, sold it all and ran the Mickery, which was the most completely experimental theatre in the whole of Europe really. Whereas before, Pip Simmons had gone to the Arts Council, he would now have to go round the world for Ritsaert, who would pay him. So a lot of the experimental groups were supported by Ritsaert, paying them and sending them around Europe, where they'd be paid more than they were here.

The whole scene fitted the mood among the Liverpool young, which was if not to discard the old, to transform it alchemically. It was a mind-based project, which is where the mind-expanding drugs, mescalin and LSD, and magic mushrooms came in. There was a sense of provocation and challenge, of a need to break out of old patterns of thought. This was also the era of the medically trained guru of lateral thinking, Edward de Bono, who defined the brain as a system that organises itself around old patterns of thought and needs to be shaken out of them to design a new way forward. The Eastern mystical Sufi influence followed and, on a more populist level, the transcendental meditation of Maharishi Mahesh Yogi, to whom the Beatles attached their wagon for a while. Jung, whose 'Pool of life' dream colours Liverpool's story from beginning to end, was also fast catching on, particularly with the artistic fraternity, where people understood his work in terms of their ability to weigh anchor on reason and logical thinking and submit to a less conscious, more intuitive, creative flow.

It was up to you where you engaged with what was going on. Peter James and his crew were the ones just before all this, operating from their theatre in Hope Street (perfect name), helping spark off the transformation.

The Scaffold, a humorous group composed of Roger McGough, John Gorman and Mike McCartney, covered both the music and arty elements and achieved some notable success with a couple of number-one hits. They emerged at a Merseyside Arts Festival organised by poet John Gorman. Mike McCartney, at the time calling himself McGear, presumably to divert attention from the fact that he is Paul's brother, was introduced to the idea in the Everyman Bistro. Peter James:

The Scaffold used to appear at the Everyman and I directed them a couple of times before they went up to the Edinburgh Festival. John Gorman, who was the funny man, said, 'You don't have to wear a suit when you come to the Everyman, but you do have to bring an umbrella, because it leaks.' They were a stand-up review team, not a pop group. Roger McGough wrote sketches about the atom bomb and stuff like that. They would write some review evenings and there were some songs, which McGear used to do, and some poetry that Roger used to like – 'Sketches for Lovers' – and there'd be a conversation on a park bench. Two people would sit on a park bench and John Gorman would come from the wings and scatter moon dust, and they would have to appear to be making love, but in fact they'd be talking about atom bombs and football teams. It was wordsmith's stuff that Roger does. And John Gorman would do the drunk Irish priest in which he mixed up stories in the Bible, a very Liverpudlian thing.

There was a sketch called 'Chocolate Eclairs', which started with a plate of chocolate éclairs on stage and you'd hear John Gorman screaming, 'Chocolate éclairs,' from every part of the auditorium. He would be a chocolate éclair addict and push these chocolate éclairs into his face. And then Roger would come out and say, 'Do you know what they are made of?' And then he would list some ghastly ingredients and John would try and clear them from his face and was very funny trying to do that.

So there were verbal things and physical things like that, and later they used to take them up to the Traverse Theatre in Edinburgh, and round the clubs. They'd sing 'Lily the Pink' and 'Aintree Iron' – 'Thank you very much for the Aintree iron' – which went to the top of the hit parade, put out by Apple just before Christmas. People sent the record as a thank-you letter.

There were others in Liverpool at this time making waves, notably a couple called Harpe, both of them outsiders, but characteristically, unpredictably, quirkily Liverpudlian. Bill and Wendy Harpe took what was going on into the poorest areas of the community, particularly among black families.

Bill Harpe found his path as a schoolboy in Darlington. Joan Littlewood, a main inspiration for what was going on at a deep level in theatre and in life at this time, was his source.[32]

A piece of improvisation resulted in my disqualification from the school play. I was one of the crowd. There was Coriolanus and soldiers defending and we were the crowd. We were to heckle. We were to say we didn't like Coriolanus. I said to the lads I was with, 'I think we can take them,' and so we took the Roman soldiers and Coriolanus!

Then, purely accidentally, next door to my school, which was Darlington Boys Grammar School, was a training college for young women, a teachers' training college. They put occasional performances on and somehow I went along to see Theatre Workshop do *Uranium 235*,[33] with Ewan MacColl and Joan Littlewood, and that's when I realised that theatre was something. That was when I thought, 'Well, this is something!'

What I remember were things like the cast saying to the audience, 'I know this seems like it's just a play. I know it's half a dozen of us up on a stage, but this is real. This is about something you need to think about. We are not just pissing about on stage to entertain you, you know.' Stepping out and saying that, and then going back into it, you know? Theatre Workshop changed the course of what I was going to do.

Harpe won a scholarship in maths and physics to Downing College, Cambridge, because his grammar school insisted that if you were bright you should study science, and it was not until he went for interview at Cambridge that anyone took his preference for theatre seriously.

They said, 'Well, you have come here with a scholarship in maths and physics.' I said, 'I would like to read English.' The

Fellow in English was F.R. Leavis.[34] So I met Leavis and I remember he said to me, 'Well, what have you read Harpe?' I said, 'I've read Evelyn Waugh, Sir.' 'Have you read the Cannon?' 'The Cannon, Sir?' 'Shakespeare.' I said, 'I've read *Romeo and Juliet*, Sir.' I didn't have 'O' level English Literature! I had 'O' level Language, but not Literature. He said, 'They tell me you could get a First in maths or physics, and I tell you the most you will get in English is a 2/2.' I said, 'I'll take a 2/2 in English then.' And that was that, I did three years with Leavis and he was wonderful.

He was at university from 1954 to 1959, having done his National Service in Bristol with the RAF, where he persuaded them to put him through dance classes. Afterwards, he went to London, continued with his dance training and in 1961 found himself in pantomime with Tommy Steel at the Liverpool Empire.

It was then he met Wendy, whose life had been as anarchic as Bill's had been ordered.

I come from a dysfunctional family. I didn't have a father. Well, I did, but he left when I was eight. He was a bastard. That is absolutely the summary of the situation. The better things in my life happened when he left. He was literally the only amoral man I ever came across in my life. And I knew that. I knew it was good he went.

[As a child] I was very ill. I mean really ill. I had asthma and TB, and bronchitis, and they decided I was dying. I was five foot four when I was twelve, but I weighed under six stone. I looked like something out of Belsen. I looked like I was dying. So every year they would say, 'You'll not make the next year.'

I hardly went to school at all. My mother taught me at home quite a lot. She was a bright woman – you know, not educated, but bright. So I learnt to read and write, but when it came to the eleven-plus, no one could read my paper. I had this amazing headmistress who arranged for me to go up to County Hall and read it to the examiners.

I was difficult, a difficult child. Really difficult. Difficult and violent. At the time I didn't really see it like this, but . . . I was violent towards adults. I had come to the conclusion I was surrounded by a bunch of idiots. These were adults. I could tell they were idiots because they kept saying things to you that were manifestly stupid. Particularly my mother. And teachers, yes. I was a problem. When my sister went to grammar school, they asked whether she was related to Wendy. She said, 'I don't know anyone called Wendy.'

The local authority arranged for her to go to school outside London, a boarding school in Hook in Hampshire.

I pushed the Matron down the stairs. Well, she was standing in front of me. She broke bits of her body. Badly. I said to the headmaster, 'You know, she should have moved.' He said, 'If I get you an education, will you stop attacking my staff?' And I said, 'I'll think about it.'

Eventually, the authority arranged to send Wendy to a school in Yorkshire, 'Wennington Co-educational Boarding School at Wetherby – Wennington because it was started at Wennington in Lancashire. It was run by Quakers, people who had been conscientious objectors in the Second World War.'

I arrived there thinking here we go again. And I'd never been north. Well, you should have seen me. I took a torch in case they had no electricity, and I took knives and forks, because you never knew what you were going to find. And I got on this train from Kings Cross, which in those days took five hours to get to Leeds. And I knew the people were going to be stupid because I'd heard them on the radio. On the way there was all this country and I thought, 'Where's all this come from,' you know? And I got to Leeds and I thought, 'I'm not going. I'm not even thinking about getting off this train. I want to go home.' They took no notice and just yanked me off the train, and, you know, it was an amazing school. I mean, it was just such an amazing school.

I got there and I just went to bed, because I knew that would get everybody really annoyed. But nobody said a word. I mean, nobody!

At Wennington, there was a very good English teacher and Wendy read a great deal. But, like Bill, she excelled at maths. At A Level she took physics, chemistry and double maths (pure and applied), and scholarship maths, and applied to Liverpool University. The interview (you were interviewed for all universities then) shows an extra-ordinary symmetry with Bill's experience, although they had not yet met:

I came up for the interview to read maths and I took one look at these three guys sitting behind the desk and I thought, 'I don't think so.' I went across to the English department and knocked on the door of Professor Muir and said, 'I'm here for an interview to read maths. How about me reading English instead?' He said, 'Are you studying English at A Level?' I said, 'No.' He said, 'You would need to have A Level English, you know.' I said, 'Yes.' 'And you would have to have Latin. Are you studying Latin?' You had to have it to read English in those days, and I didn't. He said, 'Why do you want to read English?' I said, 'I read a lot.' He obviously didn't know what to do with me. He knew the school I was at. He knew the headmaster. So I went back to school and said, 'I need to do A level English and Latin . . .'

Wendy took them the following year, and arrived in Liverpool to find a very unsatisfactory scene.

When I came here, I thought, after all the trouble I had to get to university, I'd be surrounded by like minds and I wasn't. A lot of the people were from Liverpool. Most of them had never left home. Most of the staff . . . I mean, the guy who taught us the seventeenth-century playwright John Webster and all that lot, he had lived in Liverpool, studied in Liverpool, done his MA in Liverpool, and was now teaching in Liverpool! Y'know? My first essay for him got a minus gamma. He said, 'Well, I think it's a disgrace.' He was very upset, he thought it was pornographic. We were in this seminar, sitting around a table, and he informs me that my essay is pornographic and that people had been writing about Webster for years and never had anyone ever mentioned this. To which I said, 'Let me read you a passage from Webster and you tell me what you think it means?' Thereupon he got up and marched everybody out of the room, leaving me sitting there. I thought, 'This is going to be fun, this is going to be a laugh a minute.' This was 1961.

I was all for leaving. If I hadn't met Bill I would have left. I just would have left. When I got back from Christmas my first year, he was living in the house where I had lodgings. He was at the Empire with Tommy Steele doing pantomime. He had been in this hotel that had caught fire and they'd relocated him, so I think he just decided that I was going to be the woman for him. Just like that. I kept saying, 'You don't understand, I have a boyfriend.' But saying no to Bill is a bit like talking to Everest really. It's a waste of time. So we got married at the end of my first year at university.

In 1965 there was a Commonwealth Arts Festival in four cities – Glasgow, Liverpool, Cardiff and London. Bill went for the job as Director of the Liverpool Festival and was rejected. But then Cardiff rang Liverpool in search of a candidate to fill their vacant directorial seat, and they recommended Bill. He took the job in Cardiff, and Wendy went with him.

We did a major poetry conference, with poets from all over the Commonwealth, including Michael X[35] and the beat poets, Pete Brown and Michael Horovitz from London. The Gulbenkian gave us £5,000, which was a lot of money then. Bill had this idea that we would just invite everyone we could think of from all over the Commonwealth and put a note in each room saying, 'We've got you here, now you organise the Festival.'

We brought the Traverse down [from Edinburgh] and they did a show based around the Commonwealth.[36] The Home Office phoned up and said, 'Would you mind not performing it?' They had read it! They were sure that we wouldn't want to embarrass the royal family. Bill said he would think about it. Then he phoned them back and said, no we wouldn't be taking it off; it would be performed. And they said, 'But there are all these facts, where did you get them from?' And we said, 'They all came out of government reports.' Bill had to go up to Buck House with all the other festival directors to do a speech about what they planned to do, and the Duke of Edinburgh said he would visit London and Cardiff – they were the only two places he would do.

The Cardiff festival made the *Sunday Times*. They wrote that if you weren't there, you were nobody. There was a delightful picture of Bill at the door of the Museum of Wales pointing at this Vietnamese pig, a black pot-bellied pig – they read poetry to a Vietnamese pig! – saying, 'Take it out!' And there was a guy who was 'being a living novel' . . . It was very sixties really. This was 1965 or '66. We were there for eighteen months.

When the couple returned to Liverpool, the Bluecoat, which had been an arts centre since 1906,[37] asked Bill to join them, but he had already accepted an invitation to be Artistic Director for the opening of Liverpool's new Catholic Metropolitan Cathedral, which included a commission to choreograph the Mass.

In 1933, a Catholic cathedral had been planned for the site of the old workhouse, and designed by Edwin Lutyens, but the project had been interrupted by the war. Afterwards, only the crypt was completed before building was stopped because of the expense. The new cathedral was built above the existing crypt between 1962 and '67, its modern, in-the-round design groundbreaking theologically as much as architecturally – it was the first cathedral to break with longitudinal planning. The opening attracted all sorts of controversy. Known as Paddy's Wigwam, it was lampooned in a play called *The Mersey Funnel* a short walk away at the Everyman. A model of the cathedral was created that emphasised its likeness to the Sputnik. In the play, it took off like the Sputnik and flew out of the theatre at the end. Bill's choreography for the Mass, or perhaps the very idea of choreographing the Mass, proved to be no less controversial.

With Bill unavailable, the Bluecoat asked Wendy to organise a poetry reading.

I said OK and I got Adrian Mitchell[38] and others from London – because in the meantime there'd been this poetry reading at the Royal Albert Hall, which we had gone to. We looked at the people who'd read, and invited those we liked. One was a friend of Bill's from Cambridge, Harry Fainlight,[39] who then came to live with us.

The Albert Hall event in 1965 was a huge occasion, as Phil Key recalls:

Ginsberg was there, the Liverpool poets, and lots of other poets. There was a bit of a happening going on, one of those sixties happening things. They used to have them in Liverpool. You'd walk into balloons. They did a lot of that at the Everyman. Adrian Henri was into that. It was a big poetry explosion, with Ginsberg reading poems that weren't really words, and rooms full of balloons: just one of those mad things they did in the sixties. Bit hazy,

but then the sixties, you're not supposed to remember it
are you?

Wendy's Bluecoat event was, therefore, in tune with the
times. Held in the Sandon Theatre, not only was it full,
there were people outside in the courtyard.

> The room took about eighty – 250 turned up! So everybody
> was very impressed by this. It was all young people. All the
> people who had been doing these poetry readings at Hope
> Hall were there.

Next, she brought modern art to the Bluecoat and began
to work with Littlewoods heir Peter Moores.

> I did 'Visual Arts in the Gallery' with Mark Boyle, John
> Latham, Lillian Lynne. Then we did receptions, including for
> the Royal Ballet, the first outdoor sculpture exhibition in the
> city, and theatrical performances – Mark Boyle's *Bodily Fluids
> and Functions*[40] before it went to the Roundhouse in London.
> After that I talked to a group of businessmen in the city
> who were running family concerns. Peter Rockcliffe ran
> Rockcliffe Printers; Alan Thurlow ran Modern Kitchen
> Equipment, which his father had founded; and Peter Moores.
> And they all put their time into the arts. So my promotions
> committee consisted of these people.

The association developed with an event for a Bluecoat
anniversary, to which Wendy invited poets Brian Patten,
Adrian Mitchell and Roger McGough, insisting, to
appease growing concerns of the Bluecoats Society of Arts,

that if they accepted they must behave. At one stage, a member of the Society had said to her, 'I would come to your poetry readings, Wendy, but I'm worried about what I may catch from the audience.' So she insisted that her poets wear suits.

> They were angelic. But in the audience were people from the Daughters of the Revolution from America, and the next day in the *Echo* the headline was something like 'Disgraceful Poetry Reading'. I was incensed. I thought, 'You must be joking.' They behaved so well!

Meanwhile, Bill and Wendy had been hatching an idea for a Community Arts Centre and Bill was looking for a place to base it.

> We looked at the Albert Dock. The then Town Clerk of Liverpool said, 'Can you do something with this?' We turned the Albert Dock down! That was '66. Then we found the Blackie.

The Blackie, or as it is known today, the Black-E, is housed in the old Congregational church on Great George Street, which runs parallel to Hope Street. The building is magnificent. Built in 1840–41, it is described by Joseph Sharples as 'comparable to Nash's All Souls, Langham Place, in London, but more massive and imposing . . . The columns are monoliths, said to have come from a quarry in Park Road, Toxteth.'[41]

At this stage, nothing more was done. After the opening of the cathedral, Bill went to Africa and created an all-

African, circus-style production of Aeschylus's *Oresteia* – 'the whole Greek tragedy in which Agamemnon comes back from the wars and his wife has been deceitful and kills him in the bath' – and toured it through the bush. African performers, African music, it was an amazing experience. During the tour Wendy received a letter.

> It said, 'Dear Wendy, I have thought about Great George Street Congregational church (for our project). We should buy it.' I opened the letter, looked carefully through the pages and there was no money, there was no cheque. It just told me to buy this church.

Peter Moores[42] heard about it and bought the church for them, as Wendy recalled:

> I remember I was sitting there one day. He said, 'What's wrong with you?' I said, 'Bill wants this building and I haven't got any money.' He said, 'Which building?' I said, 'The one at the bottom of Duke Street.' He said, 'What would you do with it?' 'We'd turn it into an arts centre.' He said, 'Oh, I'll buy it for you, Wendy.' And then he kept going on, 'Have you bought it yet?'

They moved in in 1967, later acquiring the ballroom floor from the nearby David Lewis Hotel,[43] 'where Joan Littlewood began. It was her first work, as it was described to us, and when they took the hotel down, we took the ballroom floor up piece by piece and brought it here, although some of it has since been "liberated" by enterprising Liverpool adventurers.'

Bill Harpe has been there ever since. 'There were two hundred arts laboratories in the country. We were choosing to do something related, but different. We were saying not, "we are an arts lab," but, "we are a community arts project. We are a mixture of contemporary arts centre, which is like an arts lab, and community centre – we have got everybody of every age." That was what differentiated us from all the other national action.'

Before long it was on the circuit of every teenage girl in the area. For Eileen Devaney it was a natural progression from the Sink, the Rumblin' Tum, and upstairs at O'Connor's Tavern.

Yeah, yeah, the Blackie is just at the other end of Berry Street. Fabulous building, and inside it's absolutely fantastic, wonderful. In the late sixties beginning of the seventies, this bloke Bill with the beard, he just said there's too much talent going to waste here and he got some money from the County Council to put on some Art Workshops and things like that in the Blackie, and a lot of the youth of the area utilised it. A lot of them didn't let on that they were going there because it was a bit . . .

Hippy?

Yeah, but when you go in there now and there are exhibitions on and they are putting together the photographs of the people who worked from the late sixties, seventies, you see what was really going on. All the information is in there, and what you see is what we used to do. We used to get into terrible trouble, because what was I doing, this young Irish girl, what did I need to go and mix with this lot for? Well, it was an exciting city wasn't it?

What brought the teenagers in initially, and attracted black kids in particular, was Radio Doom. Wendy:

We had a DJ from Southport called Dave Kaye who ran a disco called Radio Doom. We probably had the best music in the city, because we had all the soul music from America. He got all the records from the States and was way, way ahead of the competition. Girls went out with guys from Burtonwood and learnt the dances, and then came back and taught the Blackie.

People came from Toxteth and from all the way down Pitt Street, places that are gone now, all those old-fashioned tenement blocks, huge blocks, massive numbers round here, much higher populations than what there is now. They came over a series of weeks. It was one of the flukes of life. We just happened to like the same music – American soul music. First of all the girls came to see if they were going to be allowed in, and then a couple of weeks later, the young lads came to see if they were going to be allowed in. Finally, the teenagers came. That was on a Sunday night. Saturday night was the junior disco. If you were twelve and very clever, you could go to the junior one and get into the senior one as well.

Hazel George was one of them:

I always remember the Sunday discos. It was the highlight of our week. There was a gang of us, boys and girls from the

Berkley area in Toxteth. We were young and just loved dancing. We all had Afro hairstyles. The Blackie and Stanley House played the best soul music in town. We perfected all the latest dances from the Popcorn to Cha-cha. We knew we would have to face bricks and bottles thrown by skinheads as we walked up the hill from the Blackie. It became a weekly ritual of cat-and-mouse. It was kind of racist and typical of what we experienced across most areas outside Liverpool 8 in the 1970s. It never stopped us going to the Blackie – a safe haven.

Besides the disco, the Harpes introduced event art, performance art, happenings, definitive sixties fare.

We did inflatables very early, when they were quite unknown and we didn't know much about them. The first one we built we nicknamed 'the killer' because it hospitalised people. We had this huge balloon thing and if you jumped on one side you could shoot somebody sitting on the other side all the way across the room, hitting things along the way, and people did! Then we learned about putting nets over them, so you could clamber on them. Then we learnt about putting rope inside to form actual structures.

Jane George:

I always remember going on the inflatable. It was like a huge padded den. It was the biggest inflatable that I had ever seen. We only seemed to go during the school holidays. It was only after school that I realised the Blackie had much more to offer, and was to be involved in various projects.

The projects began with play schemes. Wendy:

> In the summer, we would run one every day of the week. In
> the holidays, we would run one in the afternoon and one in
> the evening, which was a killing routine. Then in the term
> time, we would do two evenings a week. Have you seen that
> game over there? Come and look at it. It's now called
> 'Dotto', it was called 'Thirty Something'.

I walked over to what looked like pieces of art. The
participant gets a sheet of paper with thirty dots on it, with
no indication of what might be made out of the dot
pattern. It could be anything. The game produces a whole
range of different solutions – owls, insects, flowers, people
– each one as plausible as the next, but all personal
solutions. Another game was called 'Bird Works':

> Participants came together in small groups and were required
> to create a bird from the materials provided. One week they
> were provided with angling materials – lines, lead weights,
> hooks, floats, and so on. The next week they were provided
> with electrical materials – wire clips, plugs . . . The following
> week they were provided with office materials – pens, paper
> . . . A series of collage works emerged, the fisherman's bird,
> the electrical bird, the office bird . . .

One result, I note, is called 'Break and Tern', and is made
out of springs from a bike. But are we talking about art?
'We are talking about games,' said Wendy firmly. This is
community arts, creative, fun. The effect was dramatic.

We had kids running through the door shouting, 'I've got another idea for the dots!' Then we did shows. The Bluecoat paid to do the John Latham show.[44] I did Allan Kaprow's menace-filled *Spring Happening*[45] upstairs, which took place in a tunnel and you could see out of gaps. It finished with your running [from] a lawn mower . . . and everyone backing down to the end [of the tunnel], and then finally the sides [of the tunnel] fell open. We also had a group in the building called Mixed Media, and very quickly we created 'lorry theatre'. We transformed the back of this lorry with large animals and things and staged performances on it. But the big thing that was very different was 'participatory theatre', which didn't exist without an audience. The first was a show called *To Hell with Human Rights*, which was commissioned by Amnesty. You came in at the front of the building and got passports, but we put different times in the passports when they would become null and void . . .

The audience was in the play, *was* the play. Clear instructions from the organiser, passports handed out with different expiry dates, well-prepared theatrical sets on three floors of the Blackie building, including a prison for anyone who overstayed their welcome in a particular country, drove the play along, making participants react spontaneously to dramatic, real-life situations invested with a moral dimension. Reactions were analysed by everyone later. It was a cleverly disguised, entertaining, educational process, which sometimes got out of hand.

What was interesting about these shows was the degree to which people got emotionally involved. We did one on housing, which led to a riot. The audience rioted in the slums and took over the middle-class house! As we said at the end of the show, were people proposing this as a solution to the real housing situation?

We did two on education. They were all commissioned by organisations. I remember Alex Schouvaloff, who used to be head of the North West Arts Board (before he started the Theatre Museum in London), he did the second education show and got locked up and a black eye in the process. He said, 'This is the only show I have been to where I got into a fight and got a black eye!'

Quite quickly, the Blackie programme became seasonal. In the summer, we would do play schemes in the building, and theatre somewhere else. In the term time, we would do performances alongside play schemes. So, we did poetry readings, for instance. It was 1981 before we had an art gallery . . .

I met Stephen Knox, who has been coming to the Blackie since he was a boy and is now fifty-three.

I was born in the block of flats next to the building, so me mum used to come and watch the performances. Lots of parents used to come in. We had a film made of us, *Time for Thought*.[46]

I asked what he had thought of the place when he first came through the door.

I thought, 'This is a bit strange.' I thought it was bit hippy. Then we got to know Bill and Wendy and saw it was *very* hippy. My memory is of seeing Bill standing on the step outside and walking up to him – me mates standing outside the gate, being scared – and me walking up to Bill and saying, 'What are you doing here, mister?' He said, 'Come in and have a look.' I go in, me mates thinking, we'll never see him again.

People came like they went to a youth club, but here you were doing different things from other youth clubs. As a kid, I found I was interested in lighting, and with the discos I began to help set the lights up. Then, when I left school, the Blackie helped raise the money to send me to study with a theatre company in Cardiff. I wouldn't have got that from the local youth club.

So the Blackie began to engage in quite a lot of education, as Wendy explained:

We did it on an individual basis. I put people through social work courses and whole degree courses. We've done maths, English, history, youth work, lighting, fine art. Parents were mainly dockers, ex-dockers, [and there was] a real lack of interest in education. It was seen that education hadn't delivered much to the parents, or been much use to them. Sixty per cent of schools in this city are Roman Catholic, taught by nuns and priests, who developed a fine sense of sin and a very limited sense of geography.

When I started with Stephen Smith, you'd leave him with a pile of books and you'd go away and come back, and he would be asleep on top of them! So I took a bowl of water and chucked it over him. There was no history of studying at all, so instead of reading a book he would go to sleep.

As I pointed out to him, this wasn't the idea that we had in mind.

Earlier I'd noticed that Stephen had contributed to an exhibition called 'Young, Gifted and On Track', which records some of what has been going on at the Blackie over the last forty years:

> Black Power film shows were held at the Blackie. I coordinated the shows with my mate Stephen Knox . . . went to London to meet Oscar Abrahama, who ran the Keskidee Centre . . . We hired films, including *Strange Fruits, The Murder of Fred Hampton, The Soldad Brothers* and *The Panthers*. The Blackie funded me to go on an educational cultural trip to Africa. It was there that I really saw poverty and realised the value of education. We take a lot of things for granted in England. I visited Nigeria, Kenya and Zambia.

I asked Joey Jocl, who was standing next to me, whether 'Black Power had been a big issue in Liverpool?'

> From 1968 on, but not in the way you understand Black Power now. Not black racism. Not black nationalism. Now they are very nationalistic, but in Liverpool ours was a very old community. You've got [black] kids with Chinese brothers and sisters, white, whatever. So, the whole national thing was out the door. It was about black autonomy, the right to make a decision that will affect your life. And with the help of people like Wendy and Bill, believe me, the South End [Toxteth, the Dingle] was much better off. We can boast the very first play scheme that ever went up to Stanley House,

293

which was THE Colonial Centre, on Upper Parliament Street.
It became the Sir Joseph Clearey Centre.

When trouble occurred it was with the skinheads, as
Hazel had already observed, but even then the battle lines
were not racially drawn. Wendy described the most
terrifying occasion:

In 1971, they came *en masse* and we were running a disco.
These kids came in and said, 'The skins are coming.' I said,
'Fine.' Then a second one came in and said, 'The skins are
coming,' and I said, 'Fine.' When a third came in I thought
I'd better go and look, so I staggered out and saw them
coming down Great George Street, a mass of people with
dogs and chains. So we locked the door and then we
phoned the police and said, 'We are being attacked.' The
police said, 'We know.' I said, 'But in half an hour we'll be
letting the kids out. We can't keep them in all night. They
need to go home. They sent panda cars up and down
Great George Street and we marched home on the other
side of the road. They lobbed missiles over the cars from
their side. This went on then for months.

Joey: This is a very cosmopolitan community. To say it was
anti-black doesn't mean that everybody who was on our side
was black.

Wendy: The thing is that even with the skins, you would have
some black kids who chose to be skins. This is one of the few
cities where you can choose your colour really. In a city where
colour is so integrated within families, you can choose which

side of that divide you are going to stand on. That doesn't mean to say it's not racist. It is, but you can be black and choose to be a skin. This is not a choice you will get anywhere else. Who was the guy who lived round the corner who went to Manchester, had the black curly hair and ran with the skins? He looked white unless you looked very closely at him. He went to a meeting in Manchester and he heard all these people yelling, 'Get the nigger!' So, he looked around for the nigger to get and it was him! He came here and said, 'It was me!' I said, 'Yeah, well have you looked in the mirror closely recently?' He was very shaken by it.

Joey: To understand it you've got to go back to when I was at school, at Windsor Street [Liverpool 8]. I found out I was a black person, because as usual kids across the block, St Martin's, St Patrick's, Protestants and Catholics throwing bricks at each other, all that – and one day it was me and we started to fight our way in and out of school. Into secondary schools, teachers had to fight their way through the melee every day, three or four hundred people waiting for you.

Joey's battles and those of other members of the Blackie have not been limited to the street. Later, I discovered from Wendy that serious life-threatening disease is a too common feature of middle age.

That's the other thing that happens: people die. You are born in poverty, you die early. We are surrounded by people whose minds or bodies are [blighted by poverty]. They may be ten, fifteen years younger than I am and they are in worse shape. That's poverty for you.

We are standing alone in the Blackie's massive hall, a wonderful space, beautifully made with the help of members over its forty-year history, immaculate wooden floor, two beautifully reproduced galleries running around it and lighting to give every conceivable effect on all four sides. 'We are just waiting for the chairs, for the audience,' Wendy said.

What the Harpes did was to show how art related to life, and how their blend of play and art could transform life in the bleakest communities. They were moving things on a stage from the Everyman as it was, but the Everyman had meanwhile been transforming itself on its own account.

It is generally agreed that the Everyman's golden era came in 1970, after the original ground-breaking triumvirate of Peter James, Terry Hands and Martin Jenkins had left and Alan Dossor took over. He discovered among many others Willy Russell and Alan Bleasdale, two seminal Liverpool writers who dealt with the social and political realities of working-class people's daily lives in a way that attracted these same people and others to the theatre. It was a move forward from Liverpool's Left Theatre of the thirties and forties, and the subsequent Unity Theatre, not least because of the level of talent it unearthed, and the nationwide reaction it provoked.

The Everyman's first big break came when Willy Russell's *John, Paul, George, Ringo and Bert* made it to London's West End, and if Alan Bleasdale's only contribution to art had been Yosser 'Gizza job!' Hughes in BBC TV's *Boys from the Blackstuff*, the playwright, whose parents were natives of the Dingle and Scotland Road, would be remembered forever. Then there were the Everyman actors in Dossor's day, Jonathan Pryce, Alison Steadman, Antony Sher and Julie Walters among them.

Alan Dossor's wife at the time, Dinah, an English scholar and artist who followed her husband to Liverpool from Nottingham University to lecture at the art college, remembers the first time she and Alan saw a play at the Everyman, shortly after the Metropolitan Cathedral opened in 1967.

> We came to see a show on a Saturday night, a very characteristic Everyman show. It was written by a local writer. It concerned feelings about a new building they had nicknamed the Mersey Funnel, which was what the Catholic Cathedral was known as at the time. It was the Everyman's first attempt at a musical documentary based on interviews with Liverpudlians. This was a Saturday night and there were eight people in the audience, of whom Alan and I were two, and five more were friends of the cast. So there were more people on the stage than in the audience.
>
> The Everyman was not getting the audiences, even though the play was fantastic, it was relevant, the performances were great. What Alan did was to take that tradition of local playwrights writing plays of significance to local communities, and he actually made it work by getting audiences in.
>
> He was very influenced by Joan Littlewood, she was the culture heroine, but he was also very good at publicity, getting the local press and local radio on his side, and exploiting every opportunity he could.
>
> The theatre was saying something important then. Alan

was passionate about working-class politics, although he is not working class himself, he is lower middle class. But it was the politics that was rooted in local communities. So, for example, they did *Cantril Tales* (1974), a version of *Canterbury Tales* in which Geoffrey Chaucer arrives at the worst pub on the post-war Cantril Farm estate in Knowsley[47] and tries to get the customers to tell stories. The art school happened to be involved, because I did the costumes and sets with students from the fashion textiles and fine art departments.

So, Alan takes this energy. He uses the everyday lives of people in the local communities. He gets in good, solid playwrights from Liverpool and other parts of the country – Willy Russell, Chris Bond, Alan Bleasdale – to shape that experience into something that the people it is about really want to come and see. And I think that is radically different from *Look Back in Anger*,[48] where somebody is using working-class, or supposed working-class, experience and shaping it in a way that middle-class people will want to come and see.

I think one of the reasons it was able to happen in Liverpool and not other cities was the huge energy that went into local grass-roots activity, which struck me as soon as I arrived. You could feel it. You could smell it. This wasn't happening in other places. Everywhere you went, everywhere you looked, there were community-based organisations, there were local things happening. It is fascinating, striking. There is nothing recent about it. It was there in the 1970s when I arrived.

So Liverpool was the place where Alan was able to take this energy and shape it, due to this huge talent and the richness, and because the people in Liverpool were ready to talk about themselves.

This was partly because it's a tribal city, and part of that tradition is to do with the number of Irish people. The Irish tradition is that there is always a story to be told, or a story to be picked up. When Alan was dealing with the social and political realities of people's daily lives, the people who came to the theatre were working-class people from those communities, not bussed in, not a piece of PR.

The tradition that carries on from that is the Everyman pantomimes. They started in Alan's time, great big pantomimes . . . which, instead of using only the traditional features of pantomime, brought in a particular kind of actor, people who were also superlative musicians, and good dancers, and drawing on relevant local issues in this unique, and again relevant, pantomime style. It's so exciting! I mean, I've booked my tickets already. I did it months ago. People simply won't miss it. These pantomimes are so successful, and always have been real box-office successes. Although critics may feel that pantomime is not culturally important, this actually builds on all the elements that made theatre a real live exciting transformational place that changed people's perceptions.

Alan's father had been a timber salesman up in Hull and lost his job in an early recession, and came down to Nottingham, so he was someone who had suffered directly from the ill-effects of capitalism. Alan took him to see *Death of a Salesman* by Arthur Miller, which deals with all of those themes, the damaging things that capitalism does to ordinary people in their ordinary lives in the name of profit and progress. But his father didn't connect his own situation with what he saw on stage – his father didn't make that connection! I remember Alan being very struck by that.

What he drew from it was that he had to find a way to make what happened on stage spring from, and be directly relevant to, and transform and change people's lives. He was very keen on Brecht and did some fantastic productions of Brecht plays[49] – Brecht's notion of not allowing the audience to go off in a state of catharsis, but holding people in a state of paradox, of unresolved ideas, so that people had to work for themselves to make sense of it in their own lives.[50] And that line went from Brecht through Joan Littlewood to a lot of regional directors. Alan was one who made this mission his own and did it most successfully.

Meanwhile, there had been a further development, this time at the art college. In the early seventies, Bill Drummond had followed in the footsteps of his hero, John Lennon, and enrolled. Later, he managed Echo and the Bunnymen and famously burnt £1 million as founder of the guerrilla art collective, J Foundation, which takes some beating as a statement of intent.

What people in Liverpool remember better is his role as a kind of magical mystical master of ceremonies in 1974, in collaboration with local entrepreneur Peter O'Halligan. They took over a warehouse on Mathew Street, by the bust of Carl Jung, and opened the Liverpool School of Language, Music, Dream and Pun. The site was hiked as coexistent with Jung's 'Pool of life', and lying in the direction of a ley line, which, as I mentioned at the beginning of the book, is supposed to run along Mathew Street. Phil Key:

Peter is a bit esoteric and discovered the quote from Jung.
So they used that. The school was a meeting ground. They
had a number of arty crafty shops there, and a rehearsal
room and performance area, where Ken Campbell
produced *Illuminatus*. This was in the mid- to late seventies,
certainly before Ken Campbell came to the Everyman as
artistic director. He had his road show, and came to
Liverpool with his then wife, Prunella Gee, and set up shop
in this place in Mathew Street, not a proper school, more
an arty meeting place. He did *Illuminatus* in parts, on
separate days, then on a Sunday you could come and see
the whole lot. You'd turn up about eight in the morning
and stagger away from some wine bar they had there at
about midnight! You see, they had a break every twenty
minutes or half an hour and the whole audience would go
to the wine bar. You'd knock some back, and go back and
carry on watching.

Ken Campbell was artistic director of the Everyman from
1980–81. He produced *Illuminatus* in 1976, adapted from
the cult trilogy of anarchic science fantasy novels by Robert
Shea and Robert Anton Wilson. It later moved to the
National Theatre, and was the first production of the new
Cottesloe Theatre in 1977. Sir Peter Hall, director of the
National at the time, writes of Campbell in his *Diaries*, 'He
is a total anarchist and impossible to pin down. He more or
less said it was a crime to be serious.'

Key remembers only that, 'It was all very weird, about
this secret society. I think it's probably mentioned in one of
those books by Dan Brown. The Beatles' first manager,
Alan Williams, played a singing whale. He could have been

an opera singer. He had a really good voice. He was one of the real Liverpool characters then.'

Dinah Dossor was involved in the production, doing some of the props with the art school.

Illuminatus was amazing! At that time, I lived in a big house in Grove Park. It had been the Bishop of Liverpool's palace and when I bought it, it was so riddled with dry rot that the Rentokil guy came round and wouldn't even give me an estimate. I looked despondent. He came a week later with several cans of dry rot killing fluid and a book on dry rot, so I started to do it, and I did the whole house. Now this house was so big that I could only live in it on a communal basis. I lived there with Alan after we separated. He took a flat in the attic. By then I lived with my next partner, Terry, who was the musical director of the Everyman for some of the shows that Alan did. So it was a real family business. A lot of the people who worked at the theatre came and stayed there, too. Initially, Chris Bond and his wife and their children came and shared it with me and Alan and Terry, and then Roger Phillips, now the star of Radio Merseyside, moved in, and at some point he was running Vanload, which was the theatre's outreach. He was the power behind Vanload. And then various actors came and went . . . It was great, and it was great for me, because it meant that the world came to the house. There was always someone around and there was always something happening in the house. And then one day Ken Campbell came up with *Illuminatus* and George, Ken Campbell's old Latin teacher, who adapted it for the stage, came and stayed in my house. David Rappaport was in it and he came too. He had dwarfism and I remember he

sat in my daughter's high chair up at the table. I also
remember George's son coming to stay at a time when I
wanted some of my chickens killed, and while we were
eating and drinking he just went out into the chicken run
while they were asleep and did it beautifully, stroked them,
and wrung their necks. So there were some bizarre
somewhat surreal things happening in this very well-
organised domestic setting, which had to do with my
contact with the theatre.

Bizarre, surreal, certainly all in the mind . . . but barriers
and boundaries were down and there was unity in this city
like never before across classes, across tribes, across art
forms. There were positive vibes, resolving forces at work.
It was a good time to live in Liverpool, for Liverpool really
was *alive*. Where could such a change be made except in
the mind, the very seedbed of change. Change in the
collective unconscious Jung likened to alchemy. The
power of art – music, theatre, humour – to resolve
imbalances, to revitalise and to transmute at the deepest
level was made clear in the sixties in Liverpool, and it has
never been forgotten by those who were there. It was a
special moment.

The keenest identifying element in the Liverpudlian
psyche – *the* distinguishing mark – is that art is now of
interest across the class spectrum. Currently, this is evident
in the level of interest shown in a Biennial organised by
Lewis Biggs, a former director of Tate North, a project that
involves the Walker Art Gallery, the Tate Gallery, FACT (the
Liverpool-based cinema and art gallery), Open Eye
photographic gallery, Bluecoat, and others in hundreds of

over seventy venues and commissions such
as Antony Gormley's *Another Place* on Crosby
ch, mentioned in Chapter One. It is a major event in
the city to which everyone goes. But similar enthusiasm has
been shown in the arts for half a century, as Phil Key
observed when he arrived from London in 1967 to work on
the *Liverpool Daily Post*:

I always found it intriguing. Yes, they go round the Tate, and
the National Museums of Merseyside have about nine
different galleries, and there are some private and small
galleries. Liverpool is very art conscious. When the Tate
opened in the Albert Dock in 1984, named after Tate of Tate
and Lyle, which had closed down three years before, there
was a big scene here already. For example, they had the John
Moores Exhibition at the Walker Art Gallery every other year,
probably the biggest competition exhibition for
contemporary art, which kept things bubbling away. But
once the Tate opened there were artists everywhere.
Whereas artists connected to the Art College used to return
to London, now they decided to stay. I think that's principally
due to the Tate opening. They are always surprised how
many people they get there.

Again, I used to go to the ballet and the opera at the
Empire. In fact, I was there this week at the ballet, but the
people who go there are not your toffs. People don't dress
up for it in Liverpool. I always remember a printer in the
Liverpool Daily Post office, a bit of a rough diamond – 'Oh
'ello Phil. Yes, I saw you at the opera last night. Bloody good
wasn't it?' I was thinking, 'What the hell were you doing
there?' Because outsiders don't imagine that people like that

would go to the opera, but in Liverpool they do. There is a great interest in high art as well as in low art in Liverpool, which always intrigued me. In fact, I got the job of Arts Editor on the *Post* in the end, because the Editor asked me, 'How do you see your job?' and I replied, 'I don't see it as a panelled off arts page. I see it as part of the general mix, because in Liverpool art is just part of the general life.' And he said, 'That's right.'

I remember writing that 'in the sixties in Liverpool on every street corner there was a musician, and now on every street corner there is a playwright'. They went from music to writing plays and there was an embarrassment of riches.

The grass-roots interest in the arts is endemic across the board and at all levels – as subject, writer, and audience, a tradition continued in the Capital of Culture celebrations in 2008, which Phil Redmond was called in to run, when it was clear that the programme had lost its way. Redmond is another writer who makes authenticity a virtue, drawing on his own experience of growing up in the fifties and sixties in Huyton, to bring television into the real world of urban childhood and teenage experience of school, college and council estate, in series such as *Grange Hill*, *Hollyoaks* and *Brookside*. In the Capital of Culture he made 70 per cent of the events free and went to the local communities first for his material. As Eileen Devaney points out:

He made it work because he was deep rooted in Liverpool, and the reason that we got the Capital of Culture was that the bid was very, very deeply rooted in the community.

Dinah Dossor ties this to the Everyman Theatre's philosophy in the early 1970s of 'using the everyday lives of local people and shaping that experience into something that the people it is about really want to come and see. Some of it has moved into the art galleries, some of it has moved into cinema, places like FACT in Liverpool. Some of it has moved into the community centres, like the Dingle production of *The Ragged Trousered Philanthropists*, where the people are doing it for themselves, rather than paying to watch professional theatre do it for them. This very much fits with the way Liverpool society has evolved.'

There is no doubt that the Everyman played its part, but the spark came earlier than that. The transformation began with the music, which found its way into the city's psyche from the forties and fifties, initiating an alchemical reaction in the minds of the people, across all classes, colours and creeds. *That* was the time people remember.

Brian Patten has alluded to 'a point, just before the Beatles left, when it really did seem as if we were the centre of the universe'.[51] It doesn't matter who you were, poet or dock-side café proprietor, no one forgets the fifties and sixties in Liverpool. It was the happiest time. Said Frank Smith, 'From 1966 back to the fifties was all the same, fantastic. Everybody was happy.' Rogan Taylor and Andrew Ward wrote:[52]

Wherever you went, people wanted to know Scousers, and Liverpudlians had belief in the city. We couldn't go wrong. We succeeded at whatever we put our hand to. Boxing, we had Alan Rudkin. Comedians, singers, football. The biggest thing was the Beatles, but the football team had its part in the success, and the excitement was right across the city . . . They'd sing Beatles songs for two or three hours before kick-off.

The hobby horse was released from the High Cross stocks in the 1960s. The Liver Pool broke its bounds, and the acid test of the authenticity of the great change is what it meant to be a child in Liverpool then, as John Bailey recalls:

Everyone had smiles on their faces. It was a great time to grow up. All you wanted to do was play on the streets, hear your dad shouting for you to get in at half past seven – 'Just wait fir the winner to go in, Dad!' – and you'd get a clip round the earhole, run up on to the landing . . . You'd wait for the last bit of light, when the sun had gone down and it was getting dark, and you'd still be playing, and it was fantastic.[53]

CHAPTER TWELVE

Miss Liverpool

While the artistic transformation was proceeding in Liverpool's Bohemia, the area to the north of town was undergoing a different kind of change – wholesale demolition.

The action, which doubled with a plan to clear out some important architecture in the city, amounted to the ethnic cleansing of the working-class Irish ghetto of Vauxhall and Everton, the old waterfront communities, site of the original nineteenth-century conurbation, and of the tribal culture that had shaped life over the preceding two hundred years.

The Corporation's idea was to clear the workers' houses, the slums and rubble from the Blitz, buy up areas such as

Kirkby, far to the north-east (actually 4,070 acres in all), and move the working classes lock, stock and barrel on to new estates built for the purpose.

The density of human habitation in Scotland Road, which was to become a multi-lane highway bereft of housing, the lack of civilised bathroom and sanitation facilities, the ill-kempt courts and scruffy old wash-houses, the bomb-damaged streets and the now disused air-raid shelters, encouraged the Corporation to take action. No doubt these factors combined with certain conditions attached to the American money that was bulging their pockets[1] to convince them to adopt a strategy that would smash whole working-class areas and launch a comprehensive redevelopment of the city.

Early publicity persuaded many people that they were seeing a new dawn, as a council insider, who preferred to remain anonymous, tells:

The wisdom of the age was that, well, people shouldn't have to put up with slum conditions any more and the ideas were of a better life.

But in fact, when the bulldozers moved in, perfectly good pubs, schools, churches, shops, cinemas, business premises and houses, the fabric of real live communities, were destroyed. It was a wholesale cleansing.

Principally, they cleared the pre-1919 housing which was structurally unsound, or so small that you couldn't really put in modern facilities. You couldn't find room to put a bathroom in, you know? Also, a lot of inter-war tenements were cleared away because they weren't capable of being converted. Kirkby, Speke, brand new estates got built on the outskirts of the city and people moved out there *en masse* in the slum clearance, which once upon a time we thought was a good idea . . .

The nightmare didn't stop there. Poor planning and cost-cutting resulted in a lack of amenities, inadequate services, and later a high incidence of vandalism, gang violence and other social problems on the out-of-town estates, especially in the high-rise blocks that were shooting up. At no point, it seems, did the authorities realise that their responsibility to the city was not simply to provide new housing, but to reconstruct the communities they were destroying. As it turned out, they were demolishing a community culture along with the buildings and leaving a dangerous vacuum in its place. My inside source explained the planners' reasoning.

Tower blocks had worked very well, actually, in France and in other parts of Europe. So, taking some ideas from that, [they thought] we could put them up here . . . And the garden suburbs, some had a lot of servicing built in, so we would give people communal this and communal that. But, of course, the public costs rose, and it was the servicing that was taken out. You take that away and you leave people to look after themselves and it doesn't work any more. It wasn't the design by itself that was necessarily bad, it was that the design only worked if you had the servicing, and when that was taken away, through public subsidy cuts, [the experiment] failed, and then it spiralled into decline.

A lot of tower blocks have been knocked down, but
some have been converted for private occupation now.
Some in bloody good locations are extremely nice. But yes,
with today's construction techniques, maybe you could have
done something with the tenements and small terraced
houses. For example, you could have knocked two houses
into one, and converted a tenement into apartments the way
it has been done with loft apartments and warehouses and
things like that.[2]

Families in tower blocks fared the worst. People no longer
connected with their neighbours as they had in the
terraced streets and tenements. In a high-rise there was
nowhere for the women to enjoy a natter of a fine evening.
People only met in the lift. The whole social, communal,
cooperative basis of living that made working-class life
special (indeed possible) was lost and replaced by locked
doors and heads turned away.

The process of splitting up and uprooting communities
and dropping them into estates where, due to rising costs,
the services had been struck off the plans, presented
enormous challenges to the evacuees. How could they
hope to recreate a community without what the authorities
refer to as 'amenities', which are actually pubs, schools,
corner shops, churches, youth clubs and centres where
people get together and live life?

One of the principal post-war destinations was Kirkby,
mentioned in the Domesday Book as Cherchebi. It was
home to seventy souls in 1086 and didn't find a foothold in
the modern world until the coming of the Liverpool and
Bury Railway in 1848. The Kirkby Urban District was

created fifty years later, the completion of the A580 bringing it further into line in 1935, whereupon the beady eye of industry fell upon it and a Royal Ordnance filling factory (munitions) was established there in 1939.

After the Second World War, Kirkby recommended itself immediately as part of the final solution for Scottie Road and surrounding areas. The idea was that the evacuee migrants would work on the local industrial estate, which indeed did expand gradually and, at its peak, provided 80 per cent of all employment in the area. Says Frank Vaudrey:

> Kirkby is a massive estate. Originally, it was a village basically. Then they started to move people to work in the huge arms factory, where they made Lancaster bombers and stuff like that. It was a big armaments place as well. People moved and worked there, and then they made it into an estate. Called it Kirkby New Town. Remember the old TV series *Z Cars*? That was all based in Kirkby.

In 1951 the population of Kirkby was 3,000. Ten years later it was 52,000. Although other cities were engaged in similar strategies to Liverpool's (notably Glasgow, which moved the whole of the Gorbals out to Easterhouse and other outlying areas), no other town in Britain expanded at the rate of Kirkby.

The first estate in Kirkby was set up in 1952, but the first shops were not completed until 1955 and the first pub did not open until 1959.

In Cantril Farm, a new-build estate farther south, closer to town, the first homes were settled in 1965, but the first pub didn't open until 1968, around the same time that the first bus routes were established. Small supermarkets were erected in the late 1960s and the Withens Shopping Centre opened in 1970.

Norris Green developed earlier between Anfield and Walton. A certain Mr H Robinson, interviewed in 1987 aged eighty-one, remembers that in spite of a lack of amenities, Norris Green had at first seemed to have great potential:[3]

> I'd put my name for a house with the Corporation . . . I was so keen to move. I was keen on gardening. I lived in a terraced house before, but this had a nice large side and back garden, and we were quite happy there. I was there for fifty years . . . There were about six cottages opposite me – very old, they were.

Two daughters and a son were born to the Robinsons here. School was a corrugated iron hut in Townsend Lane – 'It was rather strange and we used to call it the tin school.' There were no shops when the family arrived in 1937.

> Transport was negligible. It was a question of Shank's pony . . . the trams finished by the bridge at Broadway and you had to do a lot of walking . . . The trams went up Townsend Avenue and right up to Breck Road, turned down Everton Road, then came down by the Dale Street or Church Street way, depending on what you wanted . . . It was about tuppence then for the whole journey. Cars were negligible. People couldn't afford a car in those days.

But people were closer to nature in Norris Green then, and there was trust among the inhabitants:

One morning as I took in the milk, there was a cow with its head right at the front door. It had walked up the path from where they used to feed in the fields. It'd come through the gate. The gate must have been left open by the milk boy. It just walked up the path and stood there.

There was no violence at all. I didn't see any trouble . . . I never came across it . . . In those days you could go out and leave your door open and no one would bother or try and break in. Everyone was very friendly.

Even so, a common problem was a feeling of exile. These people were being moved from the city they loved and with which they closely identified. Who could they tell that 'we miss Liverpool'? Children didn't notice the loss as much as parents, who had put roots down in the old city. As a child, Eileen Newman and her family were moved east of the city centre to Dovecot.

Dovecot in the fifties was absolutely wonderful, compared with where I had come from. This was like being out in the country. It was on the boundary of Knowsley, which was then Lancashire. We had a garden front and back, and a farm behind our house, which had only been built in the 1940s. Quite a few of my friends kept chickens. It was quite normal to have a chicken running about. I always felt that people who did that were somehow a bit above us, because they had the nous to think of that. It always felt like they were a bit more competent. It was a huge change. We had a horse leaning over our back fence! It was only a small farm, but there was a big field. I was a right tomboy. I played out in the street all the time. My mum would have to drag me in at bedtime, whenever that was. We just got over the back fence and we played! People from the street, everybody used to come over our back fence. And we had about five parks as well, all very different, and swimming baths just down the road.

But my dad never settled. His heart was still down in Vauxhall Road by the docks and he used to go there every Sunday, to his mum's. He'd go and have a singsong down at the pub at lunchtime. He never really settled in Dovecot. He still went to line up for the docks every day. He used to go on the bus, but then he had to get a bike because he couldn't afford the bus. I remember there were times when he had bad weeks and didn't get any work.

When George Lund was a young boy in the fifties, his family was moved further east, to Huyton:

I suppose at that time it was like winning the pools, because the council house had an upstairs loo, downstairs privy, two gardens – a big one at the back – and at that time it was quite suburban, you see.

During the war, Huyton wood was used for evacuees. There were prisoner of war camps there as well. The Alamein Estate there is named after the North African campaign. When we were children in the fifties, I actually stumbled on these camps, saw these like wooden villages made by the prisoners of war, but I got out quick because I became quite frightened. It was so quiet in what was left of the camp.

We moved to Huyton in the early fifties, but I used to come back [to Toxteth] when I was about fifteen, well maybe even earlier, fourteen. There was a grocery shop called Bob's

on the corner of Mill Street, and Mum used to get her
groceries on tick. She still sent me there from Huyton to get
the groceries, so I used to go on the bus. It took me
probably a good hour. It took so long because of the roads,
you see, they weren't so wide. I think Bob the grocer, he lost
his wife and I think he had a bit of a, er . . . for me mum.
My mum had lived in the area and she probably got to know
Bob and, well, he was married at the time, and anyway she
wouldn't have an affair.

I said that Bob must have been a bit disappointed to see
George every week instead of his mum.

At the beginning, he used to come and deliver to her
personally and then she had to stop that, you see, because
me dad . . . even though there was nothing going on at all.

One of the great sorrows of the clearance was the loss of
friendships. Eileen's father's obvious distress at leaving
Vauxhall, and this unrequited relationship of George's
mother and Bob the grocer, I think poignantly sums up the
people's sadness and loss.

But that wasn't all. By the eighties in Kirkby the poorly
built houses and flats were themselves slums and many
stood empty, ready for demolition. Today, unemployment
is massive, thousands there have never worked, about one-
third live on the dole, conditions that were blamed for the
1993 abduction and murder of Kirkby toddler James
Bulger by two 10-year-old boys, Jon Venables and Robert
Thompson, a case that touched the nation.

Cantril Farm decayed just as fast, both the fabric of the

place and the community. Even its name was changed to Stockbridge Village in an effort to eradicate the image of what it had become from people's minds.

The Croxteth Estate between Kirkby and Stockbridge Village was another new-build. By 1965 it was home to 10,000 people. Recent research by Christine Gibbons[4] concludes:

> The top down approach led by planners and politicians meant that many of them had little or no knowledge of the needs of the populations that would be re-housed. Many people did not want to leave the areas due to the family and neighbourhood networks that had been established over generations. The general lack of amenities coupled with the increase in distance from the city centre was also a problem. In addition to this, the buildings themselves were of questionable quality. The standard of concrete used was poor, walls were too thin and damp conditions became a chronic feature. Lifts were frequently broken and vandalism became common. The upkeep of these dwellings was proving to be virtually impossible for the council, even for the most basic repairs . . .
>
> By the late 1960s Croxteth was suffering from severe housing, environmental and numerous other social problems. This led to the following motion being proposed by Councillor E. Loyden to a meeting of the city council on 7 October 1970.
>
> 'Because of the general decline in the standards of the Croxteth Estate, due in part to the lack of amenities and services and due in part to bad planning and the unfinished

OUR LIVERPOOL

> nature of the housing estate, and bearing in mind the
> consequential effect that this will have on the present and
> potential tenants in the area, the estate be declared for
> "special attention" for the purpose of examining the physical
> problems of the estate and the social and other problems
> that flow from this situation and that the appropriate
> Committees submit a report.'

The authorities' manipulation of the working-class tribe in Liverpool, both before and after the war, for some new estates appeared in the 1930s, was not just ill-advised, it was an unmitigated disaster. By 1983, 81 per cent of Croxteth residents were on state benefits. The story is similar for all the migrant estates. Today Norris Green is synonymous with gang violence, part of the town actually closing down to show respect for the funeral cortege of gang leader Liam Smith ('Smigger'), as if this was the East End of the Kray twins. Meanwhile, feuding between gangs from Norris Green and Croxteth identifies Sky TV's *Ross Kemp on Gangs* series in the mind of the nation.

There were those in the sixties who sensed that the demolition of the old city was in danger of getting out of hand. One of these was the sculptor, Arthur Dooley, who took action into his own hands when the authorities published plans to demolish the Albert Dock. He feared that if they had it all their own way, Liverpool would soon be without many of its most historic and architecturally important Victorian and Georgian buildings. Said Stephen Broadbent, who knew and worked with Dooley:

Arthur was a ferocious defender of the city's architectural
legacy and I recall that he tied himself to the railings of the
Albert Dock when, in the 1960s, the city authorities
published plans for this marvellous collection of Jesse Hartley
buildings[5] to be demolished to make way for a car park.[6]

Dooley was the quintessential Liverpudlian and an artist whose sculpture relays the spirit of Liverpool for all ages. He was born in Liverpool 8, son of a docker, in 1929. As a teenager he worked as a welder at the Cammell Laird shipyard in Birkenhead, then as a tug boy. Then he became a boy soldier in the Irish Guards, and later a cleaner at St Martin's School of Art in London, where he applied his welding skills and discovered an amazing talent for sculpture. He grew into a warm, funny, serious, unpredictable, dodgy, highly politicised, argumentative, loving, provocative, enormously physical, deeply sensitive, spiritual, caring and generous person. There was not a considered thought in Dooley's head, nor did there need to be. He roamed free, and dealt from somewhere deep inside the collective unconscious of the Liverpool working classes.

As a young man in the Army he took a couple of tanks and went AWOL in Palestine. Sentenced to three years in the glasshouse in Egypt, he was released early for good behaviour. Posted to Tripoli, thence to Chelsea Barracks, he met a priest, 'the first professional man [as opposed to working-class man] to treat me as an equal.' Father Michael Casey described Dooley as 'deeply sincere and sound about the things in Christianity that really matter'. Dooley asked Casey to receive him into the Church.

Casey recalled that as one of the battalion pipers, Dooley was detailed one evening to lead out the Bank picket from Chelsea Barracks. The form was that you marched along the embankment and swung left over to the Bank of England. 'When they all turned left, Arthur didn't. The last that was seen of him was playing 'The Boy from Colerne' up King William Street.'

Having bought himself out of the Army, and taken the cleaner's job at St Martin's, he realised that the students, 'mostly debutants and middle-class wasters' as he described them, knew nothing that was worth knowing about life, which meant that they knew nothing about art. Besides offering him the opportunity to sculpt, he said, this was the worthwhile thing that art school did for him. Henceforth, he knew where he was going, where his art was taking him, and that it was time to go home.

Back in Liverpool, he took a job as a part-time policeman, but, as his much younger friend, Jean Roberts, recalls:

> He was too fond of using his fists. He was somewhere where they had a band playing and some people were making fun of the band. As far as he was concerned, he was enjoying the music, so he just thumped them. He didn't think twice about getting hold of them and giving them a pasting.

Dooley returned to Liverpool not only a Christian but a communist.

> It was 'us and them'. They were the rich and it was a big lie. He wouldn't tolerate the capitalist system. He was a

communist. Very much. You just don't get characters like
that any more, do you?

Roger O'Hara, at one time Area Secretary of the Communist
Party in Liverpool, called Dooley 'a free spirit . . . a real
communist . . . He treated people well.'[7] He returned to the
city as art was on the up and the communities were being
pulled down, and above all he cared for the people in what
was happening. Said Broadbent:

> He always banged on about Liverpool being the victim of a
> deliberately managed decline; that it was undergoing a
> process of shipping out the 'grot' and gentrifying the town.
> He would see today's development and regeneration as the
> fulfilment of his prophecy, and it would probably fill him
> with rage.[8]

For Dooley 'the grot' were 'the little people' of Liverpool,
whom he loved. The apprehension he felt about the
Corporation's activities and his 'us and them' attitude was
now beginning to be reflected right across the working
classes in Liverpool, for the dockers had found their
political teeth, much to the distaste of some old stagers,
among them Frank Smith.

> I worked the docks for forty years . . . When the Second War
> was over, you got a new brand of docker. Cowboys we used
> to call them – 'Come on . . . Not working that! Out!' And
> that's what ruined the Liverpool docks: strike, strike, strike. If
> you didn't have your [Union] button, you was not employed.
> When I was working for T. & J. Harrisons, a [Union] delegate

came on [the stand], a man named Hunt, and a putter-on[9] ordered him off the Dock Estate. This putter-on, he thought he was smart. He ordered the delegate off the stand. 'Get out!' He called the police and the police told him to get off the Dock Estate. Well, with him doing that, we all walked and formed a stand on the other side of the road, where the putter-on had no power to do anything. The [river] side of the overhead railway was dockers land. Well, once we got over the road, the police couldn't touch you. He [the putter-on] had to come and take us on.

The Union started to build up then and get strong. The dockers saw the Union as protecting them. The Union and the dockers were very strong, very, very strong indeed. In the older days it helped, but latterly I think it went away to hell.

To begin with, the dockers' union certainly helped. It had picked itself up after the defeat in 1926 [the General Strike] and set about improving workers' conditions. During the war, under the control of the Ministry of War Transport, 'casual' labour in the docks was suspended. Naturally enough at the end of the war dockers pressed for a permanent end to it. In 1947 the National Dock Labour Scheme started a register and the NDLS became responsible for the proper registration, allocation, payment, training and medical care of dock workers.

But now, if you weren't in the union, you didn't get work. You had to show your union 'button', and if you didn't have it, you were told to get out. If you didn't get out, 'the bother men'd get you out'. As union power grew there was division between unions, between men within unions, between unions and bosses. Everything was about divisiveness, and in 1964 Lord Devlin's Commission of Enquiry into ports concluded that to organise a strike in Liverpool, all you had to do was walk down the quays and shout, 'Everyone out!'

Both in 1945 and in 1949, the Labour Government had to use troops to break strikes, and in 1951 Transport & General Workers Union (TGWU) officials were to be found in court giving evidence *against* Liverpool dockers. Strikes followed in 1955 and in 1960, when 8,194 dockers came out after 600 were refused an 'attendance approved' stamp in their books for turning down the offer of night work. They had already voted to ban all overtime and the argument was about whether night work was overtime.

People talked about 'a wonderful flowering of working-class solidarity', which was fine so long as there was work to sustain the industry. In the fifties and early sixties, the volume of goods handled at the docks exceeded all records. You couldn't wish for a better set-up, as Tom Best remembers:

> There was such a prevalence of work you could get three jobs a day in 1957, because they were rebuilding after the war. You could move from job to job.

Ten years later, the Dock Company came into being, its purpose to give all dockers a permanent employer and to outlaw the 'casual' system of employment. Work was to be shared between registered dockers on a rota system. They were all on the same rate of pay with differentials for special skills, and if there were no ships to load or discharge, they still got paid, albeit on a lower rate.

On the face of it, this was a major victory, but strikes persisted, leading Bill Smathers and others to speculate that there was something sinister going on:

> Strikes really came after de-casualisation, and they had nothing to complain about when they were striking. I'm convinced that they were led out on strike not by their apparent leaders but by the Government [to subdue them].

Or were anarchic elements within the unions working to overthrow the whole capitalist system, as Robert Tressell might have advised?

Conflict, within a relatively prosperous industry, had indeed cranked up the action to a higher level, but then de-casualisation turned out to be a pyrrhic victory. The dock industry was about to change beyond recognition. The future meant containerisation and deep-water berths. Whole lorry-loads of cargo would be craned off at a sweep and with a tiny proportion of the man-power that had previously been required. Today, there is a greater tonnage through Liverpool docks than at any time, but virtually no employment for dockers or warehousemen.

Tom Best's job as warehouseman disappeared overnight:

> Containerisation was a massive change. One container did the job of ten or twenty men. The container came off the ship and [was taken] straight to a distribution depot, which could be five, six, ten miles away or it could be the other end of the country. That was the death knell of Victorian style warehouses. There was no need for hoists or things like that now, or for me. So, from there I went to work for

Ford's in Speke. It's still there, Halewood. It was a huge change for me.

Thousands who had depended on the docks were forced to turn to the manufacturing industry. Tom Best continues:

I was on much more money there than I was as a manager in a warehouse, believe it or not, but I didn't like the work and I worked nights. Noisy, repetitive, boring. I worked there for eighteen months. I was on a production line at first. After eighteen months I left and went to British Leyland, which is not far away from Ford's, and I worked there until the demise of that. I used to work on the TR7, which was hand built and there was a sort of pride in building them. We maybe only built nine a day. In the end, they started building fifty a day, mass producing them. I think that's why they lost the trade.

These factories, to the south, out by the airport, underpinned whole communities.

Well, there was Ford's, there was Leyland, which was Standard Triumph before it was nationalised, and there was Dunlop in Speke. Halewood of course is part of Knowsley, where I live. There is no bank in Speke, people have to travel. There are schools, yeah, a few church clubs, a few churches. There is a big retail park, which is very popular. I know footballers and whatnot go there, so they must have fairly up-to-date shops. I've not been in it. But now of course Speke is a desert. The British Leyland factory wasn't closed down by Thatcher, by the way. It was the Callaghan/Healey government closed that down, but then shortly after, Thatcher took over and everywhere was closed. Factories everywhere were closed. She supported, as you know, the financial industry rather than the manufacturing industry.

This was Tom Best's dry wit. Margaret Thatcher is loathed in Liverpool for what she did to the manufacturing industry in this city. Tom must have made a fine union negotiator. He joined the TGWU in 1971 when Jack Jones was its leader, and they became personal friends. Jones was responsible for the de-casualisation of the docks. Tom is now seventy and still chairman of his local branch of the TGWU.

'So,' I say to him, 'you felt the hand of Thatcher pretty personally in Liverpool, did you?'

Absolutely, yeah, in Merseyside.

Tell me a bit about that.

It was 1979 she come in. By then, the factory had closed and I had moved into being Welfare Rights Officer in the trade union. There was massive unemployment, and in 1981, I think it was, we had a march for jobs. Michael Foot and Elsie Tanner – Pat Phoenix from *Coronation Street* – they started that march, and it went to London. A massive march it was. I didn't go all the way, I did the Liverpool part. There was a core group that walked all the way. Two hundred odd miles, but they would stay overnight in church halls. They were echoing the Jarrow March.

In October 1936, MP for Jarrow Ellen Wilkinson had organised a protest march of 200 unemployed workers from Jarrow to London, a distance of 300 miles, and presented a petition for jobs to Parliament. Now, on 30 May 1981, more than 100,000 people from across Britain marched to Trafalgar Square in London. In June 1983, another People's March for Jobs reached the capital from Glasgow (a six-week adventure). But Margaret Thatcher's power only increased. She won the General Election on 9 June with a massive majority of 144 seats, and the most respected MP for the left, Tony Benn, lost his seat. Three days later, Michael Foot resigned as leader of the Labour Party.

The final chapter in the Liverpool–Margaret Thatcher story was, of course, Derek Hatton and the Militant Tendency in the 1980s, for which there is little reverence today among the old stagers – 'Derek Hatton was middle class wasn't he? He went to the same school as John Lennon and Edwina Curry: the Liverpool Institute!' Nevertheless, a rather quirky interest in Hatton comes from some women, one suggesting that, 'the story of Militant is a parable in its own right, it could have been written by Brecht, and has yet to be written.'

After all the harassment, there was certainly excitement when Militant took on Thatcher, and Tom Best tells me the feeling lingers that for all their smart dressing and gift of the gab, 'they did build wonderful houses, which are still there in the north end of Liverpool.'

They did that, but the thing about Militant was they got too full of their own importance, and they actually were caught

by selling assets to Japan. They went into hock to the
Japanese and had a visit from a minister, Patrick Jenkins,
Thatcher's minister. He did a deal with them [to get them out
of hock] and they were supposed to say nothing about it.
But Hatton came out and spilled to the press, and Thatcher
wasn't going to have that, was she?

Between 1981 and 1991, 50,000 jobs, 20 per cent of
Liverpool's total, disappeared. The young responded to
the destruction all around them with a new wave of music
all of their own. It was centred on Eric's, which opened, on
Mathew Street of course, in October 1976. Talk of Eric's
and the mind moves along a list of influential artists, Echo
and the Bunnymen, The Teardrop Explodes, OMD, Pete
Wylie's Wah! Heat, Deaf School, Big in Japan, the
Lightning Seeds, Pete Burns' Dead Or Alive, the KLF and
Frankie Goes To Hollywood. Eric's may have survived only
four years but was unique and seemed to combine everything that had gone before with what was new, offering
jazz, reggae, folk music, performance art and poetry, while
punk was indelible to its identity.

Then in 1986 Phil Hayes, with the enthusiastic backing
of Yoko Ono, Elvis Costello, Paul McCartney, Oasis, Joe
Strummer of The Clash, and Pete Townsend of The Who,
established The Picket on Hardman Street, nurturing
emerging talent such as The La's, Cast, Happy Mondays,
Travis and Space.

It is not the purpose of this book to trace the subsequent
extraordinary development of the Liverpool music scene
through James Barton's acid house revolution, which
emerged with Daisy at the State in Dale Street in the late

eighties, erupted in the second so-called 'Summer of Love' in 1989 (with more than a little help from Ecstasy), and found its international expression in Cream at an old warehouse in Wolstenholme Square, overtaking London's Ministry of Sound at some point in the 1990s. But now nothing happened in this city without the arts, especially music, being in some way responsive to it and often commanding an international stage.

Another sudden, spontaneous and significant creation at this stage was the film *Letter to Brezhnev*, set in Liverpool, made by Liverpool people on a budget with local talent, most of it amateur, and backed by such as Willy Russell to be released with unprecedented success across the world in 1984. It is, of course, a love story across national and political boundaries, which touches not only the heart of romance but something quintessential at the heart of Liverpool itself.

In the eighties the political situation was so dire that Environment Secretary Michael Heseltine felt bound to make amends for what had befallen the city, to this day seeing his action as one of his proudest moments in office. He took three weeks off and galvanised Liverpool into redeveloping Albert Dock, now an artistic and historical focal point, which preserves and utilises all its magnificent architecture. Simultaneously he inaugurated a Garden Festival on a derelict industrial site south of Herculaneum Dock. This festival, the first of its kind in Britain, exhibited more than sixty gardens, including traditional gardens from Japan, China, India and other countries, a Festival Hall, public pavilions, a pub (The Britannia) and a Pathway of Honour for Liverpool celebrities. The Queen opened it and over the following six months more than three million people visited it. Everyone I spoke to, irrespective of political persuasion, remembered it with joy. Mavis O'Flaherty was one:

> Heseltine was very good, I mean we were the first city to have a Garden Festival. Oh, it was a wonderful time. Me son would be about 7, he's 32 now. He would come home from school and I would take a couple of his friends and other children with me. We would get the bus at the bottom here and walk through. We would go to it on a day like today and spend the evening there until about 9.30, 10 o'clock. It was wonderful. It was one of the greatest things ever.
>
> I think Mr Heseltine wanted people to be happy. I think he realised that Liverpool had had so many knocks over the years. He just wanted people to enjoy themselves for a few months in the summer. It was on reclaimed land, which he filled, and it brought a lot of people, people of all nationalities, and it brought a lot of work, you know, and a lot of wealth into the city.

The political struggle was far from over, however. In 1989 the National Dock Labour Scheme was abolished. The dockers went on strike to defend it, but the TGWU hesitated and the dockers lost. The evils of casual labour began to reappear – under the counter deals, no sick pay, no holiday pay, no pensions, and then came the final blow. In 1993 a new contract was imposed, abolishing overtime and instituting regular shifts of up to twelve hours a day to be served at the whim of the

Dock Board within an overall 114-hour band of shifts every three weeks.

Rising stress levels brought matters to a head on 25 September 1995 with the sacking of five men employed by Torside Ltd, one of the independent stevedoring companies operating in the docks. A ship had had to sail that night and the contract couldn't meet this requirement. The men, who, so it seems, were happy to work the necessary overtime, were nonetheless sacked, and other Torside men refused to go in to work until their colleagues were reinstated. Then, over three hundred men employed by Mersey Docks and Harbour Company were sacked for refusing to cross the Torside men's picket line.

For the next two and a half years the strike gained support not only from workers and unions in Liverpool, but across the country, and worldwide. It was the greatest show of solidarity ever achieved, a victory in itself, but it also showed clearly that there were two levels of purpose. There were those who wanted to reinstate the sacked men and get back to work as soon as possible, and those who wanted to make the most of worldwide support and work towards a more ambitious end.

For later, in his evidence to the House of Commons, Bernard Bradley, the man who originally sacked the five Torside men, wrote that he had, 'conceded to Jack Dempsey [the Liverpool Docks Officer of the TGWU responsible for handling the dispute] that, to stop the strike, the five men dismissed could be reinstated, and Jack Dempsey said that he would go out to the men and see what he could do.' If so, no one on either side pursued the alleged offer and Dempsey was cleared by the Union of wrongdoing.

In Ken Loach's brilliant documentary film about the dispute, *The Flickering Flame* (1997), this is the killer punch to those dockers who, for the sake of five of their colleagues, had suffered real hardship, struggled to put food on the table and pay the mortgage for almost three years. Like the men in *The Ragged Trousered Philanthropists*, who couldn't see Frank Owen's point that only the overthrow of the entire capitalist system would suffice, one docker shook his head in dismay. 'It's so hard for our people to comprehend that this dispute should never have happened and wouldn't have happened if Jack Dempsey had imparted the knowledge that he had.'

The era saw the population of Liverpool fall from a high of 700,000 in the 1960s to somewhere around the 400,000 mark. The disintegration of the exiled post-war working class communities, which I have described and which occurred at the same time, has got some people thinking constructively about the future in a spirit of integration rather than confrontation. Liverpool is of course a jigsaw puzzle of borders and boundary lines waiting to be crossed. For a hundred and fifty years or more the port city was a mosaic of tribes, all of them with their own lodging houses, and often with their own places of worship. The Greeks, the Swedes, the Norwegians, the Germans, the Catholics, the Protestants, the Jews, the Muslims have or had their own synagogues, mosques and churches.

Some tribes still have their own geographical territory today, the Chinese for example, their original settlement around Pitt Street and now Nelson Street. The Liverpool Chinese are one of the oldest established Chinese communities in Europe, and at one time one of the biggest, thanks to the Blue Funnel Shipping Line, which ran steamers directly from Liverpool to China from 1866. To an extent the Jews also still have their own areas, and are a tight-knit culture. The Jewish community in Liverpool claims to be the fifth largest and one of the oldest in the United Kingdom; its history dates back to 1750. The original settlement was in the Brownlow Hill area, which became, 'a self-imposed ghetto comparable to Whitechapel in London, the Gorbals in Glasgow, Chapeltown in Leeds and Cheetham Hill in Manchester. By 1850, Liverpool had some 2,500 Jews, and it was then the largest Jewish community in England outside London.' As the Jewish tribe prospered, it moved out of Brownlow Hill and spread into suburban Liverpool to the south – Sefton Park, Childwall, Allerton and Gateacre.

Such tribes as these are bound together by language, in the Jews' case Hebrew, the language in which their religion is expressed. It is still taught at school. Similarly, the Welsh, who came in their thousands as the eighteenth century turned into the nineteenth, spoke their native language until surprisingly recently. Whole areas of Everton, Anfield, the Dingle, Kensington and Wavertree were Welsh in speech and in culture. The streets were often given Welsh names, and Welsh was spoken more than any language other than English then. The language bound the Welsh communities together and distinguished them from the dominant Irish population.

In Toxteth, I met Meg Whitehead:

I spoke Welsh until I was five. It's funny isn't it? The street that I was born in, which is only five minutes away by car from here, down at the bottom of Park Road, the whole street was Welsh, because the chappie who built the houses was Welsh and he only let the houses out to Welsh people. It was really strange. In the mornings everyone in the street was talking in Welsh, and I didn't know there was another language until I went to school really, because I went to a Welsh chapel and everything was in Welsh there, too.

Language identifies a tribe and helps maintain its unity, but paradoxically it is also isolating. Somalis have lived in close-knit communities in London, Cardiff and Liverpool for more than a century and have found this to be the case. The Somali population in Liverpool numbers around 6,500, according to Ismail Hersi:

In some areas dominated by white people, the relations with Somali can be difficult. They give the Somali a bit of hassle. If you get a house in the Dingle or Anfield or Kensington, yeah, you know, no-go areas.

Language is at the root of the problem. Lack of English inhibits the education process, which in turn hinders integration.

When the children arrive, the white schools say, 'How old are you?' It is not, 'How is your English?' A Somali child of fourteen who has just arrived should not be going into a class of English children of fourteen. Then they see the future is bleak.

There was a school to teach Somali children English in Liverpool, but it was vandalised and burnt down. On another front the Somali community is making progress, however. 'The men always say that women change when they come to England,' has been the complaint of some Somali men in Liverpool, but when women find their feet, as was proven in the settlement of the Irish community in Liverpool, anything is possible. This is certainly also true of Jewish and Italian settlements. Now, when the Somali women's group in Liverpool were threatened with eviction from their headquarters on Lodge Lane, amazingly they managed to raise £100,000 to buy the premises. The women did this on their own. They are finding their feet.

Says Nunzia Bertali, who has been instrumental in the integration of many Italians in Liverpool:

I am a great believer that if the woman is integrated, the children will integrate, and then the relationship between the children and the host society will be easier and better. How does the woman become integrated? Through the learning of the language first of all. So, once they speak the language they will be able to mix with members of the society at large. One of the problems that Italian women had was that 70 per cent of them were illiterate. If you are illiterate, you cannot integrate. Research shows that the English educational system didn't penalise the second generation. The mothers were illiterate, but the daughters had the minimum at GCSE and the majority of them had further education and even higher education.

Children have a natural ability of absorbing English. They play with other children. At home they may not speak

English, but they watch the English television and their environment is English. Only if the father or mother forces the child to talk in the native language, because, say, they believe that the learning of the English language goes against their culture or dilutes their culture, is there a problem. This is the aspect that needs to be discussed, because I know that there is a lady doing a PhD on the maintenance of the native culture, the mother language, against the English language. She is saying there is violence in imposing English on children – that's crazy.

The science of integration is an open book in Liverpool, but as we have seen, the tribal culture operates not only at the level of nation but also at the level of social class, religion, and territory. Now, there is a growing sense of its paradoxical nature at any level, a sense that conflict and confrontation occur in the tribal model of society as often as cohesion.

There is still fierce working-class solidarity, and moments when outsiders feel as though they are in a time warp. For example, I spoke to a woman in Bootle, who said, 'There's a high level of unemployment, generations of it. I believe you've got the scabs to blame for this.' But also, the sense of belonging that people cherished in the tribal culture of working-class Liverpool before the uprooting of the fifties and sixties, while warmly remembered and feeding Liverpool's identity still, is now yielding to a new awareness that it can *exclude* as well as *include*.

Liverpool has a fair record of not letting its tribal culture exclude. Its sectarian history, for example, when the Orange tribe confronts the Catholic tribe, is nothing like as bloody as in Glasgow, where, while I was interviewing people for that book, there was a sectarian murder. There, it is unthinkable that a father should support Celtic (the Catholic tribe) and his son support Rangers (the Orange tribe), whereas it happens in Liverpool that parents and their children may support either Everton or Liverpool. The blue-and-white and the red-and white are seen walking on the same side of the street, even mingling and travelling together on a supporters coach. I haven't seen this, but former Everton player Terry Darracott remembers it happening for an FA Cup final at Maine Road against Liverpool.

The Church in Liverpool did much to prevent sectarian and other forms of strife. Famously, David Sheppard, who played cricket for England and became Anglican Bishop of Liverpool in 1975, forged an ecumenical alliance with Derek Worlock, who became Roman Catholic Archbishop of the city a year later. When Worlock arrived to take up his post, the first thing Sheppard did was to turn up on his doorstep with a bottle of wine. Joan Gibbons tells the story:

> Archbishop Worlock moved into his house, and straight away there was a knock on the door, and he opened the door and there was this man in clerical, you know with the collar, and he was holding up a bottle of wine! And he said, 'Let's have a drink together,' and the Archbishop said, 'Oh, are you David Sheppard?' And he went in! Well, that was unknown, even in the late seventies. The two of them, during the Toxteth riots [1981] when everything was burning around them – my gosh they had guts! – they walked arm in

> arm up one of the main streets. In the end they had to
> escape because of flying debris, flaming buildings!

Apparently, the two bishops were responding to a call from black leaders for megaphones, so that they could appeal to their community to go home. The bishops were carrying them under their apparel, before they found a boy to carry them to the leaders. There is a memorial to the two men by sculptor Stephen Broadbent, half way down Hope Street.

On the race front, there have been two colossal confrontations in Liverpool, never to be forgiven or forgotten. In one incident in the race riots of 1919, a twenty-four-year-old black man named Charles Wootton was at home in Mrs Gibson's lodging house at 18 Upper Pitt Street when a large gang of whites began roaming the area, beating up any blacks they could find and wrecking houses where they knew blacks lived. The windows of No. 18 were smashed. Mrs Gibson's children were screaming and the doors were barricaded, but the mob broke in. Wootton met them with an axe, wounding eight, two seriously. The mob retreated. The police arrived and, in spite of pleas from Mrs Gibson, arrested Wootton. As they walked him out of the house, the mob pressed forward and dragged him away from police custody. Wootton managed to wrench himself free and ran towards the docks with the mob in hot pursuit. It is not known whether he then jumped into the river or was thrown, but it is clear that he could have been rescued, but was not. Wootton drowned.

Earlier, in 1915, Germans were the quarry in similar race riots, following the torpedoing of ocean liner RMS

Lusitania by a German U-boat. The ship sank in eighteen minutes, 15km off the Old Head of Kinsale, Ireland, killing 1,198 of the 1,959 people aboard. In the next few days, an anti-German reign of terror raged in Liverpool, with people roaming the streets, savagely beating anyone who could possibly have a German connection. Many victims, it was discovered later, did not.

The Toxteth riots of 1981 were not in fact a black–white race conflict, but a discriminatory one between the police and the people of Toxteth.

In '81 I was working for Liverpool Housing Trust, not very far away from where the riots were taking place. The tensions, it has to be said, arose from policing methods in this area. You had fairly heavy handed policing methods and an 'us and them' attitude between the community and the police.[10]

Eric Lynch: This idea that Liverpool 8 was a black community is a load of nonsense. There have always been more white people than black people living in Liverpool 8. More black people have lived outside Liverpool 8 than in it.[11]

Josie Burger: I am white and was actually living on Granby Street. They were very naughty, the police in them days, they were terrible people for bullying. Discrimination, bullies, searching. Like, 'Where did you get that?!' and jumping out of the car. There was a lot of tension.

We were mixed, you see, then, black and white, but the young blacks were all born here weren't they? They were all eighteen, nineteen, twenty. We were double their age. We were the age of their fathers, weren't we? We had gone to school together, white and black, so they are going to stand [up] for them, aren't they? They started it, but outsiders came in, thousands!

Lodge Lane was on fire – it was burning, blazing. Lodge Lane was hit the worst and you could see the blazing from here. It was very, very frightening. And after the riots, them people who didn't belong here looted terrible, you know? They had fridges from the electric shops in Lodge Lane. That was a big shopping area up there. Everything was taken. Do you know, they boxed and boxed one another! 'I got that!' 'No, you didn't!' And then they started stealing cars. The joy riding started, and that got really out of hand. There must have been seven killed here in about four years. Three children collecting for Guy Fawkes, sitting over there on the steps of the school, on the far side of the street, they were hit by a stolen car, but them that did it didn't come from round here. The little girl died, Adele Thompson, and one little boy. A third child was badly injured. They had already killed an elderly lady weeks before, and a Somali man was killed on Mulberry Street. It was horrendous. We re-named the streets after the children who died, Adele Thompson Drive, Daniel Davies Drive. That's the little boy.[12]

So this was not a tribal conflict, it was not about racism, but about unrest over police methods, sparked by a particular arrest. However, black racism will not be denied in Liverpool. There's too much recorded history of it.

I thought it was disgusting the way coloured people were treated: they were ignored and people wouldn't drink out of the same cups as them in cafés or Vimto shops. You didn't see them in shops because of bias and they couldn't go into clubs and ballrooms. My first girlfriend wouldn't share a cup with Jews or blacks but they were smashing as far as we were concerned.[13]

But there is plenty of evidence of integration, too. Josie Burger, who was in Liverpool 8 during the time of the black-music scene and all the famous black clubs, remembers:

The ones that we mixed with then, they had lovely parties and carnivals. Steel bands – fabulous! Motown, jazz – lovely. Dinah Washington, Brook Benton. Lovely, lovely era, that time.

But Eric Lynch had a point, too, when he steered me into the following exchange:

Lynch: And the short time you have been in Liverpool, do you think that Liverpool is an integrated community?

Dudgeon: Yes I do.

Lynch: But what you mean by that is that when you walk around the streets, you see people of different nationalities, different skin colour . . .

Dudgeon: Together.

Lynch: Yes, but if you go to a bank and you go to the desk, where are the black people behind the desk?

I put this to Phil Key, who comes from outside the city-tribal boundary, but has been here for forty years.

> I'd like to say that there was good integration, but even on our paper [*Liverpool Daily Post*] I think we had only a couple of black faces. Nice blokes, but they must have really felt out of it. Just didn't mix. I'm not being critical about it. It's what it is. Again, the Chinese have their own bit. It's all very separate. I'd like to say it's a big melting pot, but . . . It's not really racist, despite the odd thing that happens.

Children of Irish descent born in the late sixties and seventies who were not part of the big Irish community thing in Liverpool are generally not so imbued with the tribal culture of their ancestors as their parents or grandparents were, and sometimes have a sharp sense of its paradoxical nature and question its value in the modern world. One woman, who wanted to remain anonymous – let us call her 'Miss Liverpool', because she embodies many of the tensions of the modern city – felt the claustrophobia of the heavy duty, Catholic Irish tribal culture into which she was born and actually left home partly on account of that. One imagines that her experience is not unique.

> You were asking me at the beginning, did I ever know that I was reaching out beyond that, and it's interesting because I knew in childhood that's what I wanted to do. I knew when I was really little, and one of the things I always remembered from childhood was standing at the window and looking out, and wanting to get out. Like, there's two sides to Liverpool. There's really insular, closed, narrow-minded, small

Liverpool, and then there's the fact that it faces the outer world and there's people who have always come and gone. I didn't know that then, but I knew when I was little I just wanted to grow up so I could get away.

Anne Thompson was born in the same year as Miss Liverpool, 1969, and as it happens both had connections with Bootle, an area that has been cast out of Liverpool and made part of Sefton.

Today, Bootle is like no man's land. No one wants ownership of Bootle. It's like there's this big imaginary line, even if you want to get the police. Because three streets away is the Liverpool border and the police won't cross over. At the end of the day the badge is Merseyside, but it's territorial and that goes right across everything.

I was born and brought up in Bootle. My dad was in the Merchant Navy, and came out of it and worked in the cold store down on the Dock Road after I was born. He was born here in 1946. And my dad's mum was born in Derby Road. So you're going back four or five generations and that's quite usual. At one time there were eight from one family in different houses in our street. My husband works down on the docks now.

This is tribal culture stronger even than in Chinatown and regulated territorially just as clearly. Anne feels that she is the custodian of something fundamental culturally. Even as she watches the fragmentation of the old community around her, she has had the courage to set up, completely off her own bat, a community centre which was bubbling with life when we met. 'This here is fabulous, completely voluntary,' she said proudly as she showed me around.

> We won a competition on the radio, we wanted to get the kitchen done up, so like when you come in here you feel there is some community spirit. We started one day a week, then two . . . It gets people out of the houses. It's building up and we are about to employ our first manager of the Centre.

Yet outside in the street, the community itself is under siege.

> It is awful. The police are saying now that the statistics for crime are getting better, but it is for fear of crime that decent people do not venture out at a certain time. A lot of the crime is a lack of parenting, because if you look at the parents, they are either alcoholics or drug users. I've got a fourteen-year-old son comes home from school and doesn't go out again until he goes to school the next day. I know that's not healthy. I know that he's frightened.

So here, in the experience of these two women of the same age and from a similar working-class background, is clearly spelt out that community spirit, the tribal culture, can both be the balm of life and its bane. Interestingly, Miss Liverpool, who left home at nineteen to escape the tribal culture and stayed away for eighteen years, recently returned and has thrown herself into it with a vital, more mature vision. This is an important issue, to which I return at the end of the book. There is also the other issue, yet again, of the failure of society to come to the rescue of places like Bootle, so that even Anne, who could not be more committed to the community, can confide in me:

> I would love to move – I never ever thought I would be one to move – but I would want my family to come with me. Because the area has gone that bad, crime, drugs . . .

'Immigration?' I ask.

> There's quite a few, but you know what? I'd rather them in the street than drugs: African, black people, they are nice. You feel they are more approachable than a lot of the white people out walking the streets. We have a couple who come in here and they are nice people. The white society, the drugs, the crime round here, is awful.

Education played a transformational role in the lives of many brought up in the fifties and sixties that I interviewed, experience showing that while crossing boundaries (in this case the class boundary) can be painful, they are there to be crossed:

> *Eileen Devaney:* I passed my eleven-plus and got into Notre Dame High School. This is where I came in touch with people who had money – only 10 per cent of the intake were eleven-plus, the rest of them were fee paying at this school. It was pretty difficult, and the fact that my sister followed me meant it was even more difficult for me mum. But there were opportunities, because if I hadn't passed the eleven-plus for example, I would have gone to St Francis

Xavier Secondary Modern Girls, and I'm not saying anything about that school because you know . . . I don't think I would have had the opportunities that I was given in Notre Dame High School, as much as I hated it. The opportunities were not only educational. I was meeting people from all over the place. I wasn't just with my own community, which sounds completely the opposite of what I was saying about community! I was meeting different people. I do think that for a lot of the sins of the eleven-plus in other ways, this was a great advantage. I just met different people. You know, the comprehensive system I think is great and wonderful, and my son and all the young boys in our family go, but . . .

Eileen Newman passed the eleven-plus and went to grammar school, and also found the class issue painful, but a tribal circle worth putting in a wider perspective.

What I found was there was a language issue. I remember being conscious of how I spoke. The other children were posher. They would often be saying, 'Say that again?' So my confidence went a bit. I didn't start improving until the third year and then suddenly I was doing well again.

I was now having to do quite a lot of homework, and I wasn't doing it [because] my mother was bringing coats home of a night [she worked for a tailor] and there'd be about six try-ons – you know, when you go to the tailor and you try on something in the process of its being made. Well, she would put it all together, so she was bringing six of these home a night. Every night we were doing the tacking, three of us on the settee.

The big difference, and this is what has really motivated

me throughout, was one of my teachers, Miss Egan. She was
concerned that I wasn't doing very well and came round to
the house, and she saw [what was going on] and took a
particular interest in me after that. She and another teacher,
Miss Burchall, her friend, really tried to support and
encourage me.

I was beginning to learn middle-class ways of being
able to mix. And when it came to it, I got six 'O' levels and
was able to go into the sixth form. That was a big thing,
asking to stay on at school. I had already stayed on at
school a year. I was too young to go to teacher training
but Miss Egan said I should try university and did all the
arrangements about filling in forms and sorting it out and I
did go to Manchester University but that wouldn't have
happened without Miss Egan. Then Miss Burchall suggested
I should apply for a Winston Churchill scholarship to
improve my French. She made all the arrangements and I
got the scholarship and lived and worked with a family in
France – unheard of in our family. These two teachers and
the support they gave me have been a lasting inspiration in
all my work.

My friend, Martha, she and I actually took to learning
middle-class ways together. There was nowhere to study at
home, anyway, so we used to go in to the central library –
William Brown Library – straight from school until 9 p.m.
That was middle class, and going to the art gallery and
having a coffee at fifteen or sixteen, just kind of discovering
. . . Martha and I were discovering this together, because her
dad was a docker as well. We are still really close friends. We
have been friends since we were five, and we're still both
dealing with quite a bit of it, and how we balanced one

[lifestyle] against the other and integrated the two so we could still be part of our families' lives.

I remember reading Michael Young's book, *Education of the Working Class*, when I was doing sociology. It helped me to explain some of these feelings I was having, because I did feel some humiliation about some of the things in my past, and I felt awful for feeling that. I also felt some humiliation about not being able to fit in, in this different world.

One of the things that immediately interested me about Shrewsbury House Boys Club was that it had been started by a boys public school. Here was a classic opportunity for confrontation across class boundaries. I wanted to know how the privileged boys from Shrewsbury School related to the seriously impoverished boys from Everton, and vice versa.

The club first opened in a disused pub in 1903, in a highly concentrated slum population at the corner of Wakefield Street and Mansfield Street, below Everton Brow. Its leader, or missioner as he was called, was an old boy of Shrewsbury School, the Reverend Digby Kittermaster, who would later become a famous housemaster of the equally prestigious public school, Harrow. The *Liverpool Review* reported that on the opening of the Shewsy, as it is known, 'numerous groups of suspicious and unkempt boys poured in from the street, so that within four months of the foundation, there were already eighty members.' Four years later, it moved half a mile north to larger premises in Portland Place, off Roscommon Street. It took up its present-day position a few hundred yards away on Langrove Street at the far end of Roscommon Street, in 1974.

George Marsden, one of a group of six members of the club Archive team from the forties and fifties, which also included Freddie Ashcroft and Harry Whittaker, told me:

> We used to go to Shrewsbury School and box, and they were big lads, I tell you. Well fed, too well fed, they had the money.
>
> *Freddie Ashcroft:* Our lads used to go up there, all our little team. We weren't exceptionally brilliant, we were more football and gymnastics. We were not intimidated. We used to get in the ring and do our bit. For the annual camp at Shrewsbury School, the tents and everything went down on the back of a flat lorry.
>
> *Harry Whittaker:* We turned up probably about 10 a.m. or something, and all the cases were put round the outside of the truck and what happened then was you all sat inside. There were no sides to it. About thirty-odd kids with their suitcases on the back there. We used to go through the Mersey Tunnel in the lorry like that, with all the kids on as well, through the tunnel.
>
> Did they ever lose any children? I wondered.
>
> *Harry:* Well, we never stopped to find out!
>
> *Freddie:* Some used to cycle down. I cycled once. Sixty miles!
>
> *Harry:* There used to be an advance party to put so many tents up, so there wasn't so much work to do when we got

there. It was very well organised. It wasn't just slipshod, you know. And they had straw mattresses. We used to go for a week, and sleep on the cricket field. It was about 28 or 30 shillings. You used to pay through the year. Many of the lads used to go actually owing. I'm still paying!

Jim Kennedy: One or two from Shrewsbury School I remember. Johnny Ingram was one and Robin Downie another, who became Chief Surgeon at Walton Hospital in Liverpool. I met him at the school about '48 and I've been in touch occasionally. He did National Service with another Old Salopian,[14] called Terence Harvey, and both eventually served on the Management Committee of the Shrewsbury House Club. Someone raised the question once, were we ever jealous of the facilities there? I can never remember thinking, 'Oh look what they have got,' because we were lads of fourteen and fifteen and sixteen, and it was an adventure for us.

Harry: It was either once or twice a month the boys from the school came to us here.

So, what did the Shewsy give this generation, now in their seventies?

Harry: A direction in life.

Jim: It didn't tell us what we wanted to do, but what it did do, it gave us like confidence and a lot of standards. We learnt to meet people and respect values, and above all, to get along with people.

Even now, this summer, Jim Kennedy, who is in his seventies, was representing the Shewsy at the Shrewsbury School Speech Day, spreading word about its work and making presentations. For Jim and many thousands of others, the Shrewsbury House Boys Club is part of an extended family which will always be there, an influence for life.

Earlier I had met John Hutchison, former youth worker at the club and now chairman of the board of management. Our conversation turned to the subject of the murder of Joe Lappin, a young member of the Shewsy who was stabbed just outside the club on 20 October 2008. Another youth, James Moore, has since been sentenced to seventeen years in prison for the murder. I asked John whether kids experience a lot of violence round here, and he returned me to the confrontational realities of tribal boundary lines.

> People watch themselves a bit, but it is a complete myth that everyone is walking round with a knife in their pocket. There are sometimes battles over territory. A lot of history needs unpicking. Some of the communities live cheek by jowl, some of them are now adding to an old history of division or separation.

Roscommon Street is just off Netherfield Road, historically a Protestant artery. Nearby Scotland Road is a traditional Catholic heartland. I assumed he was talking about sectarian history.

> Well, a part of that might be involved, but there would also

be a series of divisions that have been picked up on by those people looking to sell drugs on certain patches. Then there would be some sort of informal protection and a real understanding that this is 'a patch' . . .

Twenty or thirty years ago heroin, as a new epidemic, caught a lot of people out. But the kids today are too smart, much too smart. They have learnt that heroin is the pathway to hell and they have said no to it. What they lock into though is the money that can be made through trading it, easy money.

I think it's mainly to do with money, but then the ego gets pretty inflated, so occasionally you get that flare-up, and a response to that flare-up.

But if you pick it back you can probably discover some of the reasons for it rooted, I think, in postcode issues across the city, the city being a series of little villages with big families and certain boundaries.

Ten young people who were charged with Joe Lappin's murder are all living within a mile of here, but Joe Lappin was from Old Swan. That's three miles away. There is a line. What used to be Scotland Road runs out north of the city. Originally, that would be a quite clear dividing line. Now it's absolutely not a question of Protestant or Catholic, not at all, but it is a case of identity in this community, and [territorial identity] will also involve some boundaries for those people who are dealing illegal drugs.

Nothing could state the tribal paradox more clearly or more chillingly, or so I thought until I was introduced to the Irish Traveller community at Tara Park, a settlement in Oil Street, Vauxhall, down by the docks.

I found it a bit daunting at first, with twenty-foot walls and a CCTV camera trained on the units twenty-four hours a day. Was the security to keep Liverpool out or the Traveller community in? Geraldine Judge is the family support worker who looks after the families. She was down there to meet me before I went in.

I have been working with this community now for five and a half years. This site has been here for over thirty years. We have fourteen plots, one is free right now, so thirteen families are living here. Each family has a utility block, which houses their kitchen and bathroom. They sleep in their trailers or caravans. The rents are quite expensive, it's £93 – oh, no, it's more. The women stay at home looking after the family. [It's] very traditional, traditional gender specific roles within the community.

There has always been a tradition of the Irish Travelling community coming either to Liverpool to stay, or to stay temporarily, or pass through. One of my roles is to ensure that the families maintain their licence agreement, which is like a tenancy agreement, and that they access health, education and whatever benefits they are entitled to, and that they are also engaged with any community development that is going on, or any social activity. There are a lot of families with poor literacy levels. If they get mail, they may ask me to read it and then explain what it is and see if there is any work or action that needs to be done arising from that letter.

Unfortunately, there are a lot of people even within government for whom it's, 'Oh God, here's this Gypsy/Traveller issue, here we go again.' It's something they don't know or they don't understand or they don't want to have to deal with.

You know, Gypsies and Travellers have been around for hundreds and thousands of years, and particularly English Gypsies. Irish Travellers have been in this country for ages, and unfortunately some people display an appalling ignorance and prejudice towards this community. When I was growing up in Dublin, there were always Travellers around, whether they were in camps up on the field, or whether they were knocking at your door selling their wares. This was in the seventies and eighties. There would always be a Traveller, always, always, always, begging either on the Halfpenny Bridge or the Common Bridge.

I asked Geraldine what led her to the job.

Something in me makes me want to protect their right to travel, because there's a measure of freedom in what they do, which perhaps all of us have lost. Perhaps it is exactly that freedom the authorities want to curb.

I realised that in these families I had found probably the most traditionally tribal of all those whom I interviewed – strong family focus, traditions that go back centuries, women who stay at home while the men go out to work, just as was the case when the Irish dominated Liverpool's dockland population in the eighteenth, nineteenth and twentieth centuries. There had been some integration among those who had been here some time. 'Some of their family have actually married Scousers, their children are Scousers and they have grown up with Scouse accents.'

My time at Tara Park was spent in three family homes through which Travellers passed in and out constantly, just as they would have done in any terraced street in Liverpool a hundred and fifty years ago. I saw only one man. The place was totally dominated by womenfolk. The first, Lizzie O'Driscoll, drew me into the scene.

> Well, I was a child when we moved into a house with my parents back in Ireland, right? But what I used to remember was the bell-top wagons, and we used to have camps, and an open fire, over which we would cook and boil water to wash with. My father was a carpenter, very highly educated, could speak three languages. He used to make the spoon and he'd make the knife . . .
>
> Poverty was there right, but we didn't scavenge, like they have Travellers in that film about us. We would meet up at fairs, a lot at horse fairs.

Mary and Hannah O'Driscoll chipped in, 'We were at a horse fair the other day at Appleby.' I know about that one, and mentioned it's in Cumbria. There's been a horse fair there for hundreds of years.

> *Lizzie:* They still gather there every year and sell all kinds of things. They'll sell horses and then buy more and bring them on and sell again. That's what they do in Ireland. They race them, two-wheeled carts called sulkies. It's brilliant. Now, in our family at least, life was very strict. We weren't allowed to go out at sixteen, seventeen. I was married at seventeen. People today, some Travellers, get married at fifteen. Mine wasn't an arranged marriage, or a made marriage. I chose

the guy myself. From Donegal. I was a widow at twenty-four.
I was one of fourteen children! I wouldn't have them I
stopped at five! I was the sixth oldest, so I stayed with my
mam until my father died. He was forty-six. I had to be there
to take the kids to school and bring them back from school.
The house was three-bedroom. There was four boys left and
five girls there then. We were happy. We would always have
enough to eat. Potatoes, vegetables. Were we ever hungry?
I would say no.

I moved on to meet Bridget Doran with her young son,
Michael. She is a dark, naturally beautiful woman, but
deeply sad. At that stage, I didn't know why. We speak
about these early weddings:

Always a big wedding, horses and carriages. That's our best
day, the day we get married. That's what the father and the
mother want. It's the only thing that can give a good send-
off, a good wedding.

We could be speaking about life a hundred years ago. I
then meet Bridget's daughter, Bridget Ann, who has just
graduated as a youth worker. Earlier Geraldine had told me
that she was also the winner of a Princess Diana Award for
the way she had dealt with an orchestrated spate of racist
bullying at senior school and risen above it in a really
positive way.

As we continue to talk I see that with the younger
generation there is going to be a difference. They have got
access to a lot more opportunities and when something
good happens, something positive, everyone in the

Traveller community shares in it. When they see one of their own do something for themselves, achieve a goal that they know they are well capable of, but possibly people thought would never happen and unfortunately due to circumstances they are going to find difficult, there is real pride among the Travellers.

I discover that Bridget Ann is a member of the Shewsy, which has been open to girls since 1971. I mention the sad case of Joseph Lappin, and the atmosphere changes. Bridget tells me that her daughter's friend is the sister of John Delaney, a boy in Tara Park who has also been murdered. I meet his broken-hearted mother, and Bridget shows her true feelings for the first time.

> He was murdered. He was kicked to death. Ellesmere Port. They kicked him to death. There were eight of them. Three of them might have done it. They called him a redhead Gypsy bastard. That's the only reason they done it. He was fifteen, two weeks before his sixteenth birthday.
>
> Johnny was my nephew. When Johnny got murdered, they only got four and a half year as young offenders, and they never even done two year. So, where was the justice there? Johnny's father died trying to get justice for Johnny. He drunk hisself to death.
>
> Two got charged, two out of the eight.

I asked what happened.

> Johnny was going over to Ellesmere Port [on the Wirral] to invite some friends over for my sister's birthday party. I remember that day Johnny went out, we were going

shopping. His mam said, 'Johnny, don't move over that side.' Johnny said, 'Would you buy me a trousers and jumper? I'm going to see my Aunt Mag's birthday party.' That was my sister. And we went to town and she rang back and she said, 'Where are you, Johnny?' 'I'm here on the site, playing football.' So that was all right. So we rang back again, but he wouldn't answer his phone. We kept ringing all that day, he wouldn't answer his phone. We come home from town, about half three. There was no sign of Johnny. Kept ringing, kept ringing his phone. His sister said, 'Keep ringing his phone. If he'd got into trouble in town and he'd been arrested, the police will have to answer his phone.' The next thing, same day, we got a phone call, said to come to Chester hospital, Johnny's going down for an emergency operation. We went over to Chester. On the way over, there was a crowd of us in the car, we were about halfway to Chester, wondering what had happened, and my other sister who was with us got a phone call saying that Johnny just died.

My sister opened the car door and threw herself out. Had to jump over the side and pull her in. My sister-in-law was driving. She kept flashing her lights and beating the horn going through traffic. And we got to the hospital. There was a big crowd at the hospital. But he was gone. He had died before we'd got to the hospital.

We had a very big funeral for him. He got buried in Ireland. We took him back. Bagnestown, Tipperary. There were that many people you wouldn't be counting them – boatloads, some on the plane. They come from America, Yorkshire, Wales, Leicester, Birmingham. All the Travellers.

A lot of Travellers was going to go to Ellesmere Port and

cause a big riot. But where's the justice in that? There could have been innocent children in those houses. What would have been the point in doing that? That's not going to bring Johnny back.

Trevor Phillips, Chair of the Commission for Racial Equality, responded to the case by saying: 'The extreme levels of public hostility that exist in relation to Gypsies and Travellers would be met with outrage if it was targeted at any other racial group.' Bridget Doran cannot begin to understand the nature of a community that would support such hostility.

I don't think a Traveller would ever do that. Yes, they'll have a fight, tomorrow, the next day, forgotten about. But no enemies. Never known for to kill some boy. My dad, he's a fist fighter. He used to box all over the country. Dan Rooney. Best man walks away. What they done to Johnny is entirely different. Why go round killing innocent children? My sister went through hell when her son got murdered, two months after her grandchild died. Two months after that her husband died. Three months after that her mother died. And people say you have to carry on. If you have children, you have to carry on.

When the boys set on Johnny, it was like they were playing a game of football. So this girl ran back to her daddy who was washing a car, starts screaming, 'Please Dad, help him! Help him!' The man ran over, shoved them all away, and Johnny lifted his head up and the boy ran back and kicked him. That's when Johnny died.

The man actually did CPR with him. He actually did bring

him back to life, I think. When he tried to, he had nothing to hold onto [to stop the air escaping], no nose. He tries to put his hand over [where the nose should have been] to give him mouth-to-mouth, and when the paramedics come, when they see Johnny on the ground, Johnny looks that young they bring the child shocker. When they realise that he's a bit older, they use the bigger shocker. It was no good, he died.

Two-and-a-half year is all they served. When you're a Traveller, you know about it. When you ask the police to help, it's 'What's your name and where do you live? Oh, what's your country? All right, I'll get back to you.' Probably wouldn't see him for three or four months after.

I staggered out unable to say anything that would be of use. Like the Joseph Lappin killing, the murder of John Delaney had been territorial, tribal. His mam had said, 'Johnny, don't move over that side.' She knew. What was almost more of a shock was that the attack bore a horrific resemblance to the 'High Rip' killing of Richard Morgan in 1874, although this was, like Lappin's, a youth murder.

The sign of a sick society is when its children are its victims. Where do you go from there?

The answer was already clear to me and I wasn't surprised to find that Arthur Dooley had found it twenty years or more earlier. Themes of 'pain', 'suffering', 'feed the starving' and 'peace' are often felt to characterise the best of his work, such as 'Dachau' (his Christ in rags on the cross), or the 'Stations of the Cross' in St Mary's, Leyland. But there is a more important theme.

Love is in the Liverpool soul, as I said at the start. Dooley saw that. He had supped at the altar of the goddess.

Stunned by her 'natural mind', as true and ruthless as nature, he couldn't stop re-creating her. The essence of the moon goddess – the inspirational, maternal, loving and protective feminine principle[15] – is the essence of his famous Madonna[16] unveiled in Liverpool's Scandinavian seamen's church, and of his 'Miss Liverpool', which today is in private hands, and his 'Four Lads, who shook the World', which found a home in Mathew Street and is not a representation of the Beatles, just the initials J, P, G, R and within them his ragged Madonna, possibly a personal allusion to the tragic loss of mother figures in the lives of Lennon and McCartney – both their mothers had died, McCartney's from cancer, Lennon's in a car accident outside his childhood home, when they came together and discovered their song-writing talent.

Today, as ever, it is the caring women of Liverpool who guide the city into the future, people like Eileen Devaney, who until recently spearheaded the UK Coalition Against Poverty (UKCAP), which connected with every organisation for the poor in the city, and Geraldine Judge,[17] who has found 'the something in me that makes me want to protect the Travellers', and Eileen Newman, who took it upon herself to engage with the community of Dovecot, where she grew up, while its local youth gang culture became the pointlessly self-serving focus of the BBC TV documentary series *Panorama*. And in the future, people like Bridget Ann Doran.

Newman, who besides this voluntary interest has a full-time job as a Senior Lecturer at Liverpool John Moores University, applied for funding from the Faculty of Health to research the needs of people living in Dovecot and to facilitate the development of a community-led strategic action plan to improve the quality of life and open up new opportunities. She pooh-poohs those 'people in the agencies who fill their diaries with meetings when they go back to their bosses, but exude almost a fear of the community they represent because they know it's pretty bad in there'. So what is she trying to do?

> We are trying to engage with the community and discuss with them what we think has happened – 'Do you agree with this or do you have a different slant?' I kept the meetings open, so everybody was welcome. Then I started to explore within the community what I call 'social worlds'. The children have a social world (as I know from my experience living there); young people have a social world; pensioners have a social world; adults with children have a world. All these little worlds are all kind of whirling around separately, because, for example, in Dovecot at the moment there is no place for recreation, there are no pubs like there used to be, there are no clubs where pensioners would meet up regularly and talk about the history of their families to each other and how so-and-so is getting on. It is through that sort of dialogue that you make headway . . . You see young Peter in the street and you know he has had a few problems, so you make a point of saying hello to him, how are you. Those messages aren't being transmitted, and therefore an awareness of the place is not being articulated.

Eileen is an academic with a passion for Liverpool. Her vision is like Jung's perfect mandala,[18] a succession of concentric circles, her social worlds, connected to a common source. The shape represents a city in harmony, wholeness and balance, functioning perfectly. After the politicians pulled the plug on working-class society in Liverpool in the 1960s and again in the 1980s, it has to be the way to go.

Liverpool is alive with women prepared to lose themselves in the collective unconscious of this city and work their vision into a reality, and, as in the case of Wendy Harpe, we have seen that the city draws in such women from outside too. Breege McDaid[19] is aware of the advantages which the strong community values of Scotland Road gave its children, but aware too that those days are long gone:

The community has gone, that mutual support, that mutual respect, and I personally think that that affects everything. You might have the biggest, fanciest TV, but you can't go next door and ask your neighbour for a cup of sugar. That is the level of the change. People become quite insular you know . . . I feel, and I think other people who came over in the '80s and '90s also feel, more isolated, and a bit like outsiders compared to those who were here in the '50s and '60s, who went straight into the community and were part of it immediately.

The important Irish Centres and the Community Centres have their role and have their place and a real rightful place, but I think it's wider and broader than that now. It's about making sure that a culture is actually endemic in every community, however diverse it may be. We are a community care organisation picking up on lots of community care issues. But while most of our older Irish people would be aware of, and would use and have used, St Michael's [the

Irish Centre] in the past, many of our younger people would not. They would be more into maybe links within the [multi-cultural] community that they live in. A lot of our work is breaking down barriers within the community.

So, the drift is away from tribalism now, and that's positive as long as through that, people's cultures are valued, respected, and sustained as part of the hub and the beauty of the city.

It's about a world in one city.

Ultimately, Dooley drew on the intuitive strength of women like these, as well as on their beauty, loving some of them in a confusion of inspirational and sexual energies, for he needed them as inspiration for his work. For example, as Jean Roberts remembers: 'Arthur was madly in love with Eileen Marney and her sister Kathleen. They lived on our road. He would never take no for an answer. When they were out he would call on their mother, who was a widow. He'd sit there all night chatting to Mrs Marney.'

Eileen was in her twenties. She got caught up with Dooley, she became his muse, and in spite of her beauty she never married.

The Mrs Marney aspect of the story is no less inspirational, and brings us back to the more nurturing maternal face of the moon goddess. It reminded me of an interview with Stan Cummings[20] about Dooley:

I met him at the Communist Party Bookshop early in the 1960s. He was in the throes of working on his stations of the cross. But the first thing I saw was 'Potato Woman'. I have to say that the body did look like a potato, but it evoked for me the eternal woman, the mother earth figures that I knew all my life down Mill Street and in the Dingle, these middle-aged and elderly women with their shawls around them and the babies in the shawls . . . [The sculpture] wasn't a sort of documented history, but it was in my soul and I understood that. It led me to believe that what Arthur had hit on – and he didn't know this, because I don't think he really knew what he was doing – was this power, this energy that if you are sympatico to that, it comes all the way with you.

Throughout Liverpool's history it is its artistic, inspirational, maternal, loving and ruthlessly protective aspects which have seen the city through, and will balance its other aspects to transform it again and again into a modern city at ease with itself.

The vision is a clear one – 'a world in one city', a city in which people from any tribe (from any country, any religion, any class) can stand up and say, 'We are Liverpudlians,' with the same pride as people from any tribe in its equally multicultural sister city across the ocean can forever proclaim, 'We are New Yorkers.'

Acknowledgements

I would like to acknowledge the contributions of the many people whose memories and opinions appear in this book, and to the many archivists who have helped me track down first person material from centuries ago. At top I would like to thank my wife who transcribed the many hundreds of thousands of words, as I brought them in. The scale of this work is not easy to imagine.

In particular I would like to thank those who helped me into the project, Frank Boyle of Oxfam, and Julie Gibson and Eileen Devaney who were the UK Coalition Against Poverty in the city when I began my research. They set me on the right lines, put feelers out into the community and suggested people I should meet, as did Rosie Jolly, then of

Comtechsa, Breege McDaid and Geraldine Judge of Irish Community Care, John Fillis in Bootle, Frances Jones and Colette Moore in Toxteth, Eddie Bowen in the Dingle, Tony Boase, Lesley Black and Joan Higham of the Welldoers, and Tommy Walsh, Maureen, and the producers of *Craic* at the Irish Centre, and Chris Conway, John Hutchison, Jim Kennedy and the Archive of the Shewsy. These are all people who know the ground and were generous with their advice when it was most needed.

Among the many archives I consulted I'd like to mention in particular the help I had from the Liverpool Library in William Brown Street, especially Simon Whitby and Roger Hull of the Liverpool Record Office there, Andrew Schofield and his staff at the North West Sound Archive in Clitheroe, Alex Wilson of the British Library Sound Archive in London, and Emily Burningham of Liverpool John Moores University, who introduced me to the Everyman Theatre Archive and the Arthur Dooley Archive. My thanks go too to National Museums Liverpool, in particular to Christine Gibbons of the 'eight hundred lives' oral history project and to Helen Threlfall of the Merseyside Maritime Museum Archive in Albert Dock, site of the International Slavery Museum, which with Eric Lynch has had its own special impact on my book.

I am indebted also to Tom Best for generously opening up his personal bank of knowledge of the political history of Liverpool, and to the project to which he turned me: *Radical Route through Liverpool: A Walking Tour of Liverpool, City of Protest*, a two-hour walk around fifteen sites of demonstrations, strikes, protests and commemorations in the city. Information from this has been included in the book by kind permission of Trades Union Congress, Orleans House, Edmund Street, Liverpool L3 9NG. I would also like to thank the Shaw family and the many publishers who have granted permission for me to quote from the books on which I have drawn, all credited in 'Sources and Endnotes'. Every effort has been made to trace the holders of copyright in text quotations and photographs, but any inadvertent mistakes or omissions may be corrected in future editions.

I would also like to thank my friends from an earlier life, Dinah Dosser and Ramsey Campbell, and his friend Phil Key, for the welcome they gave me, and of course to all those whose testimony lies at the heart of *Our Liverpool*: Barr Adams; Albert Ash; Freddie Ashcroft; William Bannister; Ritchie Barton; Mike Berry; Joan Bevan; Veronica Blyth; Mike Berry; Nunzia Bertali; Tom Best; Lesley Black; Bobby Blues; Eddie Bowen; Eddie Braburn; Jack Brotheridge; Josie Burger; John Burns; Lil Cameron; Ramsey Campbell; Jimmy Caples; Garnet Chaplain; Anne Clarence; Eric Coffey; Theresa Connolly; Mollie Connor; Jack Coutts; Edie Crew; George Cross; Stan Cummings; Sugar Deen; Eileen Devaney; Joe Devaney; Margaret Donnelly; Bridget and Bridget Ann Doran; Dinah Dossor; George Doyle; May Duke; Mr Farundos; Mike Finnegan; Edith Flanagan; Marie Francis; George Garrett; Hazel George; Jane George; Christine Gibbons; Joan Gibbons; Stanley Grounds; Bill Harpe; Wendy Harpe; Bill Harrison; Mavis Harrison; Ismail Hersi; Molly Huggins; John Hutchison; Peter James; Vera Jeffers; Joey Joel; Geraldine Judge; Albert Kane; Jim Kennedy; Phillip Key; Stephen Knox; Caroline Langley; Lol and Vera from Wavertree;

George Lund; Alan Lynch; Eric Lynch; Pat Maloney; George Marsden; Breege McDaid; Molly Monaghan; Gordon Murray; Eileen Newman; Lizzie O'Driscoll; Mavis O'Flaherty; Pat O'Mara; Clifford O'Sullivan; Lil Otty; Bill Owen; Glyn Parry; Sam Perry; Roger Phillips; Jonathan Pryce; Harry Scott; Frank Shaw; Wally Shepard; Bill Smathers; Frank Smith; Mary Smith; Stephen Smith; Sonia Strong; Anne Thompson; Bob Tooley; Peggy Tully; Angelo Vaccarello; Frank Vaudrey; Tommy Walsh; Meg Whitehead; Harry Whittaker; Mary Wilcox; Doris Windsor; and Billy Woods.

Finally, permission to reproduce the photographs in the picture section came courtesy of those witnesses who kindly provided photographs of themselves suitable for reproduction, and Mrs Stan Royden of the Scandinavian Seamen's Church in Liverpool, Terry Mealey, Peter Leeson, Colin Wilkinson of Bluecoat Press, Ingrid Spiegl of Scouse Press, Nathan Pendlebury of Liverpool Museums, Christine Gibbons, Tony Russell of the Arthur Dooley Archive, Frances Jones of the Southern Neighbourhood Council in Liverpool, Dinah Dossor, Peter Kaye Photography, the Shrewsbury House Archive, and the Lee Jones Collection, the Welldoers League. My thanks, too, to Tim Peters of Head Design for drawing the map on page 16.

J. P. Dudgeon, July 2010

Sources and Endnotes

[1] 'Johnny Todd' is a traditional Liverpool children's skipping song. Fritz Spiegel, sometime flautist with the Liverpool Philarmonic Orchestra, and his ex-wife, Bridget Fry, used it to arrange the signature tune for the television series *Z Cars* in the style of an Orange march.

Preface
[1] From *Memories, Dreams and Reflections* by C. G. Jung, edited by Aniela Jaffe, translated by Richard and Clara Winston, translation copyright © 1961, 1962, 1963 and renewed 1989, 1990, 1991 by Random House Inc. Used by permission of Pantheon Books, a division of Random House Inc.

Chapter 1: The Pool of Life

1. Founded in 1360.
2. Postcodes for the Wirral Peninsula (CH41-CH66) were transferred in 1999 from the L (Liverpool) postcode area, thereby alienating them for good. The tenth anniversary of the postcode change inspired Dave Kirby and Nicky Alt to write *Brick Up The Mersey Tunnels*, which played to packed houses during the 'European Capital of Culture' celebrations in 2008, and again at the Royal Court Theatre in Liverpool in 2009.
3. In January 2010 Michael Portillo used a copy of what was described as a Bradshaw's guide (in fact, not the timetable book but *Bradshaw's Tourist Handbook*) for *Great British Railway Journeys*, a BBC Two television series in which he travelled across Britain.
4. The other two, Little Eye and Middle Eye, are actually walkable from West Kirby.
5. Commonly known as Shrewsbury Abbey and founded in 1083.
6. Evidence of a monastic connection to settlements at Wavertree and Childwall can also be traced.
7. They are called Welsh streets because they have all got Welsh names and they were built by Welsh builders, not because Welsh people lived there, although in many of them all-Welsh communities existed. Two-up, two-down and no backyard – a lot were rented accommodation for the workers, late nineteenth century, turn of the century onwards.
8. Lathom is a village about 5km (3 miles) north-east of Ormskirk.
9. Carl Jung, ibid. See Preface.
10. J. L. Griffiths, American Consul, in Ramsay Muir's famous *History of Liverpool* (Liverpool University Press, 1907).
11. www.smuggling.co.uk/gazetteer_wales_14.html
12. William Fergusson Irvine, *Liverpool in King Charles Second's Time* (Henry Young, 1899).
13. R. J. Broadbent, *Annals of the Liverpool Stage* (Edward Howell, 1908).

[14] A collection of stories concerning ancient Britain but couched inspirationally in the romantic, magical landscape of Wales, sustained orally since earliest times and transcribed in the fourteenth century.

[15] Robert Graves, *The White Goddess* (Faber and Faber, 1961).

[16] Caroline Langley, born 26.03.1894. Ex-nurse at Parkhill Hospital. Interview undertaken 01.12.82. Courtesy of National Museums Liverpool (Merseyside Maritime Museum).

Chapter 2: The Heart of Darkness

[1] F. E. Hyde, *Liverpool & the Mersey* (David & Charles, 1971).

[2] Ibid.

[3] Tate amalgamated in 1921 with Lyle's of Greenock.

[4] Liverpool Record Office 942 HOL 10, 357-375, 419-477.

[5] See www.btinternet.com/~m.royden/mrlhp/local/salt/dungeon.htm

[6] T. S. Willan, *The Navigation of the River Weaver in the Eighteenth Century* (Chetham Society Transactions Vol 3, 3rd series, 1951).

[7] Liverpool Record Office 920 NOR 2/179.

[8] Textiles from Lancashire and Yorkshire, pottery, copper and brass from Staffordshire and Cheshire, and guns from Birmingham were the main exports used by Liverpool merchants to trade for slaves.

[9] Ian Law, *History of Race and Racism in Liverpool 1660–1950* (Merseyside Community Relations Council, 1981).

[10] Elder Dempster & Company Ltd was formed in 1910, but started out in 1852 as the African Steam Ship Company, with a contract to carry mails from London via Plymouth to Madeira, Tenerife and the West Coast of Africa. In 1856, Liverpool became its home port.

[11] In *Black Liverpool: The Early History of Britain's Oldest Black Community 1730–1918* (Picton, 2001), Raymond Henry Costello writes that 'one of the largest sections of Liverpool blacks is that of the freeman black sailor . . . the Kru (Liberia)

have a seaman tradition in particular, and gradually such men settled, being laid off in Liverpool or whatever, staying from either choice or necessity.' After the Abolition 'the Elder Dempster line had something of a tradition of employing Africans and has indirectly played a large part in the settling of black people in Liverpool . . . [Also] such shipping lines as Brocklebank had long employed black West Indians as seamen'.

[12] Clifford O'Sullivan born 18.05.1913. Interview courtesy of National Museums Liverpool (Merseyside Maritime Museum).

[13] There was slavery in Cuba until 1870 and in Brazil until 1888.

[14] Louisiana slave code.

[15] Juan Manzano, Cuba (National Museums & Galleries on Merseyside).

[16] Thomas Armstrong, *King Cotton* (Collins, 1962).

[17] Raymond Henry Costello, *Black Liverpool: The Early History of Britain's Oldest Black Community 1730–1918* (Picton, 2001).

[18] Liverpool Record Office 942HOL10, 429.

[19] Ramsay Muir, *History of Liverpool* (Liverpool University Press, 1907).

[20] Ian Law, ibid.

[21] Liverpool Record Office 942HOL10,441.

[22] Some sources give 1922.

[23] *Oxford Companion to English Literature* (Oxford University Press, various editions).

[24] Ramsey Campbell, *Creatures of the Pool* (PS Publishing, 2009).

[25] This is Eric Lynch's version of 'A Man of Words and not of Deeds', supposed to have been written originally as a Puritan condemnation of Charles II, a staunch Roman Catholic who first promised Dissenters freedom and then persecuted them.

[26] The new dock has a loose personal connection, for as I discovered recently it was named after my four-times great uncle, George Canning, who was MP for Liverpool from 1812. Nicknamed 'The Cicero of the British Senate' and 'The Zany of Debate' for his oratory, he also has the dubious distinction

of serving possibly the shortest term as Prime Minister ever, all of 119 days in 1827, before his untimely death at the age of fifty-seven. The dock named after him was completed in 1829.

27 The Music Hall in Bold Street opened in 1786. Both were subsequently demolished.

28 R. J. Broadbent, ibid.

Chapter 3: The Shadow Darkens

1 Ramsey Campbell, ibid.

2 Margaret Donnelly, *My Parish Holy Cross* (Starfish Multimedia, 2004).

3 Frank Neal, *Sectarian Violence: The Liverpool Experience 1819–1914* (Manchester University Press, 1987).

4 Kitty Wilkinson's efforts were part-funded by the Rathbone family, and she and her husband Tom became Superintendents of the Frederick Street public baths and wash-house. When Kitty was presented to Queen Victoria, during a royal visit to Liverpool in 1846, her legend grew.

5 Tommy Walsh, *Being Irish in Liverpool* (St Michael's Irish Centre, Liverpool, 2010).

6 Frank Neal, ibid.

7 From *Craic*, a film made by members of St Michaels Irish Centre, 6 Boundary Lane, Liverpool L6 5JG. Tel: 0151 263 1808, www.stmichaelsirishcentre.org

8 Clarence Dock was filled in and the land sold for use by a power station, which was then demolished in the mid-1990s. There are still two dry docks in evidence.

9 Years later, Cilla Black (then Priscilla Marie White) was educated and found her voice here. The story is that she used to go after school to a play-centre in Penrhyn Street and take part in a regular singing contest, first prize 3d (approximately 1p), which she always won, causing a problem with her teachers, who thought she had an unfair advantage because her friends always came to support her.

10 Billy Woods, *No Trees in Scotland Road*, a book in progress.

See www.scottiepress.org/projects/bwoods.htm

[11] 'After the judge found her guilty, a mob a thousand strong chased his carriage up the hill to Everton. Presumably none of them could have known that a hundred years later James Maybrick would be identified as Jack the Ripper.' Read Ramsey Campbell's *Creatures of the Pool* for an appreciation of the myth.

[12] Built in 1849.

[13] Frank Shaw, *My Liverpool*, courtesy of the Shaw family.

Chapter 4: Call of the Sea

[1] Pat O'Mara, *A Liverpool Slummy* (Bluecoat Press, 1930).

[2] Michael Murphy (ed.), *The Collected George Garrett* (Trent Editions, Nottingham 1999). George Garrett (1896–1966) wrote short stories and essays rooted in his experience as a mariner, docker, and transatlantic labour agitator. Often blacklisted by employers, he struggled to support his family in the 1920s and 1930s, and devoted what time he could to political work.

[3] James Johnston Abraham, *The Surgeon's Log* (Chapman & Hall: London, 1913).

[4] Pat O'Mara, ibid.

[5] Glyn Parry. Born in 1929. Entered the Conway in April 1944. Interview courtesy of National Museums Liverpool (Merseyside Maritime Museum).

[6] Grossi's Trocadero was a sailors' 'boozer-bordello' in the basement of the Hotel St George on Lime Street.

Chapter 5: A Life in the Pens

[1] Bill Smathers. North West Sound Archive, Clitheroe. 2001.1076.

[2] The dead body of an animal that died of anthrax can be a source of anthrax spores, lethal to humans, but presumably wet hides dulled the spores.

[3] Well-known Liverpool shipping company.

[4] Bill Owen. North West Sound Archive, Clitheroe. 1986.0028. Some 4,000 head of cattle were kept within the Liverpool boundary at the beginning of the twentieth century.

[5] Bibby's was a famous shipping line that operated out of Liverpool. John Bibby (1775–1840) worked as a ship broker and an iron merchant in Liverpool before he set up in business as a shipowner with his partner John Highfield, in 1807. By the time he died, murdered in a mysterious attack, John Bibby was a wealthy and influential man with a sizeable fleet and a thriving metals business.

[6] Frank Smith. North West Sound Archive, Clitheroe. 1999.016.6.

[7] Frank Shaw, ibid.

[8] Mike Berry. An Oral History of the Post Office. British Library Sound Archive. C1007/75/01-12.

Chapter 6: Macho Liverpool

[1] For more on 'the money trick' read Chapter Nine and Robert Tressell's *The Ragged Trousered Philanthropists* (Grant Richards, 1914; Penguin Classics, 2004).

[2] Spencer Leigh in P. Willis-Pitts, *Liverpool The Fifth Beatle* (Amazon Press, 2002).

[3] Joan Gibbons.

[4] The knocker-up used a long stick to knock against upper bedroom windows from outside to wake people for work. It was still going on in some places in the 1950s.

[5] www.old-merseytimes.co.uk/index.html

[6] Albert Kane's memories come to us courtesy of the Kane family, by way of Kev, the manager administrator at www.yoliverpool.com/forum/forum.php

[7] The Demerara colony in Guyana, the original source of Demerara sugar.

[8] Michael Macilwee, *The Gangs of Liverpool* (Lytham: Milo, 2007).8 Set in France in 1880 – a series of murders is attributed to a Wolf Man.

[9] William Herbert Bannister, born 1890, interviewed by Audrey Hoskinson (1969). Family Life and Work Experience before 1918. British Library Sound Archive. C707/49/1-2.

[10] *Our Story: Memories of Gay Liverpool* is a community history project managed by the Unity Theatre, Hope Place, Liverpool 1, and supported by the Heritage Lottery Fund and the Liverpool Culture Company. The quote is from the reminiscence of Yankel Feather, born in 1920.

Chapter 7: Walking Free

[1] George Alfred Doyle, born 1901, interviewed by Audrey Hoskinson (1969). Family Life and Work Experience before 1918. British Library Sound Archive. C707/43/1-2.

[2] Joan Gibbons.

[3] Mollie Connor. Cruel Sea Reminiscence Project (2005). Liverpool Record Office 387/CSR/6/1.

[4] Terry Cook, *Scotland Road: The Old Neighbourhood* (Birkenhead: Countyvise, 1987).

[5] Clifford O'Sullivan, ibid.

[6] The Southern Neighbourhood Council Community Group in Upper Mann Street included Molly Monaghan, Anne Clarence, Meg Whitehead. Mary Wilcox, Edith Flanagan, Pat Maloney, and the late Theresa Connolly, variously credited elsewhere in the text.

[7] Frank Shaw, ibid.

[8] Bob Tooley, the Dingle History Group.

[9] Eileen Newman.

[10] The Dingle History Group.

[11] St Martin's Market dates back to 1840 when it was known as North Haymarkets and traded from land on which St George's Hall now stands. From its new position, and known as Paddy's Market, it launched Matalan (John Hargreaves had a stall there), Solitaire (the Liverpool fashion retailer) and Jeffs of Bold Street among others, and was a principal feature

of the Scotland Road community. Today, in its position on Great Homer Street, it is known as 'Greaty'.

12 Frank Vaudrey.

13 Frank Shaw, ibid.

14 George Cross.

15 Mollie Connor, ibid.

16 Frank Shaw, ibid.

17 Pat O'Mara.

18 Mike Berry, ibid.

19 The 'free boxing lesson', the dread of any miscreant, is just a verbal upbraid: 'If you don't behave, you get a free boxing lesson.'

20 St Sylvester's School was built at the top of Ashfield Street. In December 1911 a plot was acquired at the corner of Silvester Street and Latimer Street.

21 Johnny Morrissey started as a junior with Liverpool FC, signing professional forms when he turned seventeen and making his debut in September 1957. In 1962 he moved to Everton for a fee of £10,000. Manager Bill Shankly didn't know about the deal until it was done.

22 Anfield was one of the original grounds when the Football League was formed in 1888, but it was Everton Football Club that played there. When, in the early 1890s, Everton had a dispute with the owner of Anfield, Tory MP John Holding, Everton were evicted, Holding and his friend William Barclay decided that the city had room for two clubs, and Liverpool Football Club was born. Everton has been based at Goodison Park since 1892.

23 Billy Woods.

24 John Burns.

25 May Duke, born 1912.

26 The Dingle History Group.

27 George Cross.

Chapter 8: Mother Liverpool

[1] Date of the Poor Law Amendment Act.

[2] May Duke. North West Sound Archive, Clitheroe. 1986.0029.

[3] Joan Bevan. North West Sound Archive, Clitheroe. 2006.0397-9.

[4] Doris Windsor. Cruel Sea Reminiscence Project (2005). Liverpool Record Office 387/CSR/6/1.

[5] Responsible for putting the metal sheets on the sides of the ships.

[6] *Blood Brothers*, a cult musical by Liverpool born and bred Willy Russell, is one of the longest-running shows in history. It premiered in 1983 and the 1988 West End production is still running. It tells of twin brothers, separated at birth and brought up in families at the opposite ends of the social spectrum, who fall in love with the same girl . . .

[7] Lil Otty and Vera Jeffers. Cruel Sea Reminiscence Project (2005). Liverpool Record Office 387/CSR/6/1.

[8] Pat Maloney of the Southern Area Council Community Group in Upper Mann Street.

[9] Marie Francis, a member of the League of Welldoers.

[10] Bill Owen, ibid.

[11] Joan Gibbons.

[12] Mary Smith, Sedgemoor Residential Home, Cruel Sea Reminiscence Project, 2005. Liverpool Record Office CSR/6/1.

[13] Doris Windsor, born 1917.

[14] Joan Gibbons.

[15] This fading, but in many ways still magnificent, hotel (there are remnants of original marbled floors and sycamore panelling, inlaid with rare woods, finished to a silver grey) is redolent of the romantic, early twentieth-century era of huge Atlantic liners. It first opened in 1827, but its Sefton Suite is a replica of the first class smoking lounge on the White Star Line's ill-fated *Titanic*, which sailed out of Liverpool for the first and last time in April 1912.

[16] On 15 April 1989, a disaster at Hillsborough football ground,

Sheffield, resulted in the deaths of 96 Liverpool supporters. The occasion was the semi-final of the FA Cup, Liverpool against Nottingham Forest.
17 Tommy Walsh.
18 Joan Gibbons.
19 Veronica Blyth, Cruel Sea Reminiscence Project (2005). Liverpool Record Office. 387 CSR/6/1.
20 A confraternity is a Roman Catholic organisation of lay people approved by the Church hierarchy.
21 Joan Gibbons.
22 From *Craic*, ibid.
23 The beach across the Mersey on the Wirral.

Chapter 9: Solidarity
1 Eric Lynch.
2 Eileen Devaney.
3 Joan Gibbons.
4 Anne Thompson.
5 The *Irish Independent* vigorously supported its owner's interests in 1913, with news reports and features hostile to the strikers and their leader, James Larkin. It did the same in 1916, describing the Easter Rising as 'insane and criminal', and took a pro Unionist stance in 1919. For most of its history, the *Irish Independent* (also called simply the *Independent* or, more colloquially, the *Indo*) has been seen as a nationalist, Catholic newspaper, which gave its political allegiance to Cumann na nGaedhael and later Fine Gael.
6 Tommy Walsh.
7 The Fenian Brotherhood, named after the Fianna, the legendary band of Irish warriors led by Fionn mac Cumhaill, was an Irish republican organisation founded in 1858 by John O'Mahony and Michael Doheny. It was a precursor to Clan na Gael, a sister organisation to the Irish Republican Brotherhood.
8 The Irish Volunteers, led by Patrick Pearse, the Irish Citizen Army of James Connolly, and two hundred members of

Cumann na mBan, seized key locations in Dublin between 24 April, Easter Monday, and 30 April 1916. The aim was to end British rule and establish the Irish Republic. The leaders were executed, but in the 1918 general election the Republicans won 73 out of 105 seats, and declared independence in January 1919. Following more than two years of guerilla fighting, the Irish Free State was established in July 1921.

9   The attack on the Post Office was a key moment in the Easter Rising. Led by James Connolly, Republicans marched to O'Connell Street, charged the GPO, expelled customers and staff, and took a number of British soldiers prisoner. The tricolour and green Irish Republic flags were raised on the GPO roof. A short time later, Patrick Pearse read the Proclamation of the Republic outside the GPO.

10   From *Craic*, ibid.

11   Anonymous female.

12   Dinah Dossor.

13   Linda Grant, *Guardian*, 5 June 2003.

14   Harold Hikins, *Strike: The Liverpool General Transport Strike 1911* (Merseyside: Toulouse Press, 1980).

Chapter 10: War

1   The Beginning of the Reckoning, Radio City recording narrated by Bill Bingham. Written by Arthur Kelly. British Library Sound Archive. C12/5/6.

2   Mavis Harrison and Dorothy Curl. Cruel Sea Reminiscence Project 2005. Memories of wartime Liverpool by people from Sedgemoor Residential Home. Liverpool Record Office 387CSR/13/3.

3   The Argyle Theatre, where some of the greatest stars of British Theatre and music hall played, itself received a direct hit in September 1940. All but the office and foyer was destroyed.

Chapter 11: Sixties Transformation

1. Jean Roberts. Arthur Dooley Archive. Courtesy of North West Sound Archive, Clitheroe Castle. nwsa@ed.lancscc.gov.uk.
2. Peggy Tully.
3. The Pavilion Theatre, known as the Pivvy, was in Lodge Lane, Liverpool 8.
4. Cruel Sea Reminiscence Project 2005. 'Wartime Liverpool' by people from the Joseph Gibbons Day Centre. Liverpool Record Office.
5. Wilton's comedy emerged from the tradition of English music hall.
6. Mavis O'Flaherty.
7. Angelo Vaccarello.
8. Lil Cameron. Cruel Sea Reminiscence Project 2005. Liverpool Record Office. 387 CSR/6/1.
9. Edie Crew. Cruel Sea Reminiscence Project 2005. Liverpool Record Office. 387 CSR/6/1.
10. Lee Jones Reminiscent Group. Welldoers, Limekiln Lane.
11. Mike McCartney, *Thank U Very Much* (Granada Publishing, 1982).
12. Frank Shaw, ibid.
13. All the top sixties Liverpool groups and solo artists played at the Mardi Gras Club – the Beatles, the Big Three, Gerry and the Pacemakers, Cilla Black. Originally a church, the building was demolished in the mid-seventies to make way for a car park.
14. Frank Shaw, ibid.
15. The Merseysippi came out of the Wallasey Rhythm Kings. Formed in 1948, they backed many great jazz names, and brought George Melly to Liverpool for the first time.
16. Mike McCartney, ibid.
17. Bill Harrison and Ritchie Barton interviews, courtesy National Museums Liverpool (Museum of Liverpool – eight hundred lives project).
18. P. Willis-Pitts, ibid.

19 P. Willis-Pitts, ibid.
20 Sugar Deen interview, courtesy National Museums Liverpool (Museum of Liverpool – eight hundred lives project).
21 '*Mach schau*' was what the German fans shouted to bring the Beatles full on.
22 The Merseycats' venue is now the Aintree Conservative Club in Lancing Drive, Liverpool L10 8LN. The Merseycats have raised £300,000 for kids in the Merseyside area.
23 Rory Storm and the Hurricanes were one of the most popular bands on the Liverpool and Hamburg club scenes.
24 Wally Shepard said, 'We all looked up to Bob, he was the original DJ. At twenty-eight, thirty, he was a real old man. He'd worked on the railways. He became a DJ at the Cavern, worked with Brian Kelly and was instrumental in bands getting a start.'
25 P. Willis-Pitts, ibid.
26 P. Willis-Pitts, ibid.
27 Roger McGough, http://en.wikipedia.org/wiki/Liverpool_poets
28 Interview with Jonathan Pryce by Alfred Hickling in the *Guardian*, 6 October 2009.
29 With thanks to Roger Phillips and Peter James. Their interviews courtesy of the Everyman Theatre Archive at Liverpool John Moores University Special Collections and Archives. Roger Phillips is the star of Radio Merseyside. Peter James FRSA has been Principal of LAMDA (The London Academy of Music and Dramatic Art) since 1994.
30 For the benefit of non-Liverpudlians, Speke is a well-known part of Liverpool on the No. 42 bus route.
31 Groundbreaking sixties experimental theatre troupe.
32 After the Second War, Joan Littlewood (1914–2002), a paid-up member of the Communist Party and under surveillance by MI5 from 1939 until the 1950s, formed Theatre Workshop, which toured until 1953 when it settled at the Theatre Royal in Stratford. The company gained international fame, performing plays across Europe and in the Soviet Union.

Seminal productions included Bertolt Brecht's *Mother Courage* (1955), *Fings Ain't Wot They Used To Be*, which ran from 1959 to 1962, Shelagh Delaney's *A Taste of Honey* (1958), and *Oh! What a Lovely War* (1963).

[33] The atomic energy play developed at Joan Littlewood's famously creative Stratford East Theatre Workshop.

[34] Hugely influential academic and critic, author of *The Great Tradition* (1947).

[35] Michael X was a black revolutionary and civil rights activist. Convicted of murder in 1972, he was executed by hanging in 1975 in Port of Spain's Royal Gaol.

[36] Jim Haynes's Traverse Theatre opened its doors in 1963 and developed its worldwide reputation for politically relevant contemporary fringe theatre. See www.jim-haynes.com/life/theatre.htm for the full story.

[37] In 1906 the Bluecoat School had moved to larger premises in Wavertree. The Port Sunlight soap magnate William Lever, later Lord Leverhulme, bought the building and let rooms to the Sandon Society, a Bohemian group of Liverpool artists led by Augustus John, who lived in Sandon Street in Liverpool. Thereafter the Bluecoat became a focus for the arts in Liverpool.

[38] Perhaps *the* anti-war poet in Britain, one of the politically conscious revolutionaries who made the pivotal 1965 Albert Hall poetry event so significant. His often angry output included anarchistic anti-war satire, but also love poetry and stories and poems for children.

[39] The late Harry Fainlight, contemporary of Ted Hughes (and Bill Harpe) at Cambridge, was the younger brother of poet Ruth Fainlight, who is still writing today. Ruth Fainlight, widow of Alan Sillitoe, is an important connection between Hughes and Robert Graves. A member of the beat generation, Harry Fainlight spent time in America with Ginsberg, who referred to him as 'the most gifted English poet', and took quantities of drugs in an experiment to enhance his gifts, returning in 1965 to live in Liverpool.

40 *Bodily Fluids and Functions* was an amazing happening, involving the projection of sweat, tears, blood, saliva, sperm, etc., and even vomit onto a screen, accompanied by sound effects. (See www.boylefamily.co.uk/boyle/texts/journey2. html).

41 Joseph Sharples, *Liverpool* (Pevsner Architectural Guides, 2004).

42 In 1964, Peter Moores, a member of the family that made a fortune originally from the Littlewoods pools, mail order catalogue and department stores, set up a charitable foundation to further his interests in the arts, particularly in music and the visual arts. From 1971 to 1986, the foundation sponsored the highly popular biennial contemporary art exhibitions at the Walker Art Gallery. For a short time, Moores was chairman of Everton Football Club. In 1993 the foundation bought Compton Verney House in Warwickshire, and in 2004 opened an art gallery there. The foundation also sponsors the Opera Rara classical music label.

43 David Lewis, a great philanthropist, was born in London, but Liverpool was his great focus. Settling there in 1840, he saved enough in sixteen years to start up the first Lewis's retail store in Bold Street, originally an affordable clothes store for men and boys only. This was the first step towards his famous department store (not to be confused with the John Lewis chain), one of the largest retail businesses of its kind in England, erected just south of Lime Street station, opposite the equally famous Adelphi Hotel. Similar stores were founded in Manchester, Sheffield and Birmingham. The Liverpool store closed just as I was finishing writing this book.

44 The artist John Latham played with the theory that the most basic component of reality is not the particle, as in classical physics, but the least-event. The ideas of event-based art were the context in which performance art and happenings took shape in the sixties.

45 A New York event artist whose work helped develop performance art and happenings.

46   The film was sponsored by Wills, the cigarette people, and was based on four centres, of which the Blackie was one. Another film featuring the Blackie, *On the Eighth Day*, was made by Granada. You see the kids breaking through the front door. *Time for Thought* was premiered in London.

47   A council estate, known as Stockbridge Village since the 1990s following a period of regeneration. The estate was originally laid out during the 1960s but deteriorated rapidly due to crime and unemployment.

48   John Osborne's exercise in coffee-table socialism moved the action of theatre from drawing-room to kitchen and crystallised the existentialist concept of the 'angry young man'.

49   At the end of his first season, Alan Dossor asked six writers to read Brecht's *The Private Lives of the Master Race* and to write a short contemporary equivalent. From this brief, a varied programme of short plays emerged. In 1973–74 he reinterpreted Brecht's *The Good Woman of Setzuan* on the Everyman stage.

50   Brecht viewed catharsis as pap for the bourgeois theatre audience, and designed dramas to leave significant emotions unresolved as a way to force social action upon the audience. This technique can be seen as early as his agit-prop play *The Measures Taken*.

51   Brian Patten in interview with Alfred Hickling, *Guardian*, 21 February 2007.

52   Rogan Taylor and Andrew Ward, *Three Sides of the Mersey: Oral History of Everton, Liverpool and Tranmere Rovers* (Robson Books, 1993/1998).

53   Rogan Taylor and Andrew Ward, ibid.

Chapter 12: Miss Liverpool

1   The conditions concerned combatting the communist threat, the reason behind America loaning Britain the money. This threat was perceived as being seated in the working class,

which was now being thrown to the four winds in Liverpool and Glasgow.

[2] Anonymous.

[3] Mr H Robinson interviewed 31.07.1987, aged 81 years. Cruel Sea Reminiscence Project (2005). Liverpool Record Office 387/CSR/6/1.5 This was a distinct possibility. In Glasgow, plans had to be headed off that would have made the entire centre of the city a 1950s new-build.

[4] Christine Gibbons, *Effecting Change: Historical Memory, Community Activism and the Legacy of the Occupation of Croxteth Comprehensive School 1982–1985* (2010).

[5] Jesse Hartley (1780–1860) was Civil Engineer and Superintendent of the Concerns of the Dock Estate in Liverpool between 1824 and 1860.

[6] *Liverpool Daily Post*, 13 February 2008.

[7] The Roger O'Hara interview is part of the Arthur Dooley Archive, courtesy of North West Sound Archive.

[8] Stephen Broadbent, *Liverpool Daily Post*, 13 February 2008.

[9] One who decided who would get work.

[10] An insider who preferred to remain anonymous.

[11] Eric Lynch.

[12] Josie Burger.

[13] Stephen Sinnot Sedgemoor Residential Home LRO 387CSR/13/3

[14] A Salopian is an old boy of Shrewsbury School.

[15] See Chapter One.

[16] The councils of the early Christian church had to contend with much heretical overspill from pre-Christian, Pagan mythology, including the identification of the Virgin Mary, Mother of God, with the goddess, as Robert Graves points out in *The White Goddess* (Faber and Faber, 1961).

[17] Irish Community Care.

[18] See Preface.

[19] Coordinator, Irish Community Care.

[20] The Stan Cummings interview is part of the Arthur Dooley archive, courtesy of the North West Sound Archive.

Index